MW01226870

White Lies Dark Truth

by
Mony Singh

Robert D. Reed Publishers • San Francisco, CA

Robert D. Reed Publishers
750 La Playa, Suite 647
San Francisco, CA 94121
Phone: 650-994-6570 • Fax: -6579
E-mail: 4bobreed@msn.com
web site: www.rdrpublishers.com

Editor: **Ruth Schenkel**
Typesetter: **Barbara Kruger**
Cover Designer: **Julia Gaskill**
Pictures: **iandistudio – www.iandistudio.com**

ISBN 1-931741-22-0

Library of Congress Control Number 2002107259

Manufactured, typeset and printed in the United States of America

To contact the author, visit the book's website at: www.WhiteLiesDarkTruth.com.

Dedicated to the supreme Father and divine Mother for giving me another chance to explore this human life. My infinite thanks to my parents for becoming a gate to this physical world. To my Guru, Shri Anil Jain, who awakened my Kundalini Shakti and with whose blessings I have come to understand the Science of Body Features. Also, my loving gratitude to Doc and his wife for their love and support and for helping me to break the fetters of my past lives and allowing my energies to explore their full potential in this body. My hearty thanks to all my friends, who have proved to be wild cards in this game of life. Whenever I got stuck in this capitalist world they helped me move on with my passion to bring a change in mass consciousness; without them this project would have taken a few decades. Finally, my love and gratitude to my family, who have given me their love and care no matter how rough the times were.

Contents

Introduction

A child is born; we nurture the child to the point where he can walk and talk, then we send the innocent kid to school. At school he learns all the basic tools of survival, i.e., language, science, mathematics, politics, capitalism, etc., but do we ever teach him how to live this life? What this life is all about? What his role is in society? Why he has taken birth and why he will die one day?

When you go to the Grand Canyon or any state park, at the entrance you are handed a map, a list of do's and don'ts. The map tells you where to go, where to camp, what areas you should stay away from and what areas are the most interesting. But do we ever give a map to our kids as to what areas are interesting in life and what areas they should stay away from?

If we are traveling from one city to another, we plan our trips in advance and we have road maps, highways and signs to help us reach our destination, but do we ever plan our life path or have any maps to take us from one birthday to another?

When our children become ready to walk on this road called life, we never teach them to map their lives where they can enjoy the cities of peace, harmony, love, compassion, caring, awareness, meditation and faith, but we make sure that they do not miss the cities of capitalism, competition, egoism and jealousy, which lead them to the dark and unknown lands of pain and misery.

All our lives we are focused on one issue—how to make more and more. People grow up to become good earning machines, and although the majority do not like their profession, they continue their everyday struggle in bumper-to-bumper traffic trying to reach their destination of financial security, thinking that one day they will relax and enjoy this life.

If parents and teachers are aware, they can figure out a life plan for a child based on his habits and interests at a very early age. All they have to do is keep track of the child's interests and the areas in which he excels, and a map can be drawn about his growing years. But parents are selfish and ignorant. In order to satisfy their own wishes and desires, they make their children as their scapegoats. A kid may be good at art and love to paint all day, but his parents want him to be a doctor; although the kid might become a successful doctor, his life is wasted. He took birth to satisfy his inner self—to be a painter, to express himself through painting, but his parents kill the painter within him when they force him to become a doctor. You will be surprised to know that Hitler wanted to be an artist, and if his parents had helped him express himself through art, perhaps the world could have been saved from so many killings.

To live in harmony one must love one's profession; otherwise, one may make money and live in a mansion, but one will never be at ease with one's self. Just recently, psychologists have started saying, "Do what you love and the money will follow." Yet the majority is following the same old principle of working in a field where they can capitalize.

We teach kids vocabulary but never teach them the deeper meanings and associations of the words or the emotions behind them. But kids are smart when it comes to associating words with emotions. A kid may be riding with his mom and dad in the car when someone cuts them off; the dad says, "You SOB," and the kid sitting in the back enjoying his milk stores "You SOB" in his databank along with emotional sound waves of hate and anger. Some day he will be out in the world and will repeat the same episode with others. It is no wonder we have so much hate on our planet.

Do we have any guides in the society who can teach us how we should live our lives? No! Because it is taken for granted, just as when you own a car there is no need to know the mechanics behind it because in the case of a breakdown, there are hundreds of auto shops around. To compensate for our lack of knowledge about ourselves, we employ psychologists, doctors, counselors, and priests, and if they fail to help, we can make use of our mental institutions and jails.

God knows how many innocent people are rotting in our mental institutions and jails.

This all happens because of one simple reason—we never teach our young ones how to live this life. We have not explored our own lives, so how can we expect to teach?

Governments are willing to spend billions on drug education, but will not spend a penny on going to the root of all miseries—the lack of understanding to live this life beautifully. We have the resources, the information, and the technology to make this world a place to enjoy, experience, and understand, but the statistics show that the majority have to live a life of scarcity, insecurity and poor health. Every human life is wasted just trying to survive or amass.

All humans are born with equal potential to laugh and enjoy their lives, but very few chosen ones fall in the category of the successful ones;

the majority live in misery and die in misery, as they are always in survival mode, trying to make ends meet.

The tragedy is that one who was born to be a Buddha is working as a bartender, and one who was born to be a Jesus has ended up being a janitor. We all come for one reason: to grow and go beyond this misery called life. But 99% end up in the same crusher of unawareness because they are never taught to center themselves so that one day they find their real selves to go beyond this "Maya," or illusion, which is another word for misery.

We have had abundant spiritual masters and teachers and the majority talked about the body, mind, and soul connection, and many talked about God. Most of them were and are mere businessmen, just here to capitalize on man's ignorance in the capitalistic west. Have we reached anywhere by knowing about the connections between body, mind and soul? Many have claimed to reach enlightenment but their experience cannot become ours, as all understanding must come from one's own experience or vice versa. Have we gotten anywhere or reached enlightenment ourselves by merely listening to them or reading their words? There is a strong need to know the basics of human existence as to who we are and why are we here.

I have devoted one chapter to this 5000-year-old science from the Vedic era; it is known as "Sharir Lakshan Vigyan," or the Science of Body Features.

Every child is born with unique physical features as a result of the DNA contributed by both parents. Genetic coding shapes one's physical features and these physical features are the indicators of one's thinking ability. Both these factors play a very important role in our lives because we are judged by the way we look and the way we walk, talk or act. All our actions depend on how we think and what we think as our minds respond to the millions and billions of thought waves hovering in the universal consciousness. The thoughts one receives from the universal consciousness are in perfect resonance with the quality of one's physical features, just like the components in a radio or TV. Our physical features are the indicators of the quality of the components found within our body and the power of our bio-computer. If the quality of the parents who contributed their genetic coding is high—with respect to awareness, sharpness of the mind, their past karma, their knowledge database, the quality of the blood, etc. — and if they are in deep love with each other, their own selves, and with the world around them, a child who will take birth from the union of these two individuals will supersede the quality of his parents in all areas. This science has enough potential to revolutionize the way we think about others and ourselves.

Just look around and you will find that the majority of people are products of disharmony and the eyes of these people will never be the same size and shape since the left side of the body is an indicator of the mother, and the right side an indicator of the father. The imbalance in the shape, size and appearance of one's eyes are clear indicators of disharmony among parents at the time of conception.

If ever you wanted to know how close your parents were at the time of your conception, just stand in front of the mirror and have a good look at yourself. If your father was in harmony with your mother from the time they started knowing to the time you were conceived, and they have both loved each other and have showered that unified love on you in your growing years, you will grow up to be a very balanced and attractive person, and the shape, size and appearance of both your eyes will be in exact proportion even if you are not born with good features.

On the other hand, if your father was not joyous about your coming to this world, you will carry that ugliness on your face even if you are born with the best quality features. The same is true of the tops of your feet, which are related to your mother's state of being. If you have ugly feet where veins are showing on the top, then you can be assured that your mother's circumstances were not harmonious at the time of your conception or in the period preceding it. As a result, you were deprived of your mother's love.

Imagine the quality of the components used in a common radio compared to the components used in the probes that are sent into space to explore the universe. The quality of the components used in these probes are of the highest quality science can produce, since these probes are designed to perform specific functions and the results have to travel millions of miles in order to reach the base unit; no chance can be taken with the quality of the components used—once the probe leaves earth it cannot be brought back.

Just as some humans have the ability to be good teachers, some have the ability to be good singers, good artists, doctors, healers, mathematicians, engineers, carpenters, and so on, based on their genetic coding and the science of their body features. The creative and destructive forces lie dormant within us until we dive deep into these mysterious forces and use them according to our limited awareness.

It is such a powerful science that if someone involves himself in an inhuman act, such as killing another human out of grudge, hate, or anger, and not in self-defense, or if a woman aborts her fetus at a very late stage, or even if a person is instrumental in killing someone due to negligence, within a few days of such an act certain signs will show up on the person's physical features. It is the way of existence to let us know that we have gone against the laws of nature. I have disclosed this secret in this book for the benefit of mankind. This little secret can help the justice system to be fair and honest, as not all homicides are preplanned crimes of hate. Some happen to protect the self.

This science can help healers and therapists as they look into the inner state of people and know where their life is being held at bay. Using this sacred science one can see how much happiness a person has, whether a person enjoys his food or not—since what we eat and how we eat today will determine the state of our being in the future—and the quality of a person's energy system, how much sexual energy the person has, as well as the state of the immune system. There are tons of secrets one can know just by knowing the science of analyzing one's body features.

Since this is not a book on "the science of body features," I have only disclosed what is of importance to a common man in order to know himself and start living this life in harmony.

I have also dedicated one chapter to healing because healthy individuals are a rare find; most people suffer from chronic health problems. I have also disclosed some ancient therapies that can pull the masses out of some chronic diseases like cancer, depression and AIDS, provided their immune system has not been completely torn down and their five elements have not started to disintegrate, something which can be determined by looking at a person's temple area (the indicator of the state of a person's immune system).

Humanity is at a crossroads as we enter the 21st century; people are poorer than they were a few hundred years ago. The lack of revolutionaries who have the awareness and the guts to bring a change in the system are making the lives of people unfulfilling. People are confused and their lives are a mess.

The concept of marriage, our family system, the justice system, our ability to forgive, our religions, our peace of mind, our patience—all are collapsing.

Money, religion and politics have caused more damage to humans than has any other dogma. Interestingly, all three are based on creating illusions at different levels.

Money creates illusion on the material level.

Politics creates illusion on the mind level.

Religion creates illusion on the emotional level.

Mankind is losing itself in the jungle of intellect. The intellect is as vast as this cosmos. The energy of the heart is like a leash for our consciousness, and if the leash is not strong enough we will lose touch with our being.

Considering the direction in which humanity is heading, there is little time left. Man is turning into woman and woman is turning into man. Women are losing softness and men are losing strength. We must change our course or the result will be disastrous. Masses of women will choose to be lesbians and masses of men will take to homosexuality, transvestitism, or transsexualism. This emotional shift and the forced physical shift will distort the subtle balance of the mind and will result in homicides, civil wars, mass suicides and genocides. If we look at the current state of humanity, most people are unhappy, angry, impatient, selfish, rude, and judgmental. The number of people losing their balance of mind is on the rise.

Two essential elements to live this life as a normal human being are evaporating fast. These elements are love and hope. People are feeling helpless, clicking frantically on the mouse in search of something potent, something which will give peace, love and clarity. But that something is not out there—it is within you. You need to pull your eyes away from the picture tube and start looking inwards on the dark screen of your forehead; you need to click on your consciousness and tap on the keyboard of your heart, because that is where the divine music will be orchestrated. These ears will not hear what you desire to hear. The universal sound of "AUM" is within you.

What you can see with these eyes are just **WHITE LIES,** a mere illusion that falls apart at the moment of death. Just as you came into existence out of nowhere, you will dissolve into nowhere—it's only a matter of time. Whatever you can see, touch, feel, taste, or hear is going to dissolve one day. The clock is ticking and the day is not far when this beautiful pulsating gift of life will have to be abandoned.

The **TRUTH** is hidden in the darkness of your unconscious mind. Look within and you will find all. Do not be confused by the lies outside of you.

I have covered those areas of life where the maximum confusion lies. Mankind has been chained to those issues for millennia. After you have gone through the book, you will be able to break those chains that have kept you imprisoned for a long time. Once you start walking on the road of awareness things will start clearing up, and no longer will you find yourself in confusion.

Many times I have used the comparison between the east and the west, without which this book would have been incomplete. As the east has half the knowledge and the west has the other half, the east and west are like male and female. They are very opposite and complementary to one another. The east is emotional while the west is logical.

If your upbringing has been very emotional, this book will help you open your logical mind, and if your upbringing has been very logical, this book will help open up your emotional center.

This book is an honest attempt to help mankind start a new millennium, one in which we can be happy with our existence and make this planet into the heaven that was the original intention of the creators. It is an attempt to turn this planet into a school of life, a research center for the cosmos, a vast library or database of knowledge as described by Barbara Mercenick in her book, *The Earth*.

I have tried to make society aware of where we have been lacking, and attempted to open some hidden secrets science does not know, that the poor doctors and psychologists have not ventured into because the trend has instead been "the blind leading the blind." No one has had the guts to look around, experiment, learn and give back experience to the world. Yes! People have passed on information, but they have not passed on knowledge or wisdom, which is lacking on the planet despite the fact that we hanker for it all our lives.

My aim in this book is to help humanity reach a stage where it becomes easier for people to know who they are and what their purpose is. After reading this book, you will have all the tools to move on in the search for truth and no longer will you have to give up your families, your property, or your hard-earned money to these so-called "gurus" in the search for the knowledge that you have been seeking for ages and lifetimes. After knowing these secrets, you can start your own journey inside of you and if, along the way, you stumble across a real master or guru, it will be your good luck and you should feel blessed. I have also given secrets from the science of body features as to what you can see in a guru so that you will know if he is a real guru or just another con man who has read a few books on philosophy and is merely a good talker.

I would like to end the introduction with this wish for the future: In the coming times, society becomes so aware that money is more of a tool to play with than a power, although it presently rules the world. No longer need one pay for any sort of guidance, whether it be spiritual, physical or material. Guides and doctors are created for the benefit of society and they are supported in their needs by a group of people. They do not need to worry about their daily necessities, allowing them to spend their time gaining new insights into human life and sharing these insights with society.

My sincere wish is that after reading this book you should apply these secrets to your life to make it wholesome so that one day you may stumble upon your holiness.

1

Our Life! A White Lie

Welcome to Earth! The only planet that we know of in our solar system that has life. The land of the rising Sun and the shining Moon. Day and Night, Life and Death, Richness and Poverty, Laughter and Tears, Happiness and Sadness, Anger and Compassion, Love and Hate—welcome to the land of duality. Buddhas were born here as well as Hitlers. You are born with power to be both. Accept it or be mad, live happy or die sad; the choice is yours.

"Please, someone, help me. All I want is something small. Nothing big. I just want to be happy." (Kristin Kinkel)

These are the words of 17-year-old Kip Kinkel, an Oregon native who gunned down his parents and then opened fire in his high school cafeteria, killing two students. He was sentenced to nearly 112 years in prison in November of 1999. Shocking, isn't it? This poor soul could have been the next Martin Luther King or Gandhi; sadly, he will spend the rest of his life behind iron bars living his life no better than an animal: caged, helpless, and hopeless, just waiting for the day when his being will leave his body in search of a better one. **All he wanted was a little bit of happiness!**

We are all seeking happiness in some way or other. Are we not? Our search for a better car, a better house, and a better spouse, all boils down to a search for something within us, something better than that which we know at the moment. Believe it or not, we are all searching for our inner self, our true self, not the one we know—our name, the brand name society has given us, the software we have created within our bio-computers, or the software that has been installed by the society or religion in which we were raised.

Most people are living a stereotyped life created for them by others, and all the programming one has is based on lies, half-truths, false notions, religious dogmas, and racist and judgmental emotions. Take a good look at yourself and see what belongs to you.

The truth is that you are brought up on lies and you live your life based on notions and dogmas that have been stuffed into you. Nothing is genuinely yours within your mindset. Pro-religion or anti-religion, it does not matter. Christian, Hindu, Jew, Sikh, Muslim—all carry a mindset which does not allow the other.

All our belief systems are mere thoughts borrowed and garnished with religious, political, and racist emotions. We are beggars of information, thinking that one day we will be kings. Yes! Some do end up being kings of information, but they become the kings of beggars. When death knocks on the door they have a bigger load to let go of. All the so-called religious, political, material, racial beliefs, notions, and thoughts are trashed at the time of death.

Our belief systems have created nothing but bewilderment on this planet. Our religions have created nothing but racism, and our political systems have merely created more prejudice, making people poorer on many levels. Every few years a new person pops up who condemns his predecessor, promises a new future, enjoys his perks while being the head of the country, and leaves behind a badly scarred and disillusioned society. Crime and corruption continue; some win, some lose, and the majority are left to experience anarchy, violence, and hate. The list goes on.

The other day when I got off the BART (Bay Area Rapid Transit) at the Berkeley Station, I saw a sign that read: **"There was just one hate website on the Internet at the time of the Oklahoma City bombing; today there are more than 2100."**

We all want to be the rulers because it hurts to be ruled over. If you look deeply you will start laughing. We all live our lives based on primary and secondary thought patterns. These thought patterns have been contributed by our parents and the people who have lived around us all our lives. If someone was brought up thinking that he wants to be a painter, then he or she will be living off the collective consciousness of the best painters who have existed in the past; he might or might not have heard of Picasso, but his goal is to be the best painter. Others will have the goal of being the best singer, the best actor, or the best politician. My personal feeling is that politicians are the best actors and the best actors are those who fail the most often at real life; if you look at the lives of these so-called "stars" among us, their personal lives are a total mess. This personal mess is beautifully portrayed in movies, shows, and songs, and further contributes towards a messy and destructive society. Very few of these artists contribute towards the growth of our society using their talents.

The first goal is to be known by the masses. These are the primary thoughts that run our moment-to-moment life, and when we forget about our primary thoughts the gaps are filled with secondary thoughts. Let's call them goblins. I just love goblin movies. Don't you? Funny-looking illusionary characters. They have so much in common with the thoughts we get, each thought having its own personality, coming from nowhere and going into nowhere but leaving a huge imprint of its feet on the surface of our unconscious mind.

So let's come back to the stage; the gaps which appear when we are not thinking of our primary goals are filled by these goblins of fear, insecurity, lust, anger, resentment, greed, and so on. Day-to-day simple problems, such as how you will make the next car payment, next month's rent, your job, or thoughts of a rich spouse, winning the jackpot, your parents leaving a large estate for you, and so on—they all make it seems as though life is playing a word game with you.

Maybe you have risen above all that insecurity about money and you have reached a stage where your predicament has changed, and instead of worrying about the rent you worry about losing money in the stocks, or about someone trying to rip off your recently accumulated wealth, or about someone denting your brand new Lexus, or about your sexy partner cheating on you. Whether you are rich or poor, it does not matter—the goblins of fear, jealousy, greed and insecurity play their own games within your thoughts. For a poor man these goblins are meager and shabby looking, and for the wealthy they are rich and well dressed.

The end result: you struggle, survive, or are successful based on how you handle these goblins, and whether you fill the gaps with the goblins from the Angel group (willpower, positive thoughts, love, etc.), or goblins from the Devil group (anger, hate and resentment, etc.). But again the end result is the same: you are acting based on the primary and secondary thought patterns which are controlling your each and every moment, from the time you wake up in the morning to the time you doze off in bed at night.

For the majority of people, life is missed out on and messed up by these primary and secondary thought patterns. Even before you realize what life is all about, you have joined the list of people who have departed.

Has the following ever crossed your mind? How old are you now? Where were you before taking this birth? Do you remember when you were a six-month-old baby or a one-year-old toddler feeding on your mother's breasts? Where have all these years gone? Do you realize that time is flying by and every single day you are getting a bit closer to the day when life will end for you? Every breath you take brings you a step closer to death.

But don't feel pessimistic, as that is not my purpose here. You will die when the time comes for you to die. The clock is ticking and the truth of the matter is that you were nonexistent at one time and you will be nonexistent again. Even before you realize it, seventy-plus years will have flown by and death will be knocking at your door; the way you have missed life in a hurry you are bound to miss death too. All your power, control, ego and possessions will drop like a dead leaf along with this body.

Have the following ever crossed your mind? **Who** are you? **Why** are you here?

If you are bored with what this material and physical life has to offer, I will still give you seven out of ten marks because you have realized that life is nothing more than a ho-hum repetition. I suggest that you watch the movie "Groundhog Day." But if you are not bored and instead find that you do not have enough time to meet your goals, then you are in a hurry and chances are you will end up being a loser no matter how much material worth you may have accumulated. No matter how successful you become, you will realize in the end that you have gained what has no value and lost what was of value.

Have you ever noticed that by age five or six years kids are already in a hurry to grow? Why? Their egos have developed and they have realized that bigger is better and that power is the key and control is the fuel that nourishes the ego.

Sadly, one day they will realize that childhood was more precious, worry free, and fun; life is no longer the bed of roses they had thought it to be, and they must struggle in order to survive. Very soon they realize that the struggle they have endured and the torture they have imposed on their minds and bodies have been futile. This is the story of every human whether they be rich and famous or poor and unknown. I would say only 1% of humanity realizes at an early age what this life is all about and from there on has a purpose and lives by this purpose; these 1% leave a mark on the society. The other 99% live in constant struggle to find their way in this maze called life, always looking for happiness and never realizing that as soon as they touch happiness, they have chosen unhappiness, which is nothing but the other side of the coin. Excitement ends in boredom. Attachment turns into hate. One ends up being a yo-yo.

The majority live by primary and secondary thought patterns that have already been set by society or by the TV channels they watch. Your whole life is planned by society, your mind is controlled by the mass media, and if you rebel against society, you will be terminated or dumped into an iron cage where you will no more be a threat to the politicians. You will end up being no better than an animal in the zoo.

Are you free? You might say yes! I have a house, a secure job, a good family; I have the resources to go anywhere I wish. But stop and look deeply: Where is your freedom? What if you lost all of the above—could you be in the same state of mind as you were with all the perks this material life had to offer? Your whole life would become an endless misery without the physical comforts. You are not just a slave to this outer materialism—each and every moment of your existence is dependent, a slave, to the five elements: air, fire, water, earth, and ether, and their combinations. You are not even free in your thoughts because they are caged in your bio-computer and that computer is caged in your body. Your body and your mind are both slaves to many elements, both subtle and obvious.

As we start a new millennium, life seems so unclear and foggy: health, relationships, emotional and mental stability, even divine grace. STOP; close your eyes and think for a moment: What is your life all about? You will find nothing but darkness; the only light we have at the moment seems to be coming from the picture tube of our television. TV has become our guru, our role model. We follow what this techno guru tells us. "Drink more milk, it's good for you," one research says; we run to the refrigerator and gulp a glass of milk. The next day the same TV tells us milk is the number one cause of allergies and heart attacks. We stop drinking milk. It seems we have created an inner highway of thoughts and are living a life of stop-and-go, moving towards our destinations in a hurry, changing lanes in frustration.

Every day we wake up unwillingly and drag ourselves to work. The majority of people do not like to do this, but they have no option and must force themselves each morning to work in order to survive. For most, the pattern continues until they are 65. By this time their life energies have started packing up and they end up in elderly communities at the mercy of their families or government, just waiting in fear for death to come and pull the plug of life.

We do not seem to have any definite purpose—from birth to death, the same drama has been repeated over and over again for millennia, and it is still being repeated. Our life is no more than a juggle between opposites. One moment we are happy and the next moment we are full of anger and rage. One day we feel good about ourselves and the next day we hate our own existence. Your happiness, love, affection, compassion are no more than passing clouds in the sky of your limited awareness, as are your sadness, hate and anger. The tragedy is that none of these passing clouds get a chance to soak you with the rain, and your being, or consciousness, stays barren and desert-like. Your laughter and crying are just thunders—if these clouds of happiness or sadness could rain, you would get a chance to taste the divine nectar. Your love, hate, anger, compassion are experienced by others but never by you because the "you" has never existed within you and the "you" that you have always experienced is nothing but a video made by others but watched by you. If you could ever experience love within yourself, you would never hanker for love again; if you could ever experience anger and hate within you, there would never again be space left for anger and hate within you; if people could experience hate and anger within themselves, then there would be no need left for jails because the killer and the killed are both victims. The killer is a victim of anger and rage and the killed is a victim of the killer, and when society gives the death penalty to the killer, he becomes the victim of society's vengeful nature. What a beautiful cycle we have created, where we create victims every day. If the trend continues, very soon we will be jailing nice people because we will run out of space for the criminals.

Just open your eyes and look around you. Look at the way the whole life functions. One is born, one suffers, and finally one dies. Your contribution to the system is negligible unless you are born with a strong destiny, in which case you will make a change in the system for bad or for good.

Precious lives are wasted amassing wealth or struggling to survive, and the little bit of time left is wasted in watching TV or in idle gossiping. All we do is talk and talk. We talk about love but practice hate, we teach compassion in our schools but serve them meat at lunchtime, which is nothing but practicing cruelty. We are not only cruel to others but to ourselves. With the advancement of technology, humans have started living the lives of machines; in today's "technologically advanced" world, machines are better cared for than humans. If our car is running sluggishly, we run to the mechanic; on the other hand, if we have a headache, we do not leave work and relax so that the inner mechanic can fix the problem; rather, we throw in a couple of pain-reducing tablets that intoxicate our inner mechanic and continue with our work.

We have lost our basic instincts: we cannot laugh unless we hear a good joke, we cannot cry unless we are in deep pain. We cannot love unless we have a vested interest in the person.

Humans are accumulating the social garbage within their bodies and minds, which is coming out in the form of dangerous diseases like cancer, leukemia, AIDS. There is no limit to the number of diseases on this planet.

We have tons of resources available to us on the planet, yet mankind has been unsuccessful in providing food and shelter to all living beings on this planet—every day millions go hungry, while leftover food rots in the garbage dumps of the affluent. Rich or poor, each one of us is wanting in some way or another. The poor beg for food and the rich beg for power, and people who have gone beyond poverty and riches beg for mercy from the Lord.

Despite all the spiritual masters who have existed on this planet, and despite all the religions we have and the holy books available to us, humanity is still in chaos. Society has crippled humanity to its core. We talk about compassion, love and sharing, but when it comes to our interests the vulture of greed within us takes over and influences our decisions.

If you have never thought beyond the phrase "survival of the fittest" in the jungle of capitalism, in my opinion there is no difference between you and a fox in the animal kingdom who is looking to feed itself from the "lion's share," because one day you are going to end up being someone's dinner.

Dishonesty has become a way of life. The problem is, there is no instrument for measuring one's honesty. We have instincts but sadly we have become immune to our inner voice and we are constantly falling prey to con artists, until we pay for the lies to find the truth. Our legal system is in a mess. The legal system was created to save the innocent but then we lost the legal system to dictators and criminals; attorneys came into existence to save the innocent from the clutches of the justice system, and after a while they turned dishonest too; when it comes to helping a murderer, profits overlap ethics. The present-day court system is nothing but a mockery of the judicial system—judges are paid by the government to serve the interests of the wealthy who run these governments behind the curtains of capitalism. The social structure has decayed to the point where it is hard to draw a line between ethics and survival. This whole mumbo jumbo is robbing mankind of a very powerful asset called "faith." We are not just losing faith in others but in ourselves, too.

What is AIDS? Weakening of the immune system! What is the immune system? Collective Faith of the body! That it is protected from negativities and the failure of the immune system clearly signifies in one direction that man is losing faith in his own existence. When we are physically weak we fall prey to the medical system, which is at its height of corruption as the insurance companies, the pharmaceutical companies and the medical profession have become friends in this fleshy business. Hopeless and helpless from all directions, we end up at the hands of false gurus, incompetent astrologers, con psychics, and fake healers who are ripping off innocent people of millions of dollars. How these crooks trap people is very simple. Ads run like this: "All your problems solved!" or "One question answered for free or talk to a psychic for free on this toll-free number." This one question is nothing but the bait. The battered end up becoming the bait.

From womb to tomb our life remains illusionary and futile, yet every year we celebrate our birthday by blowing out the candles; in reality, we have blown another year off our lives. We can blame it on society, our past karma or our parents, but the end result is that most have no plan to live this life successfully. We do not teach people how to live on this planet. Most suffer until the last breath leaves their bodies and they die, and all they leave behind are memories that rot in the minds of their kith and kin or gather dust in the attic in the form of writings and pictures.

Continuing on this course, humanity will not survive for more than another 50 years. If within the next few decades we do not straighten out our acts, and instead we continue the way we have been living our lives, we will have nothing but disaster on all levels—emotional, physical, spiritual, and ecological—because the planet Earth is as alive as we are. The earth eats, breathes, discards, cries, and celebrates just as we do. If we have no respect for the ecological system, our bodies, or our minds, in a few years people will lose ground and so will the weather system, as we are all linked together. We will have a series of natural and manmade disasters that will eliminate our life form from this planet, as our survival is directly related to what we feel about ourselves and about Mother Earth.

Most people are lost in the fantasies of their minds and have become disconnected and removed from the outside world. We have lost touch with our inner selves and have thrown ourselves at the mercy of logic. We are living in a world of comparison where logic has become our master.

You go to one friend's house; his wife is nasty, unsociable and a bad cook. You immediately start admiring your wife because the comparison has come in. Next week you go to another friend's house; his wife resembles the current Miss Universe, is very sociable and cooks like a chef. In an instant you become miserable and start thinking about that unlucky day when you married your wife. It seems you have disconnected your wires with divine cable and have bought a dish where the channels have increased and so has your confusion as to what channel is good for you.

We have created our self-worth based upon what others feel about us and those others are following the same course. We have been blessed with the power of thought, action, and words, but we have forgotten the art of thinking, and based on our erroneous thinking, our actions are random acts born out of our impulsiveness and talk about words; all we speak are **White Lies** because we do not want to end up being another Jesus or Socrates speaking the truth and the truth is dark: our life starts with suffering and ends at suffering, we fear the darkness and the death. Pain and fear is the first lesson a child learns when he slips out of the womb and his umbilical cord is chopped off in an instant. This pain continues until the ax of death falls on the flow of breath and relieves the individual from misery.

From Krishna to Buddha to Jesus to Socrates to the sages of the 1900s, all said that life is nothing but "Dukkha," or misery. Our liberation from this suffering lies in our awareness, which is fogged by our desires and wishes.

Even though we are blessed with the power of intellect, we are never taught to use this intellect; on the contrary, we are always taught to fight back. Our history of thousands of years is clear evidence of our rebellion; we have fought hundreds of wars—how can we not rebel? For ages mankind has thought that the problem lies somewhere outside of us— man against the world. We never use our intellect to look within to see where this rebellion is coming from because we cannot rebel against ourselves. To do so would be to run the risk of losing ourselves, and so we must rebel against the outside world.

There is a very interesting story. Once upon a time a donkey challenged a lion. Now why would a donkey challenge a lion? The simple reason is that donkeys are always frustrated with lions, and they have every reason to be angry as everyone treats them with disrespect. So this donkey blasted at the lion: What do you think of yourself, do you think you are the king of the animal kingdom? Let's prove who the real king is! Let's have a fight to prove who's the best. The lion thought for a moment and then quietly disappeared in the jungle. A fox was watching the scenario; she became speechless. Without losing a single moment she ran towards the lion and exclaimed in sheer amazement: "What's the matter, my king?" The lion replied calmly: "The donkey has nothing to lose!"

All our lives, from the time our mother taught us to speak we are gathering information; very few transform that information into knowledge. Information is nothing but filling the bio-computer with data so that one day one is able to contest on the Jeopardy show. Information can only create parrots, and parrots are always interested in associations. Just split the word "ass-ociations." The word speaks for itself. They want to be in the front, where people can admire them. The majority of politicians as well as actors are full of information. If ever actors could have intellect, they would refuse movies and shows that have a negative impact on society. If politicians had intellect they would disguise themselves and move among the masses to know what is happening in the life of a common man, but they do not have any time left from enjoying the perks that come with their position.

There is a vast difference between information and knowledge. From information we get knowledge and from knowledge we experience and get wisdom and from wisdom we move on towards awareness, which is our key to the beyond.

When they are young, we force feed our kids with information to make them productive just like machines. We always teach our kids to struggle to be number one but never teach them to relax and enjoy this gift of life.

Our obsession with being number one has transformed this planet into a living hell. If you take statistics you will be shocked that the number of people who have to appear in a court of law every day or wait for the doctor to check them have exceeded the number of people going to the churches or temples to meditate. The majority of people are mentally, morally, emotionally, and physically sick.

A family takes a wrong exit in Los Angeles and loses their child to gunshots; a man is beaten mercilessly on the streets of Los Angeles, not by gangsters, but by two dozen cops who are supposed to protect the public. While someone loses his life trying to steal a pack of beer in Arizona, the other is beaten to death for being a gay in Wyoming. Bomb blasts have become very common now as there is no fun left in killing a few, so criminals have progressed, too. Genocides, homicides and mass suicides are what humanity is left to. Kids and teenagers have also joined the adults in the game of death. Schools are transforming into assassination camps. Seven-year-old children have started killing six-year-old children. The day is not far when we will be teaching four- and five-year-old children about using guns. It all begins at a very young age.

Is this our purpose? Have we taken birth to defend ourselves in this cruel world? What has brought us here? What is this duality all about? Have you ever tried to explore the mysteries of this duality? Man and woman, male and female, positive and negative, life and death. Are we done with this jumping from one pole to another or we are waiting for the day when we cripple ourselves to the point where we succumb to the darkness without being able to reach the inner light?

Compared to woman, man is more foolish by nature, very childish and ignorant. Man is born out of a woman he calls mother and one day he rapes that very mother. Sounds like a very strong statement but truth is always dark—only lies are white. Were you not born out of your mother's womb? Didn't she nurture you every day until you were able to stand on your feet? Did she not teach you how to talk and walk? Did you not feed on her breasts? This is the small picture, but let's take the big picture. From where comes the food, water and air that we must have every moment of every day in order to survive? From the earth! So what is earth to us? She is the mother, too; are we not raping our mother every day by destroying the rainforests, dumping all those toxic wastes, and creating destructive weapons? The gloomy picture is that our biological mothers have started losing touch with Mother Earth, too. Woman is the only connection for man to ground himself with the earth, so that he can grow and grow, so that one day he is able to touch the sky and remove the veil of illusion in order to reach the supreme father.

Who is this supreme father? We know our biological mother and we know the supreme mother, which is earth, and we know our biological fathers. But where is this supreme father that all the sages, saints, and gurus have always talked about?

It seems God has gone on a long vacation, leaving fate in our own hands. Our future seems to be doomed unless we take charge, as no longer are holy prayers being answered.

There is an interesting story. When God created humanity He wanted feedback from people. Every day people would come to Him with their suggestions and complaints and ask Him to make changes. Finally He got sick of their complaints. He wanted to run away from humanity. He wanted to hide where man would not look for Him easily. So He asked for an emergency meeting with His advisors. The big question was, where should He hide? Some said go to the forest, go live on the moon, hide in the ocean, but God said man would find Him some day. Finally, one very old advisor suggested to God that He hide in the man himself, as man would never look there. He was right—we never look within.

For ages the spiritual masters have been repeating over and over again about the self, inner being, our oneness, but how many have the guts to leave their families and run to the jungle as did Buddha and many others in search of the ultimate truth?

For a common man the truth is not the search for God but the search for his hunger and his survival. Once these are taken care of he enters the realm of the desires hovering around him. Only when there is food in the stomach and a satisfaction in the heart does he get a chance to think what this life is all about.

It seems we are determined to uproot ourselves, not realizing that the vultures of anger, greed, attachment, lust and egotism are feasting on our bodies and mind at every moment and the day is not far when this body will lose its battle and the life form will leave this body in search of another body, in the hope that it will be able to find the supreme father.

Humanity is not lacking in any way; the only drawback is that most people think like sheep in a herd. My point can be proven very easily. Just gather 50 people in a hall and close all doors. Have a door with a sign that says "Not an Exit"; all you have to do is yell "the building is on fire" and run towards the door that clearly displays the "Not an Exit" sign and I can bet that the majority of the people will run towards that door following you, overlooking that sign; very few will have the awareness to think for a moment and look for the exit door.

A person who has not mastered his mind will always look for masters outside of him; as a result, most people are always ready to be followers. It all starts within us and then we practice it in the outside world. We are slaves of our imagination, taste buds, thoughts, desires, and emotions. As our focus changes from the screen of our imagination, it focuses on the world outside of us.

Again, I will give better rating to women compared to men because men are childish by nature; the reason being that men are seldom concerned with their bodies and are happy with their toy called "mind." They live in their minds and the mind never gets old; on the contrary, women are connected with their bodies and live in totality most of the time and their minds age with their bodies. Even though the trend among women has changed for the worse, still most women carry more sense than men, although where we stand today the majority of men are lost in their toys of technology and women are lost in the fascination of fashion.

Men and women do not know about their basic purpose anymore; as a result the gay population is on the rise. Man has started following the woman and women have started following the men. Women are no longer interested in sitting at home, taking care of the kids. They want to go out and make money, have power, and be free from the bondage of taking care of the home front. Giving birth to a new life form no longer amazes a woman. The day is not far when movies like "Junior" will become a reality of life. A woman will no longer be interested in carrying a baby in her stomach for nine months. Man is no longer interested in his male strength. Since World War II, his mind has been fueled by so much of the beauty created around women that all his focus has shifted and he has started imitating women. Man is still fighting because that is his nature, but he has now started fighting his masculinity.

While more and more women have taken seats in front of computers, more and more men have made themselves comfortable in front of mirrors. Do you realize which way we are heading?

Humans are not only losing touch with the outside world but also losing touch with themselves, where the potential to unmask this illusion lies. We have created all the escape routes to run away from ourselves so that we should not run into ourselves as Jesus, Buddha, and many others did. All we do is talk about our faiths, trying to market our beliefs because we do not even believe in our beliefs and we are constantly looking for others to support our belief system. If you are a Christian, have you ever found yourself looking for that Son of God in another human not belonging to your faith, or if you are a follower of Islam have you tried looking for Mohammed in a Christian, Jew, or a Hindu? No! Because within your heart, you have not allowed Jesus, Mohammed, or Krishna to be a guest and all your search is focused on looking for someone who can support your belief; what you are doing is no more than hero-worshipping.

We have not only lost the ability to relate to ourselves but to others, too. Religions are nothing but empty bottles of liquor with labels saying: "Drinking the contents will make you enjoy bliss." The people who found the divine nectar and drank it left behind the empty bottles of religion but the poor humans have made new labels saying: Drinking the contents of our brand is the only way to enjoy bliss. "Caution: Watch for imitations."

They have made their own recipes and filled these empty bottles with their own creations. No wonder each religion has been divided into so many groups; each has its own interpretation of the ancient recipes to enjoy the divine nectar.

In order to live a meaningful life, we must divert our focus inwards, towards our bodies, our thoughts, our feelings, our being, and our inner selves.

We can only achieve this if we know our relationship with ourselves because what we feel about us, we also feel about the world. Our reaction to the outside world is based upon our thinking patterns. If we have anger within us, then for us this world is full of criminals. If we have hate within us we turn to racism. If we have guilt, we take shelter under the flag of religion. Unless we know how to relate to ourselves, we will never learn how to relate to others. We need to know our type, what we are— our potentials and our drawbacks.

Let's look into who you are and what potentials you have and then it will be easy for you to move on in this life in a fulfilling way, as you will have a better understanding of who you are and with whom you are dealing, since the trouble starts when we do not know ourselves. When we miss ourselves we miss the world.

2
Know Thyself
The Science of Body Features

You are constantly making or breaking your future: Your thoughts, your words, your actions, the food you eat, and the people you move around are constantly contributing to your growth or destruction. Every breath you take is influencing a change in your physical features on a gross level and your consciousness on a subtle level. Your body is the blueprint of your inner state. How much glow you have on your skin, the aroma of your sweat, the sweetness of your breath, the shine, clarity and the liquidity in your eyes, the flow and pitch of your voice, the shape of your features, the lines on your palms, all these are the indicators of the inner state of your being. If you are kind, loving and down to earth, you will carry the vibes of a person who is a giver. On the other hand, if you hate yourself, are egotistical and cruel, your physical features will indicate that very clearly. No matter how much you hide your true self from others, people who have the ability to look through you have already read you even before you had a chance to open your mouth.

In India, we call this science **"Sharir Lakshan Vigyan,"** which was blessed to mankind thousands of years ago by a Rishi (Saint) known as **Samudrik;** this science is also known as **"Samudrik Shahstra."** We will call it "The Science of Body Features" so that it is easier for the western mind to understand.

By getting acquainted with our physicality, we can know why we think, feel and act in a particular way. Even though we are all made of the same combination of five elements consisting of air, fire, water, earth, and ether, and we all have the same organs and the same composition of blood flows through our bodies, we are still very different and very unique. We are so unique that if four people are sitting together, all four could have a different blood type.

Every part of the body is connected with a particular area of the brain. The thought waves we get from the universal databank and the thoughts that manifest in our conscious mind along with our actions influence the shape, size, color, and appearance of our physical features. Any major variation in our thinking patterns or any action that overwhelms our psyche—e.g., depression, rage of anger or hate, killing someone or watching someone being killed, or death of a close one, extreme guilt and resentment, or even winning a big amount in the lottery—can trigger a change in the shape and appearance of a particular body feature over a period of time. We are not aware of ourselves and most people hate their own existence, and thus we do not care much about the changes that take place on our outer surface; moreover, these changes can take several days to several weeks. The only way we can keep ourselves updated is by using the science of palmistry, as the lines on the palms can appear or disappear in as little as 24 hours to a few days. These changes appear in an instant on the iris of the eye. The day is not far when palmistry, iridology, physiognomy and phrenology will become necessary tools to solve human problems.

The way an individual thinks, acts, and talks, his voice pitch, his actions, and even his destiny—none of these would match with another individual. Even if two children are born at the same time, in the same hospital, to different parents, they will both live different lives even though their horoscopes will be the same—the reason being their physical features are based upon their past karma, which is in precise alignment with the parents one is born to, as the DNA of both parents determines one's physical features as well as one's mental makeup.

The father carries the seed (sperm) that is planted into earth (mother) and a child is born after nine months. Your gross (physical body) has been contributed by your mother and the subtle (soul power) has been contributed by your father. If you look deeply you carry the whole existence within you from a stone to the supreme soul. You carry the elements found within a stone and you also carry the light of the supreme soul. If you look at a drop of semen under a microscope you will find many sperm and each sperm would carry a speck of light. That speck of light is the soul power within the sperm.

The left side of your body indicates the state of your female energies and your biological mother and the right side of your body indicate the male energies and the state of your biological father. If you divide your face right in the middle, as in the figure below, the left side of your face will reflect your mother's side and the right side of your face will reflect your father's side.

Since eyes are the windows to your soul you can also notice the difference in the shape and size of your eyes. It all depends upon your parents. If they were in harmony at the time of your conception, then your eyes will look similar in shape, size and appearance; otherwise, one eye will be different than the other in shape, size and appearance. If you are a product of harmony and perfection, your face will be like a 3D picture. Your face will reflect each parent from different angles.

One's physical features are the blueprint to the functioning of the mind and body, and the life force or the bio-energy energizes us. As we grow old our physical features change in appearance and these changes are based upon the kind of life we have lived and are living.

It is very sad to know that most people know how to operate their fax machines, computers and cars, but have no idea as to how their body functions. Has science ever looked into why men have nine openings in the body and there are only nine numbers? Or why females have nine openings as well, until they reach puberty, when their tenth hole partly opens up? When women have sex for the first time, the door to recreate new life opens up. When the child is delivered after nine months, their nurturing doors open up to feed the newborn. We have created places like "Disneyland" where we pay to get thrilled for a few hours but we never pay any attention to this wonder of nature we carry all our lives, which is the source of all excitement. This whole drama called life is a game of one and zero with one being God and zero being his creativity. If you look at the erect human penis it looks like a number one, and if you look at the open vagina it looks like a zero. All computer science is based upon 0 and 1. One is light and zero is darkness; everything comes into existence out of darkness, and merges into darkness.

If you have a "touch lamp" at home, were you ever thrilled to know that you could only make the lamp function if your flesh touched the lamp, and it would not work if you touched it with your nails or hair, even though both are part of your body? If the same hair is combed in a very dry place, you can see sparks flashing out of your hair. The fact of the matter is that you are so busy with the toys technology has created that you have never even tried to venture into the mysteries of the body. It is very obvious that our unawareness towards our self is inversely proportionate to the advancement in technology. As the technology is developing we are getting more and more hooked on it, forgetting and moving away from our own existence.

We know how many moons Jupiter has and how hot it is on Mars but do we know why we have five fingers and nails on each finger and what the moons on the fingernails signify? Each finger represents each element we are made of, and nails are the barometers of the energies connected with these elements. Nails carry the log files pertaining to the functions of the body and the working of the conscious and unconscious mind.

This might shock you, but if a human kills another human out of hate, anger or jealousy, the nails on the hands of the killer will turn black in color and become deformed and crooked. Similar effects can be seen on the hands of a woman who has aborted her fetus at a very late stage. People who practice black magic or voodoo to harm others have black or rotten nails as well. During my research I was amazed to see that alcoholics who have been involved in automobile accidents, and who became instrumental in taking someone's life because of negligence, had their nails turn black as well—the reason being that the nails are the indicators of the life force within us, which runs this cosmos, this galaxy, this solar system, our planet Earth, and all life forms on this planet including our bodies. Since, as humans, we are in a higher state of consciousness, we have not been given the permission to kill others unless we are forced into a state where it becomes necessary to defend ourselves. If the same bio-energy is used to kill another human out of grudge, hate or anger, we have used our will to perform an action that belongs to the dark energies, or the right way to put this would be: we have allowed the dark forces or negative frequencies to use our body, mind, and life force to destroy another life form, and as a result our energies are disrupted within. Nails, the indicators of this life force, will display the negative effects in black and white. We can save ourselves from future negative events just by keeping track of all these changes that take place in our physical bodies.

If you go a little deeper, the awareness within us has been blessed with this vehicle called a body to explore and venture into this material life. Now when we run over another being not by an accident but with rage, anger and hate and destroy the other, we are branded as criminals by the laws of nature. We might evade the human laws with the power of money but the laws of karma do not provide us with an attorney to defend us and save us from divine justice. The laws of karma do not care whether the cap fits or not, the karmic laws are that one size fits all.

If the law can use this secret, it would help detectives focus on the right person and murder cases like the Jon Benet Ramsey case could be solved in no time. Whether the parents were involved or not could be determined just by looking at the nails of her father and mother, and the same goes for the drama of this century's O.J. Simpson murder case. The Joseph Amrine case could be decided in two minutes using the science of body features.

The murder trial of Raffi Kodikian, who says he killed his friend to end his suffering, could be solved with 100% fairness because justice is blind and this blind justice has molded our social structure to be ugly and unfair. Just by looking at the nails of Raffi Kodikian, one could determine whether his act was out of compassion or cruelty. If the nails on his hands are of perfect color, shape and texture, he is 100% innocent; but if the nails on the thumb, index finger, middle finger and the ring finger show any sign of discoloration and carry a blackish tint, the killing took place out of hate, grudge or anger, and not out of compassion as he stated.

We all carry the devil and the divine within us, and we all carry the ability to create and destroy based upon the state of consciousness we are in.

If someone hurts you emotionally, the color of your lips will change to shades of black. If you have powerful vibes, you can cause equal or greater damage to the person who caused you that hurt because we all live in a vast web of energies and are able to tap certain negative or positive frequencies to hurt or heal others based on our understanding of these frequencies. We come into this life with immense power to create or destroy. Devil and Divine are both within us and we have been given the choice to use either.

Here is another eye-opener. If you are suppressing your emotions and resisting tears, the big toe on your left foot will start bending towards the left as shown in the figure below.

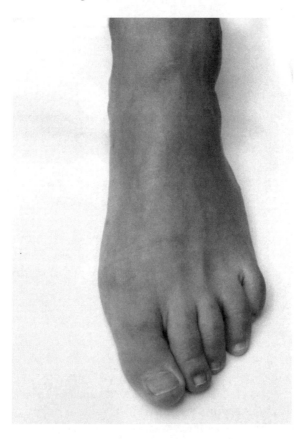

If you are not resisting negative thoughts, negative circumstances or negative people, in other words, if you are not being aggressive in saying no to the negatives in your life, your big toe on the right foot will start bending towards the right as in the figure below.

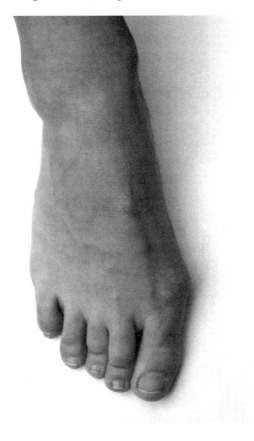

If both toes have bent in opposite directions from each other as in the figure below, you do not know when to cry or when to resist or when to be active and when to be passive, and what you have been doing is actively resisting the tears and passively taking the abuse within you, allowing yourself to getting burnt on mental and emotional levels.

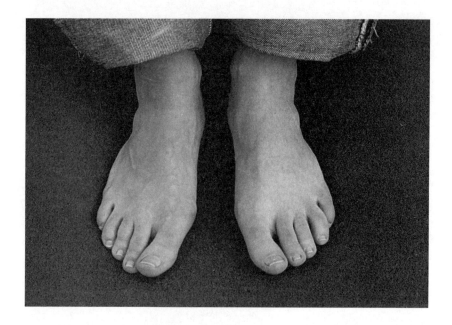

In order to dive deep into the ocean of your life, you will need some extra gear that has never been available to you before. In order to assimilate this new knowledge you must become childlike, and it is important that you do not judge and form an opinion about yourself or others using the secrets of this science, since by knowing some of the secrets you will know the type of person you are and the people you deal with. Another thing: since this book is not meant to be a book on the science of body features, I have given only those basic secrets that you will need to live this life happily and walk in harmony, and help others walk in harmony on this road called life.

My humble request to you is to become childlike: innocent, pure and creative.

When was the last time you had a chance to look at a flower plant every single day? To look at the buds appearing and then the buds opening slowly day by day and finally the bud blossoming into a flower? Isn't it amazing to see the flow of the nature? Now find pictures of when you were a toddler, a teenager, and notice the difference. Now go stand in front of the mirror and give a good look at your face. Your face is no less than a bud waiting to bloom. Our face is like an incipient flower; when we come a step closer to the bloom time, clear signs show up on our face, hands and feet. Just like a bud blooms into a flower, the same way the flowering happens on the face as we grow in our consciousness. Enlightenment is nothing but the flowering of this human life; unfortunately, the majority never reach a stage where the flowering happens. The human attachment to flowers is not a mere coincidence.

This science is so fascinating that just by looking at someone's face, hands and feet, an abundance of secrets about the past, present and the future are revealed; secrets about relationships, love life, root cause of chronic illnesses, emotional blocks, sex power, love power—the list is endless. *Spiritual Path,* whether it is meditation or devotion, spiritual masters have always emphasized choosing the right path. Using this science, we can easily figure out between a con man and a holy man. All you need is to look at an individual's face, one feature at a time, and then at the whole face in its totality.

It might amaze you but there are only three types of people found on our planet. The first kind of people belong to the "Deva Ghan"; the only translation I can have for this Sanskrit word would be the ***Angel Group.*** Look at your lips and see if they turn upwards at the ends, just like in the next figure.

These kinds of people are born with positive attitudes towards life and are good at controlling others. They always feel that they are right and it is hard for them to be wrong or take any blame. They love the material and their lives revolve around fun and enjoyment. The most fascinating thing is that a great majority of these people are found among the lighter skin colors; they have their lips going upwards. They belong to the "might is right" and the "my cup is always full" type. They are at ease with being positive at all times, but if something negative happens to them they get baffled and lose their balance of mind. They love to live their lives in illusion and they hate to fail in life as it hurts their egos, making them feel useless, since they are achievers; life should always be on the go for them, and any kind of stagnancy will be taken as suffering. On the spiritual side, they cannot believe in the philosophy of Buddha as "Duka"; suffering is not their piece of cake. Even if you find them attracted towards religion, it would be to win the game of life using the religious market. Overall, these kinds of people are here to compete, enjoy and win the game of this material life, as their sole purpose is to win at any cost. These people will find themselves more connected with Krishna's Philosophy, if at all they are interested in spirituality. I have yet to see a honest spiritual guru who has his lips going upwards. Yes! You will find heads of religious institutions, Preachers, Vedic Pundits, New Age Gurus marketing their spiritual candies using their odd (numbered) laws.

The second type is where the lips are horizontal, just a straight line which joins the upper lip and the lower lip. These belong to the "Manushya Ghan," or the **Human Group.** See the figure below.

These kinds of people carry a balance within their minds. On a deeper level they are adventurous and give an illusion of being swayed by the circumstances and people around them, but in reality they are experimenting and weighing life. They try to experience what others tell them, but in the end they find their own balance and move accordingly. These people are the smartest kind because they have taken this birth after finding their balance in past lives, having lived and experienced lives as angels and devils. These people are the real explorers. On the spiritual side, these people will want to know both Buddha and Krishna, and then find their own paths. They have experienced the valleys as well as the peaks, and in this life they have been given the ability to find the tunnel to their being. One can only grow in consciousness if one has started practicing being humanlike; the other two kinds must rise or fall to the level of humans in order to start a journey back home.

The final kind is where the lips go downwards as you see on the face of a child when the child is unhappy, angry, and in a bad mood, as shown in the figure below.

These kinds of people belong to the "Rakshasha Ghan" or the **Devil's Group.**

The Devil's Group is either Buddhist by nature or masochist. These are the kind of people who are always in a state of hopelessness and helplessness and these negative traits become their driving force to survive in this world; they use these oars of hopelessness and helplessness to row in the sea of life towards the holy realms of Christ (purity), or towards the lands of sinners.

They are very self-judgmental and their cup is always empty. They are angry with themselves and others and are either extremely cruel or extremely kind by nature, depending upon other contributing physical features. They are very good disciplinarians because discipline needs certain cruelty. Most are cruel with their own selves unless other factors support their cruelty towards others. They always look for the negative and are very comfortable with it, and it is not always easy for them to take positivity or happiness. Hate for the self is very common among this group of people as they think that they do not deserve to be happy. The more drooping the lips are at the ends, the more hopeless and helpless they are, but since their driving force in life is negativity, you will always find them struggling as struggle is their mascot.

These people are revolutionaries because they dwell in a negative state of mind; they rebel against themselves, against parents, and against society, and in the process they not only bring a change into their own lives but also become instrumental in changing the lives of masses, whether it is a positive change or a negative one. You will find Hitler and Mother Teresa among this kind.

Yogis and saints are also found in this group because the hopelessness and helplessness helps the individual steer one's consciousness towards something that is more potent than this illusory and miserable human existence. To dive deep into the world of God, one must become disillusioned and discontented by this repetitive and boring human existence, and hopelessness and helplessness are the two essential keys to opening the doors to one's inner self.

Here is a simple test you can do in the privacy of your home. This test will tell you how much you love or hate yourself. Make yourself comfortable in front of a large mirror. Look straight into your eyes and do not blink, let your eyes water—keep looking for few seconds, a few minutes; try to be as loving as possible and start whispering: I love you, I love you, while looking straight into your eyes. Now, if you really love yourself you will laugh with joy or become emotional and tears will start rolling down your cheeks. These are the tears of inner bliss.

If you are full of ego and are obsessed by your body and mind, you will think that this is crazy and you will want to move away; in that case, you are so lost playing with this toy called a mind, that you have not been able to explore the worlds of love or hate. The last thing that will happen to you is that within a few minutes you will start hating your own face and will stop looking at yourself in the mirror.

Once you know your type and the state of consciousness in which you are, it will be easier to reach that goal of being in the middle state of the human group of people.

At this point, you must be thinking: what is the function of the hair, eyebrows, eyes and nose, etc., besides their biological functions? Here are your answers:

The *Hairs* on our heads are our antennas to communicate with the universal mind, and the hairs on the other parts of the body represent the quality and quantity of energy within us.

The *Forehead* represents the quality of the bio-computer we are born with.

From the *Eyebrows* we can see the quality of the human electronics (the quality of bio-energy or the circuit board), as well as the amount of sex energy available to the man, and the state of the energy within the breasts of a woman. This might shock women, but if you pluck too many hairs from your eyebrows and make them pencil thin, you are risking the health of your breasts.

The *Eyes* are the windows to the soul. From the eyes one can look at the state of one's consciousness. Calm, clear and peaceful eyes are the best. The best way to do an eye comparison is to look at the eyes of the cow or deer. These two animals have the best eyes. Then look at the eyes of the vulture, wolf, shark or a snake. Now it will be easier for you to look at humans and know the state of consciousness in which they are.

The *Nose* is the potential meter.

The *Ears* are the indicators of the amount of cruelty and compassion a person has. Fleshy ears indicate compassion while very thin ears indicate a lack of compassion.

The *Cheeks* become the joy meter or the sorrow meter. Rounded cheeks indicate inner joy, while flat or sunken cheeks indicate unhappiness.

The *Teeth* are the indicators of sexual enjoyment as well as the state of one's stomach. Clear, white, well-aligned teeth indicate good stomach and good sex life, while rotten, discolored, unshapely teeth indicate stomach problems and a lack of sexual power. Since mankind is obsessed with sex and half of the marriages fall apart just because one partner is not enjoying sex, here is the secret related to one's ability to enjoy sex as well as to help the other to enjoy sex: The lower teeth are the indicator of female power or receptivity and the upper teeth are the indicator of male power or the potential to give. Now if the lower teeth are not aligned properly and are crooked, the person will have a hard time enjoying sex, and if the upper teeth are crooked, the person will have a hard time giving enjoyment to the other person. There are tons of hidden mysteries just in the shape of the teeth but we will not discuss them here.

The *Gums* are the indicator of the quality of the blood within the body: Pink gums indicate healthy blood, while dark red, blue or blackish gums indicate blood that is full of toxins.

The quality of male energies and female energies one has brought into this life can be seen by analyzing the *Lips,* as the upper lip is the indicator of male power and the lower lip of female power. Lips are a very strong indicator of your emotional state. If your upper lip is discolored and does not show shades of pink to dark red but instead carries blueness or blackish tint, you are not in harmony with the male energy or issues relating to your spiritual side. If the lower lip shows discoloration, then the female energy within you is disturbed causing emotional imbalance, and you are also not comfortable with your body or with your existence on the planet earth. Smokers, alcoholics, and drug users have both lips discolored because they are not only abusing their bodies and the environment but also abusing the sensitive unity between body, mind and the energy (soul), as our existence is dependent upon the oxygen that fuels the fire within us. The color of the lips is also related with the functioning of your organs: the upper lip is the indicator of the liver and right kidney and the lower lip is the indicator of the spleen, heart, and left kidney. The area under the eyes also indicates the state of the kidney functions.

The shape of your hands determines your relationship with the outside world. Issues relating to the exchanging of your energies can be seen clearly by the shape of your hands, and the length and shape of the fingers. All your fingers should be perfectly straight, especially the middle finger and the little finger. If your middle finger is bent as shown in the figure below, you are rigid and stubborn and you have a strong need to work on your "I am right, you are wrong" attitude . The angle of bend on the middle and little fingers in the picture below is an extreme example and on a scale of 1-10 with 10 being the worst I would rate the picture below a perfect 10.

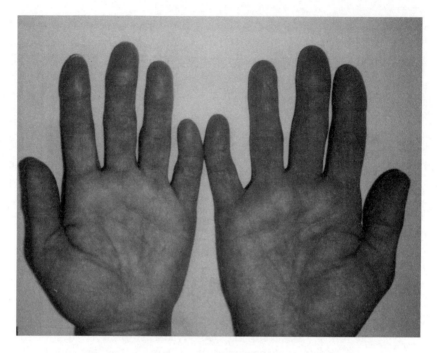

If your little finger is bent as shown in the figure above, you always think about others and in the process forget yourself. It might amaze you but the majority of people from the Angel group have their little and/or middle fingers slightly bent. The obsession for the "I" is so strong that it makes them lose their connection with their inner self.

When you travel by air and the plane taxis to the runway, the flight attendant always explains to you that in case of an emergency, oxygen masks will drop, and you must put the oxygen mask on yourself first and then help someone who is in need. People who have bent little fingers neglect themselves and go out of their way to do things for others and please them, and then they expect others to treat them the same way. Sadly, it never happens and this is one of the major causes of disharmony among humans. People with bent little fingers must stop thinking about others, and must stop going out of their way to do things for others and then expecting others to act the same way as they do.

The smoothness of your body, the shine of your skin, the straightness of your body features, the calmness within your eyes, the fleshiness of your body, the brightness and fleshiness of your lips, all point in one direction—that your quality is very superior.

On the other hand, if any part of your body shows a lack of shine, clarity or luster, you can rest assured that you are lacking in that area and need to work on yourself.

Do you want to have a high quality body and a high quality life?

Here are some tips:
1. Know and love your body, listen to your body, respect it, and take good care of it.
2. Eat healthy and eat compassionately; if your food comes from a cruel source it will contribute to cruelty within you.
3. Spend a few minutes every day looking at your body parts and rubbing them with your palm with love and compassion within your heart.
4. Take care of the hairs on your head as they are the antennas to communicate with the universal mind; if your hair is lusterless, dry, or lacks direction, your life will be no different. On the other hand, if your hair is clean, shiny and well directed, your life will also carry that shine and direction.
5. Ears: Check if your ears are fleshy (compassionate) or paper-thin (cruelty). The percentage of your ear that is fleshy will equal the compassion within you. If your ears are thin, try being compassionate towards your own self and towards others, and your ears will start becoming fleshy with time.
6. Eyes should be calm and peaceful and if you are unable to look at your own self in the mirror with love, then you are full of guilt, anger and self-hate.
7. Lips should be pinkish to bright red; pinkish means you are still in the learning stage and bright red means you have already acquired knowledge and are ready to use it for your own self or for others. If you have dark lips, then you need to relax and let go of your negative past.
8. Teeth should be clean and sparkling white. If they are yellow, rotten, dirty, or broken, you will be instantly rejected by others, either subtly or visibly depending upon the guts of the other person. If your teeth are in really bad shape, you are bound to be socially rejected.
9. Finally, eat right and eat slowly, enjoying your food. The amount of calmness and anger one has is directly related to the way one eats.

3

Thoughts

Thoughts are entities, both good and bad, and their life depends upon your "Prana" (breath) or the life force to play on the merry-go-round of your mind where thoughts are riding all the time. They are harmless until you start nurturing them with your emotions. Once they have access to your emotions, they have the power to kill or create. If you want to live happy and fulfilled you must know how to play with thoughts.

The moment we drop out of our mother's womb, we have stepped into the world of thoughts. Our present life is an outcome of the thoughts from past lives and our future existence will be an outcome of our present state of thoughts. We are born around thoughts, live around thoughts, and will die around thoughts, and the kinds of thoughts that manifest in our conscious mind are based upon our past lives and our present circumstances. The energy of thought is so powerful that we can create or kill with thoughts. Were you ever taught about the thought process in the school, what thought is? The power of thoughts and how to use them? How thoughts have a negative polarity and a positive polarity?

No! You were taught just enough to become a machine that would know how it has to survive and become usable to society.

Thoughts are electrical signals which are picked up by our unconscious mind from the universal consciousness and then filtered and sent to the conscious mind where the "I" within us either processes the thought for action or discards it; the whole process is very scientific. The kinds of thought waves we get are based purely upon the state of our conscious and unconscious mind and the state of our soul.

Our birth in a particular country, religion, family, and into a male or female body, is the outcome of the collective thought patterns that are stored in the karmic databank that we have carried on from past lives into our present life and will carry on to the next one.

All thoughts that come onto the screen of our conscious minds are stored in our unconscious memory whether we accept them or reject them; all actions and all emotions are stored in our unconscious memory as well. Whether we have thoughts of fear, anger, love or hate, all is stored. That is one reason people suffer from phobias; some are scared of heights, some from water and some from animals, as they are all experiences that took place in the past or in past lives.

The way one dresses, talks, and acts shows the state of one's thought patterns. It is not just Hollywood or Bollywood where movies are made; we are constantly making movies in our minds and projecting them on our lives.

Without thoughts one will either be in the state of a Buddha, or Buddhu (idiot in Hindi).

A poor man could think like a king or a king could think that he is no more than a beggar in his life. It's all because of thoughts; we continue taking births based upon our thoughts and desires. This world is a mere hollow-deck as they show in the new "Star Trek" show.

We have existed in the past and we will exist in the future and we will always exist; even enlightenment cannot destroy our being—all it does is to dissolve the "I" within us. What we are today, at this very moment, we have stored within our bodies; the experiences of all the lives we have ever lived, but the memory of the past is not accessible to us as we have become so weak that we cannot handle the drama of our day-to-day life. If by chance or by accident that storehouse of the past, that hidden hard disk, is made available to us, our bio-computer will crash and could become unusable, unless and until we prepare ourselves to have access to the past lives.

Let's go back into your life; just think of any episode which has impacted your life for better or for worse, good or bad experiences—they are stored equally within us—but we have a tendency to retrieve bad experiences exactly the way they happened more than good ones as 99% of humanity live in misery 99% of the time. Only 1% of the world population is happy and for them life is a bed of roses, such is their thinking process.

So this experience happened to you some 20 years ago and even today the memory is as alive as it was 20 years ago. Do you think it will fade away after another 20 years? No! It will stay as fresh as you want it to be. Unless and until you make a conscious effort to discard that episode, it will stay as alive as if it happened yesterday or only a few hours before. Even if you tried to erase it with meditation, affirmation and other techniques available to us, all you would be doing is separating it from the emotional energy and then the episode will lose power as the link between the memory and the emotions is broken forever, since you have made a decision to unplug the emotional current that was feeding a particular thought or episode.

Hypnotists and healers use the same principle. They backtrack your mind into the experience and you are made to relive that experience, and at that sensitive moment they add a few lines in the data that this software or experience is no longer needed by you and in the process the emotions connected with the episode are separated. You will not be able to cry or laugh anymore, but it will still be there in your memory with no feelings connected to it, no emotions. In your sleeping state you could dream of being a king but once the dream is broken you do not cry for the rest of your life that you have lost your kingdom. If you want to explore deeper into your mental and emotional problems, search for "Concept Therapy" on the Internet.

Our mind is a movie studio and a theater of our own, and actually a step ahead because we also use our senses of touch, taste, and smell in our real-life movies. The day is not far when the TV will transmit an aroma along with the picture, or when science will able to know the base aromas just as science has known the base colors. Your TV will come with an aroma cartridge just as your printer has a color cartridge.

Whether we survived a horrible experience in the past or past lives, or a good one, all is stored within us just like a movie stored on a DVD, and based on the power of our being, we are able to assimilate or become addicted with the experiences. If the "I" within us stays sharp and aware, we learn from those experiences and move on. Otherwise we keep on playing it over and over again, adding to our collection of miseries or fantasies.

People become addicted to drugs for the same reason as do people who are born in male bodies but are always trying to make them look female in the mirror. These are all examples of how we get addicted to our experiences. Imagine a boy who is still in the development stage left in the company of teenage girls, whom he has never experienced, and the females dress or undress, and he has never seen his mother putting on all that makeup; he gets a kick out of it. Just for fun's sake, these teenage girls ask this young lad if he would like to put on these female clothes, and if he says yes, he is in for trouble for the rest of his life because society has separated even clothes into male and female, and once that little boy sees himself as a female in the mirror he has plugged into the consciousness of females; if he likes and loves his new image, he will spend the rest of his life reliving that state over and over again.

Since our present life is a continuation of our past lives, I would strongly say that the outcome of being a drag queen or a transvestite is not always a psychological disorder—half of the time it is karmic, and is due to a unfulfilling female past life or to having too many lives in the male body, and one has taken this life in a male body in a state of confusion; he has taken birth in a male body but his unconscious mind is accessing the thoughts belonging to the female body.

Do you realize that in ancient times, clothes were never male or female and men could wear jewelry as women did? Now the social structure has changed, dividing men and women to the point of lunacy so that now we even have pens, notebooks and cars exclusively made for females or males. Now a male cannot use something that is pink, or he will be labeled "gay." The west started the concept with the sexual revolution and the east is catching up now. Back in the 1950s and 1960s, pink Cadillacs used to be the fashion among men, and now one could lose one's life, as one would be taken as gay.

Day by day humans are becoming slaves to the collective consciousness of the mass media and individual uniqueness is evaporating. Humans are growing up to be Madonnas, Michael Jacksons, Harrison Fords or Elvis Presleys. No longer are we **"US,"** or **"OURSELVES."**

We live in the world of thoughts and our actions are based on the thoughts we receive, which are entirely dependent on the state of our awareness. As long as this chain of thought exists, we will always exist, exactly the same way our memories will always exist until the "I" dissolves, at which point we have unplugged the memory from the emotional energy and have gone beyond this duality.

Let's presume that despite all the people Hitler killed on this planet, he had some good karma left from past lives and he is reborn to parents who are very spiritual-minded but have negative karma from past lives; as a result they became instrumental in bringing such a burdened soul to this world. So Hitler gets another chance to go beyond his negative past. Now the bio-computer he got in this life is very spiritual but his past is very dark. What is going to happen? He will dream of terror, live in terror and guilt, eat in terror unless and until he has made a good rapport with his existence. Just as the planet earth has an ozone layer which protects the planet from harmful radiation, we have a psychic web protecting our astral body, which filters negative thoughts. So our Hitler has been reincarnated with a weak protective web due to his negative past; as a result his unconscious mind will not be able to resist and filter his negative thoughts and those polluted thoughts will seep into his conscious mind and will haunt him day in and day out.

Here is a real-life experience, which I went through about 12 years ago. I was living in Mill Valley, California, at the time. One of my best friends, Andrea, called me one day and said that she would like me to go with her to an introductory class being offered by a chiropractic doctor known as Doc, and so I went with her just out of curiosity. About 15 people were present in the hall, and I was sitting there watching Doc as he demonstrated his extraordinary abilities to go into the past lives of people and erase their karmic blocks. When he was done with the person he was working on, he said, "Let's see who's next." I started concentrating within my thoughts to pick me, and he did, such is the power of thought. So I relaxed myself on the table and he made me say the following affirmation: "I release my addiction with coffee and sugar." I interrupted him and said that I am not addicted to sugar and coffee; on the contrary, I do not even like coffee. He said that four lives ago, I was in Rome as a merchant and I was addicted to sugar and coffee, and since my mother's family came through me, there is a family history of diabetes in my mother's family, which was 100% accurate. Just to let you know, I never had diabetes then or now, but most of my uncles and their children from my mother's side have this problem. How could he know about my family history?

I became more curious and as a result I signed up for his workshop, which was going to take place the following weekend. Next weekend came, and Andrea and I went to his weekend workshop. There were about 12 people in the workshop including Doc and his wife, a few Germans, and some Americans. I was the only person from India in the group. It was a kind of international mix destined to be there. The workshop started with general discussions about Doc's background and about his wife, who was there to help Doc with his workshop. Off and on Doc would ask people to repeat sentences after him.

We were all sitting in a circle around Doc; that's what we called him. All of a sudden he turned to this American lady in her late 40s and asked her to release the guilt she had connected with the massacre of males she ordered on the planet Venus. In an instant, she started crying from the deepest core of her heart and started saying that all her life she has always felt guilty, even as a child, and she never knew what the reason was. Doc said that millions of years ago, there was life on the planet Venus, and the planet was dominated by females. The woman was a figure of power on Venus, where she had ordered that the testicles of many males be chopped off in order to punish them.

I felt really sorry for this woman, but also skeptical; at the same time I was chuckling from within, as the scenario was very amusing for me because of the sexual repression that is very common in India. Doc gave her a box of tissues and immediately moved on to a German man and he said, "You were the one whose balls were chopped off, so you repeat after me: I release my anger…" All of a sudden we could see the fireworks of anger on his face and he screamed and cried loudly. Doc gave him a pillow into which he could release all his anger, and made him say some more affirmations to release his anger. Suddenly he moved towards me and said, "Yours too"; that was all he said, "Yours too," and my body started trembling vigorously, each part shaking on its own as if I were having a fit. In a trembling voice, I asked Doc what was happening and he said that energy was being released that had been blocked all this time; the shaking and trembling continued for almost 45 minutes as the workshop continued. During the break he told me that Andrea was my friend on the planet Venus but could not do anything for me at the time. It became very obvious to me that past lives are as true and alive as our existence at this very moment, and there can be no future if there was no past. After this episode my sexual repression evaporated and something opened within me and I started growing in consciousness at a much faster pace than before. I had been obese since my childhood and after this episode I started exercising, eating right, losing weight, and came down from a size 40 to a size 32.

As we read this very sentence, we have left the last word we read in the past but we always have the choice to go back and reread the whole book or the paragraph unless and until the book is lost and goes out of print and not a single copy can be found.

Going back to Hitler; the reason poor Hitler is feeling guilty and negative and is living in misery is because of his past records; the credit rating system of existence is very strict and you do not get a new file when you get a new body. The old records continue until the day you make a conscious effort to erase the data and ask for forgiveness from the higher source and from the souls you have hurt in past lives.

Now you can go back into your life and see if, in your life, you have experienced violence and torture from your father, your mother, your family, friends or strangers. It is you who is supposed to go through the suffering and your poor parents become instruments because of their own negative past. If money is what is giving you problems, then you must have cheated someone in the past and are now re-living your own past. If it is hard to find love, then you must have deceived someone in the past. If you are sick, then you must have become the cause of someone's sickness in the past. If you are unhappy in this life, then rest assured that you were the cause of someone's misery in a past life.

We all come into this body for just one purpose and that one purpose is to erase our past and grow so that we can come out of this cycle of birth and death. But 99.9% of people get stuck in the same old rut of survival and very few reach a state where they come to realize the futility of life and start their journey inward.

There is a very interesting story about Buddha. One day Buddha and his disciple Ananda were sitting under a tree in a small village. Buddha was meditating while Ananda was watching. A man came and spit on Buddha. Being Buddha's staunch follower, Ananda's face turned red with anger; he was about to stand and hit the man, Buddha opened his eyes and asked him to relax. Ananda, still furious, commented, "Why? This man does not even know you yet he spit on you and now you ask me to relax and let it go?" To Ananda's astonishment Buddha replied, "I had been waiting for years for this man to come and clear his karma with me, as this was the only balance left from the past lives and he has discharged me and I am a free man today," and Buddha thanked the old man. Listening to all this, something happened in the old man and he fell on the feet of Buddha and asked for forgiveness.

Are you still skeptical about past lives? Here is an experiment you can do in your real life. Next time you are thrown into a situation where the decision pertaining to your life lies in the hands of a stranger (e.g., your job is at stake and your boss is trying his best to get you fired), relax yourself in a comfortable position and take some deep breaths; breathe in deeply and hold and exhale deeply; follow this pattern about 15 times and then hyperventilate your mind by breathing in and out very fast and deep without holding; do this about 15 times. Go back to the relaxed breathing and visualize your boss. Smile at your boss in your imagination and tell him, "(Your boss's name), I release all negative experience connected with you from your past lives, on all levels of existence where we exist and have existed. I forgive you for the past and I ask for forgiveness from your higher self; I transmute and transform all negative energy into love and from now on we will be neutral as far as our past and present is concerned."

Breathe in deeply and exhale with a long humming sound. Repeat this a few times.

Take a deep breath and try to live what you said a few minutes ago; really feel for your boss and do not give him any nasty looks or send him negative thought vibrations. Also, do not involve yourself in topics at work during breaks where your coworkers are having volcanic eruptions about your boss. You are in for a surprise; in a few days the same boss who was contemplating getting you fired has become a different person, and do not be amazed if he recommends you for a promotion. Even if none of the above happens and you do get laid off, still you will find that a lot of positivity came out of this negative episode. Such is the power of our thoughts relating to our past and present lives.

Man is facing a new kind of problem called depression. One is unable to sleep at night, concentration is lost, and mood stays negative all the time. One becomes hopeless and helpless, even suicidal. If one is physically weak, the body starts showing signs of fatigue, fever, running nose, indigestion, allergies, and we can go on and on. The whole system goes into a mayday situation. What exactly is depression? Too many thoughts, too much thinking, overloading the mind, and one starts having stress, as one has stretched his mind to the extreme in the thought world and now one has a bunch of negative thoughts that take hold of the mind and one is unable to diffuse them and depression starts setting in.

It always starts with stress and then escalates to depression. Tightness around the shoulder area, on the forehead, right above the eyes, in the temple area, in the upper and lower jaws, and at the roots of the thumb area on both hands are all indicators of a stressed body. Stress gets accumulated in the upper part of the body first and then starts moving downwards, affecting the organs. When the body gets loaded with stress it goes into a depressive mode. In depressive mode the nails on the big toes on both feet lose their natural color and become black, hard, or deformed.

What transpires in depression is that one is unable to come out of the depressive state of mind, as one gets lost in the quicksand of slushy thoughts. The source of fresh and positive thoughts dries out and there is a stagnation of thoughts within the conscious mind, and as they rot, the fumes put a pressure on the mind and the mind is unable to extract oxygen from the bloodstream causing the mind to go into a depressive state, and the body goes into a mayday situation, as it depends upon the mind for its functions to operate smoothly. Modern science is very poor and outdated and it has no idea as to what causes depression.

Here is another eye-opener: earth is negative polarity and sky is positive polarity, and we exist in between earth and sky. Our head is in direct contact with the sky, just like a satellite dish, and our feet are always connected with the earth; our existence is right in the middle. When we lose the connection with the earth, which the New Age community calls "grounding," our ability to send negative and corrupted energy to the earth is lost and the communication is broken, thus causing stagnation in the bio-computer. As in a state of depression, we lose the ability to drain old thoughts or recycle them. Depression is primarily a male disease. Very few women suffer from depression; the ones who are mind-oriented and lack a strong connection with their feminine side suffer from this horrendous disease; otherwise, it is purely a male disease.

Please look in the Healing section for a simple remedy to eradicate depression.

If you can stay happy most of the time, there is no way you will ever suffer from stress.

Here is a simple method to check your inner happiness or unhappiness: if you have lived a life that has been full of thoughts of joy and happiness, you will have high cheekbones or very fleshy cheekbones. Whether you are a man or a woman, it does not matter. Your skin quality will be smooth and your face will look like a blooming flower, as shown in the picture below.

In the above picture you can see that the person has high and fleshy cheeks; people with similar cheeks and cheekbones are full of positive thoughts and are happy from within; you can feel this in their company.

Now let's look at the opposite of happiness, which is unhappiness and sadness. As you see in the picture below, the person has no fat on the cheeks—the cheek area is depressed, and his skin lacks shine and clarity. Sadness and a disinterest in life is quite visible on his face. If we compare the two pictures we can see that the woman's face blooms with joy and the man's face shrinks with sorrow. Unhappiness is the end result of stretching oneself between the past and the future rather than living one's life in the present moment. Contentment and control of the mind are key elements towards keeping one's self away from becoming miserable.

The cheek area represents the positive and negative attitudes within a person. If you look at the bigger picture, you will find that only 10% of men are happy, compared to 90% of women who are happy. It is very interesting to see that the majority of women in western countries are unhappy and have depressed cheeks. It is also interesting to see that a great majority of blacks are happy and have high cheekbones despite all the racism they must contend with. It all depends on the state of your inner mind. Your awareness has the ability to control the flow of negative and positive thoughts, but if you are not focused in life, your mind will lack the ability to concentrate on one thought or one area. In most people's minds thoughts are not concentrated but are scattered. These people jump from one thought to another and end up at the original thought they started with, and then start jumping again. They lack the concentration in life and are flops in their personal lives relating to all matters. Since they are so disoriented, and since most have no understanding, they fall for vices on the inner level as well as on the outer level. As they become addicted to negative thoughts, i.e., hate, anger, resentment, guilt, etc., they become addicted to vices like drugs, alcohol, and cigarettes on the outer level; these addictions give them some concentration because smoking is a sort of mantra, as is alcohol. The king of all vices is drugs, where the mantra becomes the master as soon as you give your power to it. The majority of drug users will get hooked and form habits because they will gain a kick in life by chemically slowing the mind and steering it towards their fantasies and illusions. By using the drugs, the "I" within the person loses its grip. But since the "I" is very strong, it fights back, and every time the person will need a higher dosage. When the "I" loses its grip the boundaries drop, so that one who is on drugs who starts laughing will go on laughing, and one who starts crying will go on crying. In the long run, the nerves start becoming numb and the neurotransmitters slow down to the point where the individual becomes dumb and blacks out quite often. One day the individual never returns to his conscious state, as the "I" has lost its war to a chemical and the body loses its connections with the mind, making it unbearable for the life energy to stay as a guest. The host dies and the guest leaves in search of a new host.

Instead of taking drugs, if one is really interested in intoxicating one's mind, the best way to achieve that is by chanting a mantra over and over again. This mantra can be anything from "AUM" and "AMEN" to "ALLAH HO." After you have chanted it a few million times, you will have mastery over the mantra and you will remain drunk in the divine nectar at all times. Not just this—you will be able to perform miracles unknown to common man, heal people, know what others are thinking—it all depends on your dedication and on how receptive your individual chakras are.

We need to use the power of thought to live happily, blissfully, and at the same time, we have to use thought to go beyond thought; it is very tricky because even the thought of going beyond thought is also a thought. But it is the vehicle of thought which will transport the "I" within us to the point where we will have to take the jump into a thoughtless state. It is very much possible, only if we practice and practice.

Remember that thought + action + grace = mission accomplished. Never forget grace, as our existence is much smaller than a microbe in this vast and infinite cosmos; we do not even exist although, interestingly, each one of us thinks that we are more powerful than the collective power of this cosmos.

Thought is our link to the outside world. From thoughts we move on to words and actions. If you are nurturing negative thoughts of hopelessness and helplessness, your future will be hopeless and helpless; if you are giving power to thoughts of hate, you will hate yourself and the world around you; as a result you will be hated by the people around you in the future.

If you are giving power to positive thoughts of love, happiness and creativity, your future will be happy and blissful. Watch your mind; be aware because the thieves of greed, anger, hate, and guilt are always looking for an opportunity to rob your bio-energies, as their survival depends upon you. If you want a good harvest of positive thoughts, you must become a scarecrow for the negative thoughts. Thought is energy, thought is power, and mankind needs to use this power for its liberation, as our only hope lies in the thought.

Use this power of thought to erase your past and try to live in the present because we always live in the past or in the future but never in the present. Use the power of thought to create a loyal friend within yourself who can remind you that you are not the "I" and the "I" within you will start shrinking, and one day, just this friend will exist and not the "I" and then you can say good-bye to this friend as you jump on the bandwagon of thoughtlessness, a state of deep meditation, where you will be greeted by your being, your inner self, the real you.

Your relationship with yourself starts with your thoughts. If you are in harmony with yourself, if you are in love with your own being, yourself, there is no way you will hate the world; then everything outside of you is in harmony including your relationships with other beings around you. Then you will smell of love, breathe love, drink love, talk love, and love is the only vibration you will spread; then you will not find the need to say to others "I love you." The radiance of your love, the power of your love will attract people towards you and any person white, black, brown, whose heart or emotional center is ready to open, will open in an instant.

Some tips to think about:

1. Just as you are aware that you do not breathe in pollutants, just as you are aware that nothing unusual gets into your mouth, just as you are aware that dangerous bacteria does not enter your body and harm your health, just as you are aware that an unknown person does not enter your house and rob you or harm you, follow the same rule with your thoughts. Be very aware that negative, corrupted and inharmonious thoughts do not enter the screen of your consciousness and start multiplying and start destroying the fate of your future.

2. Treat all your thoughts with your love because if you hate a thought you are still giving power to the thought. Love and understanding are the only power we have to deal with the negative thoughts.

3. Think and then rethink before you say or act because your words and actions could cause immense damage to you or to the other person at whom your thoughts, actions, and words are directed.

4

The Mind

Our existence can be compared with a computer: Our body is the motherboard and the mind is the CPU. Where the hard disk is our memory, RAM is our active memory. We are always connected to the universal web or the unconscious mind accessing the universal websites of love, hate, greed, sex, religion, etc. We take this birth with preinstalled software from past lives (genetics) and then our parents install their chosen software, i.e., language, religion, culture, economics, etc., and the society we live in also contributes/updates their versions of these softwares. Overall we live a robotic life where the mass consciousness controls our minds. The majority remain a slave to their minds and very few understand the functioning of the mind and use it as a tool to go beyond the mindless state.

Our consciousness is the "I" in control of this computer, but unfortunately there are many hackers who are trying to take control of our computer. Even though the purpose of our parents, relatives, and friends is to be programmers, unfortunately, many take the role of hackers due to their limited understanding of human life. If we go deeper, the game called life is a mere exchange of data and frequencies where we are creating new games of construction and destruction in a dazed mode.

Very few among us are trying to live this life in a waking state. If that were not the case, then people like Buddha, Jesus, Socrates, Krishna to Krishnamurti, and many other enlightened masters would not have been heard of, and if the majority were not living this life in a dazed mode, then we would not have been killing and spreading terrorism in the name of Allah and waging "Jihad" holy wars or crusades against other humans.

Mindsets are mindsets, whether Mohammed Atta's mindset (who was involved in the World Trade Center attacks) or Frank Silva who shot and killed an innocent Sikh in Arizona mistaking him for someone connected to Islam. One was protecting Allah and the other Jesus. Think deeply and you will laugh because neither of these idiots had a chance to taste the consciousness of Jesus or Allah.

Poor Frank, living in the world's number one country where one is born in an ocean of information—he had no understanding of who he was, not to talk of Sikhism, not knowing that between the 16th and 17th centuries, Sikh Gurus sacrificed their lives to fight the ancestors of Bin Laden, the very same Islamic militants who invaded India from the middle east and were spreading terrorism and would rape Hindu girls and kill Hindu men who would not take Islam as their religion.

For one mistake of the mind, Frank will spend the rest of his life in society's dumpster or society might discard him just like a pest and unlucky Frank thought that he was being a patriot. It seems obvious that he was brought up on **White Lies** and even before he realized the **Dark Truth,** his life was darkened by one act of foolishness conceived by his erroneous mindset powered by corrupted emotional energy.

Was it an act of patriotism or cowardice? Just imagine if someone would have stopped him from killing an innocent human and had asked him to go kill Bin Laden instead, if he was so passionate about avenging the suicide attacks on WTC. Do you think he would have agreed to sacrifice his life for the country?

My answer is a complete no!

Why?

Because patriots are created just like animals are bred. Father is in the Army, Navy or Air Force; the sons follow the same pattern because they have taken that genetic coding from the father. Patriotism is inborn and as they grow on it, it's being fed to them every day. But the nature of the mind is impulsive. Mind is a sucker of rush whether it is adrenaline or drugs, alcohol, marijuana or cocaine. Whether they are joy rides in a theme park or running to win the gold medal in the Olympics, or trying to reach a sexual orgasm, the bottom line is rush. A controlled rush becomes a pre-calculated act of creativity, compassion or violence, but an uncontrolled rush generally ends in an act of anger and/or hate for the self or for others, i.e., rape, killing, suicide, etc.

The mind is just like a monkey, and if you do not put this monkey on the leash of your consciousness or awareness, then I would say, "God bless you first" before it blesses America. If we believe in the theory of evolution: our mind comes from the animal kingdom and we still carry the animal mind or those primitive cavemen's software within our collective consciousness.

The nature of the mind is to race to extremes, to be a master or to be a slave. It is no wonder we have people who have become kings and people who choose to be their slaves. It all depends on how a person tames his mind or on how his mind tames him. Do you know how the wild elephants are tamed and their power controlled? When a wild elephant is caught and brought to the trainer, his front leg is tied with a very strong chain; the elephant tries to break it over and over again and one day he gives up. At that point, the chain is replaced with a strong rope. Now if you look at the rope you will laugh and think that this is like a thread for the elephant—why can't the elephant break it? But if you look at his past you will be amazed to know that he was tied with a strong metal chain at one time. Our story is no less than the poor elephant. We have created our chains of limitations in the past and past lives. The dilemma is that our intellect is more powerful than an elephant's, but within our unconscious we carry the thoughts of being chained for lives, and unless someone who knows the laws of nature helps us erase those thoughts, we will be carrying those thoughts of being chained to our negative past karma for lives to come.

Our consciousness has expanded, and here consciousness has two prongs: the consciousness we have brought into this life and the consciousness of the world around us. Yet the basic functioning of our mind has almost remained the same as it was thousands of years ago. The basic rule of fight or flight is as good as it was millions of years ago.

Our reactions are instant towards the actions of others. Someone hits us; we hit back, whether they are words or actions. The majority have no control over their minds and the primitive monkey is in charge of our bio-computer. The more we lose ourselves, the more control this monkey mind gets; whether it's jumping from one branch to another or from one thought to another, the undercurrent is the same.

The mind is an obsessive perfectionist. Have you ever played chess on the computer? The purpose of the chess program is to beat you and so is the purpose of your mind to beat itself in its own game. Otherwise, why is man so obsessed? You have the world's most beautiful partner but your eyes are always looking for a better one; you have an oceanfront property with a BMW in your driveway and a few million dollars in the bank but you want to have more, maybe an estate or a personal jet. The game goes on and you want to be the richest man on the planet and still do not stop because someone else is trying to compete with you in your mind game. We all play these mind games with ourselves and with others based on our level of thinking.

The nature of the mind is to possess and be in control; it's a cannibalistic slave rider who loves racism. Do this simple exercise and you will know whether you control your mind or your mind controls you: Relax yourself on the bed or on the chair and take a few deep breaths. Now select a word which appeals to you or your mind will start resisting and you have already started losing: if you belong to Islam and I ask you to repeat Jesus, your mind will rebel and start thinking that all those who do not believe in Allah are infidels.

If you are a religious Hindu and I ask you to repeat the name of Jesus, your mind will instantly associate it with a beef-eating, cow-killer white male and give you creeps, and of course if you are a Christian and I ask you to repeat "AUM," your mind will start thinking of a poor monkey-looking man holding a sitar begging for food in the slums of Calcutta. The basic nature of the mind is to be a racist; you love tea but hate coffee, and you hate Chinese people but crave for Chinese food. Even though your skin color is white but your favorite color is black, you dress in black, your furniture is black and the color of your car is black as well, but when it comes to human preferences, your favorite skin color is white and when you see a black person on the road you would like to run over him. It is absolutely not your fault because the environment in which you are born has programmed your mind into having preferences.

Even parents get trapped in the multiple choices of the mind; the son who is rich is the favorite of the parents even though he scolds them every day for not doing a good job of raising their children, and the son who would take care of the parents but is not wealthy is stupid compared to the one who is rich.

The reason the tree of love blooms before marriage and dies after marriage is because of their minds. Before marriage the tree of relationship is nurtured by both, and after marriage each one of them is responsible for their share of nurturing the tree. In the process it dies, as before marriage the choices must be blended but now they have multiple choices; one contributes more than the other or both pull away from the responsibility, or they water it so much that the tree does not die but becomes weak and sags because of too much water. By the way, water is another form of emotion.

So coming back to our test, take a word of your choice and start repeating it slowly over and over again in a repetitive mode. In a few minutes you will start yawning because you are going against the mind and it does not like orders as it is the boss and you are the slave. In few minutes you will stop repeating and become distracted because of boredom caused by repetition or will fall asleep. In both cases you have lost and the mind has won.

People who cannot sleep, people who are on drugs, alcohol, smoking, and other vices are slaves to their minds and do not know how to tame their minds. Since the nature of the mind is obsession, they are obsessed with their minds and cannot create gaps in order to take over their minds. The mind takes them on a merry-go-round where they keep on coming back to the same spot or thought over and over again, and to sleep soundly or to stop smoking one needs gaps in the mind so that sleep can take over or the obsessive pattern can be broken.

If you are very familiar with computers you will know that if you have programmed your computer to doze off after four hours of inactivity and your computer gets locked because of a corrupted screen saver, it will not be able to doze off. The human body is no different. People who are suffering from insomnia have certain thoughts creating a gridlock situation and the flow of the thought traffic is impeded. If you are one of those people who cannot sleep, the only remedy that can help you is repetition of any sound for hundreds of times every day, as it will hammer the struck thoughts and break the gridlock. As a child you must have played these games with your friends, i.e., how would you kill a Pink Elephant? And the answer was with a Pink Elephant Gun. How would you kill a thought? The answer is with another thought.

Mind is our survival tool and we need it at all times; whether it is food, sex or meditation, mind plays a very big role. No matter how delicious the food is, you will not enjoy it unless the mind cooperates; if the mind is not there, sex will turn into a stigma, and if the mind is not controlled in meditation, it is nothing but madness. If the mind is not controlled in religion, it turns into fanaticism. If the mind is not controlled in spirituality, it turns into an overblown ego. I have come across many people who read some books on spirituality, visited a few masters and did some workshops and proclaimed that they were enlightened. In fact, I am blessed to have dined with these so-called enlightened masters many times. When I met some of them after a few years, the enlightenment was nowhere to be seen. This "holier than thou" attitude can be experienced in religions and "religious people" as well.

Each one of us has a unique mind, but sadly we have automated the mind processes so much that our uniqueness is evaporating faster than we can think of and we have turned ourselves into stereotyped robots.

The mind can also be compared with a busy airport; if you are one of those people who cannot think beyond your race, culture and religion, then you have a national airport where only domestic flights of thoughts come and go.

Back in 1982, I was visiting Paris, and since I did not speak French, it took me four hours and many turned-away faces before a Frenchman guided me on the bus routes to the Eiffel Tower. I experienced the same treatment in London on a lesser scale, even though my English is better than that of many westerners. If you have traveled on Brit Rail, you will find everyone is engrossed in his or her own business, and to start a conversation with a British person is like talking to a wall. These men and women have strict rules and regulations about what thought flights land on the airports of their active consciousness.

In America the case is different; if you are in a elevator with another human, chances are you will be approached with one of the following opening lines: "This elevator is going too slow today," or "God! This snowstorm is making things impossible." Now, the elevator does not have a mind that would make it go slow or fast, or the elevator might think that I am sick and tired of going up and down and today I am going to speak my mind. Or when does the snowstorm make things possible? But the mind is a deceiver and wants to protect its identity by coming up with a game plan, which is again the outcome of the duality. If the other responds, great! But if the other does not respond, then you were talking to yourself. One needs certain guts to say the above things directly: Don't you think the elevator is too slow today? Or don't you think this snowstorm is making things impossible? But then you risk being insulted; the other might agree, disagree, or decide not to answer at all. The mind is very protective of the ego, which is the fuel of the mind.

The mind is a loner. Compared to the eastern mind, the western mind is more lonely: everything is on loan and there is no certainty; you have a dedicated partner today and who knows, tomorrow you could be searching for a divorce attorney; you are rich today and you have plenty to waste, but times can change tomorrow and who knows, you could be searching the waste to feed yourself. The loyalty factor is missing from the western mind. You dedicate the precious part of your life with a company; the company grows with your efforts, but you cannot expect any loyalty from the CEO; you could be thrown out any moment, your laughter turned into tears on the spur of the moment.

The west has a mind based on capitalism. Everything is sellable: from sperm to spirituality, the demand should be there and demand equals need, and if need is not there, then discard, whether it is your husband, friend or employee or the plastic fork, paper cup or your wife. "Emotions are for display only." A widow drops a few tears at her husband's funeral and even before the gravel gets a chance to settle itself on the grave, the woman is back in the bar getting drunk, seeking another boyfriend. While kids are left alone in their bedrooms when young, the parents die in hospitals with cards and flowers around them when old; what goes comes back. It seems the western mind is always out of stock as far as emotions go but the emotions are always displayed in the window: "I love you, honey," but within, you are sick of the sweetness and looking for the spice in your life. The blonde, oops! The bond is missing. People smile at you but the love, the caring, the loyalty is missing. In the east, people will not greet you or smile, but will be eager to help you in case you are in distress.

In the west, the left-brain has matured and has become logical, sequential, rational, analytical, and objective. It also only looks at parts, rather than at the whole. The entire western system is based on the left mind; as a result, each part is well planned. From New York City to Los Angeles you will not find much difference: highways, road signs, gas stations, pizza parlors, fast food chains, department stores, downtowns, Broadways, Main Street—everything is well organized and well planned.

The east is right-minded, random, intuitive, holistic, synthesizing, and subjective. It looks at the whole, rather than simply the parts alone. The husband dies, the wife is going to live the rest of her life crying for the departed one, and she will always find that something is missing from her life. She dies in a way with the husband. To talk of remarrying is like killing the memories of her sweetheart; logic is missing from the eastern mind. If we say that, "Emotions are for display only" in the west, we can say with confidence that, in the east, "The mind is for display only" and very seldom used. In the west people have the ability to shut off their hearts, while in the east people have the ability to shut off their minds.

The east is disoriented. In India if you travel 30 miles, language changes, dialect changes, dress changes, food changes, and so on. Very few streets have names and if you are visiting someone's house, the chances are that the address and directions will be something like the following: I live in a white house across from the fruit stand whose owner stutters, and you give these to the rickshaw puller or the taxi driver at the train station and he will take you to the right place; isn't that amazing?

The west appeals to the east; actually the east is crazy about the west because a mall is more appealing than a flea market. The mall is organized and air-conditioned, as is the western mind. But a flea market is like emotions you cannot organize—otherwise, it wouldn't be called "Flea Market." A flea cannot plan her trip every morning: "Today I will fly east 200 yards and then turn 20 degrees north and fly 500 yards before returning to the starting point." The east is no more than a flea market; people and fleas are in the majority and you will find them all over no matter where you go; an accident happens on the road, people gather like fleas. If you get sick, your relatives will swarm your bedroom in no time. You cannot be left lonely, no way. The reason Buddha left his family and ran to the forest is that he wanted to be alone. In the west, it is not possible because you need an ID card, or you could be chanting your attorney's name behind bars. In the west, no one bugs you; people are not only lonely but they are alone, too. Nobody cares whether you are sick or sane; it's a world of psychologists and physicians, and whatever saneness or sickness you are left with is taken care off by psychics or psychedelic drugs.

The east is less mind-oriented than the west; the west is obsessed with the mind, the east is obsessed with emotions. The reason India was invaded by Islamic militants and robbed of their riches was due to the illogical thinking of the rulers; life was fun, many wives, horses, palaces, swimming pools, servants, in-house musicians. The Moguls (Islamic militants) took advantage of this weakness of the mind for a couple of hundred years and then the British scraped out for 200 years what was left behind by the Moguls. India used to be called "The Golden Sparrow." The Mogul invaders and the British de-feathered this so-called sparrow and caged it too. Since Indians were taken for a ride for 400 years, they are coming out of their emotional blindness and have become obsessed on the mind level; as a result, a great percentage of software programmers are the outcome of a new mind-oriented generation. Finally the capitalistic west has sold the mind to the east but the price was huge. In 200 years of British invasion, India was cleaned out of its riches. Poor east, for thousands of years, the spiritual masters preached "No Mind," and in less than 100 years, the west has turned on the eastern mind. The only positive effect the British had on India was the language, otherwise you would have bought a translation of this book. For 18 years people have asked me over and over again: You know English well—where did you learn to speak it? Grow up, Americans: India was ruled by the British for 200 years—who do you think were the teachers in the school? Yet I have also been told many times that English is clearly not my first language. As long as I can get my message to the other person does it matter whether English is my first language? This is a perfect example of mind's dual nature. In India if one's son excels in life, his relatives would say, "We knew from the moment he was born that this boy would grow up to be a prodigy." But if that same boy is a loser, that same relative will comment: "We knew all along that he was a born loser."

Since we live in the world of duality, the mind has its two sides, too, male and female or positive and negative, and with the union of the two sides along with our free will (consciousness) and the energy from our heart chakra, we create our realities. As I write this paragraph my mind is also picturing the thoughts and the thoughts are being energized by my emotions or I will not be able to write. Creativity needs imagination and imagination needs data; the two sides of the mind are intertwined and work in harmony as long as we are aware and are in control but when we leave ourselves to the mercy of the mind, it takes over and destroys this harmony, then we either become obsessed with the male side of the mind (data) or with the female (imagination).

The lopsidedness of the mind can be experienced in drag queens; one is born in a male body and all the body functions are male oriented, but the mindset belongs or has been programmed to be a female, and one is yearning to change that body to a female body. Even though this computer called mind is installed in a male case (body), the operating system is a "Windows FE" where "FE" stands for female edition and the camera (eyes) which have the ability to exchange data with the mind is always trying to change the looks of the computer case (body) into a feminine one—thinking about dresses, make-up, feminine hairstyles, long nails, high heels, and jewelry. The whole focus of the mind is concentrated on female related things.

If God appeared and asked one of the drag queens what their wish was? You know the answer.

If our society were smart we would very much allow/help these individuals to either change the operating software to "ME" (male edition) or help them alter their genetic coding to help the body change the appearance from a male to a female one. If you are not going to like the way you look at yourself in the mirror, it is going to make you ugly from within too, and inner ugliness will only make this world an ugly place to live.

Ramakrishna was one saint of a kind who is a perfect example that the genetic coding can be changed with the power of the mind and the effects can be experienced at the cellular level. Ramakrishna achieved enlightenment many times using many ways. On one of these journeys towards enlightenment, he became a lover of Krishna and in his mind he started thinking that he was a Gopi (female friend) of Krishna and started living each moment of his life thinking that he was a female and his genetic coding started changing to the point that in few months his skin became soft and smooth and the physical appearance became more feminine; he started developing breasts, milk started coming out of his breasts and it will blow your minds to know that he even started getting periods like any normal woman. You can see a picture of him with developed breasts on the Internet at: www.WhiteLiesDarkTruth.com

I do not blame these innocent souls because at least they are being honest about themselves and trying to live their lives as per their mindsets. Since we are all products of male and female combinations, some men are more feminine and some women are more masculine. We have been fed with so much charm, fun and beauty connected with the female body that man has started losing his male balance on the genetic level. On the other hand, women have been fed with so much strength and power connected with the male body that they have started losing their female balance on the genetic level. The future is very clear; in just 20 years we will have a new society consisting of she males and masculine females, so do not be surprised if by the year 2020 the majority of men start dressing up as females. Today more men are visiting salons than 20 years ago and the services they get will amaze you; they get everything done from facials and face packs to waxing of different body parts to eyebrow shaping, not to mention getting regular pedicures and manicures. The reason permanent makeup is getting famous among women is that today's woman is career-oriented and fast-paced and does not want to waste time on make-up compared to just 20 years ago when a woman would spend hours in front of the mirror to look perfect.

Look deeply into men and women and you will be amazed that women are losing breast size and roundness of the body; they are becoming tough and rigid and muscular on all levels, and on the other hand, men are becoming rounder, plump, and have become softer by nature.

It's all in the mind, folks, and our mind is weak and frugal by nature. Advertisers know this secret and use the weaknesses of the mind to sell their products; the race for perfection continues. While life is becoming perfect and easier on the outside, it is becoming more difficult on the inside.

You could afford traveling first class on a 777 and sitting in your state-of-the-art window seat equipped with the Internet, air phone, your personal TV and music channels, and many other gadgets to make your travel comfortable, but within, you are disturbed because the thought craft of divorce has landed on the airstrip of your mind and all the passengers of greed, revenge, hurt, stigma, anger, jealousy, etc., are making your operation impossible. Maybe it is not a divorce but an antitrust lawsuit or it could be a thought implant of breast cancer or colitis by your doctor to make more money.

If you have an expanded consciousness, then you have an international airport where you get flights of thoughts from many parts of this planet earth; then you love Chinese and their food, while you start your day with yoga and Ravi Shankar, the day ends with a few beers enjoyed by black and white friends.

Then we have visionaries whose thoughts roam beyond the galaxies into different dimensions and planes to go where no mind has ever gone before.

The end result is that we cannot live without our physical minds. If our body dies, at least our soul has the choice to look for another body or stay bodyless, but if our mind dies while the body is alive, then we are like a computer without a CPU sitting on the rack of a hospital.

Be mindful and your life will be fulfilled and be mindless and you will be lost in the darkness of the mind. What is meditation? Being mindfully mindless. In order to achieve a higher state of mind, you must practice being a thought traffic controller, or you will start having crashes of thoughts with yourself, with your parents, friends and society. Do not put this bio-computer on the auto mode and do not give your password to others; become so aware that you achieve the ability to intervene in your dreams at any time because what you dream at night influences your life in the day-zed mode.

You are as unique as your mind and your glory is in this unique way of looking at things differently with your mind. Mind your own business, and if you do not know how to start your own business, here are some exercises to be the COO of your own mind:

1. Relax yourself on a chair or bed with your hands at your sides or on your lap; take few deep breaths. On both hands, bring your thumbs under the base of the little finger and close your fist as if you are holding your thumbs in the grip of the fingers; it should not be too tight or too soft. Stay in that position for at least 15-20 minutes and concentrate on your breathing. After 15-20 minutes, release the hold and relax for few minutes before going back to your routine. This exercise will not only control your blood pressure but will help you achieve mind control.
2. Massage your feet and head every day and comb your hair with a non-static comb for few minutes. Keep your scalp in good condition by regularly shampooing it and by massaging it with hot oil.
3. Eliminate alcohol, drugs, cigarettes, and red meat from your diet and drink enough water to keep the blood pH in good shape or you will feel hyper or dull.

4. Do this exercise a few times a week to harmonize the two sides of the mind, i.e., male and female. Make a vertical ∞ as shown in the picture below with the eyeballs while the eyes are closed.

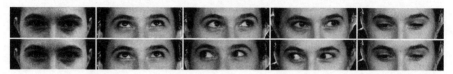

5. The mind's food is oxygen—make regular trips to the forests, oceans and places where there is no pollution and allow yourself to breathe fresh air in and out deeply. Hyperventilate your mind once a day by breathing in and out deeply and quickly for few minutes.
6. Mantra chanting (Mystical Sounds) will not only give you mind control but will open the hidden faculties of the mind.
7. If you loved "Star Trek" like I did and would like to go where no mind has ever gone before, here is a simple technique. Every day at the same time, preferably before sunrise, sit with your legs folded facing east; keep your spine erect and be comfortable; do not be in a stressful position. Now touch your palate with the tip of your tongue and breathe in deeply, hold your breath for 4 counts and breathe out with a loud and long humming sound, just as if a huge swarm of bees is passing by. Let the sound vibrate your whole face, lips and head. Do not let the air escape from your lips and do not control the loudness. Repeat this for 108 times every day. Do it for few months and be patient for the mind to uncloak its mysterious faculties.

5

The Power of Spoken Words

Words are more powerful than swords; with a sword you can kill one at a time but with words you can create a massacre. When words are fueled with emotions, they get tremendous power to create or kill. Use words with caution because you are liable for what you say, as each word you say is recorded in the universal databank and your karmic balances altered.

There can be no words and no action without thought. We get a thought and then we can express the thought through words or through action or use both words and action to express ourselves. As long as we stay within the thought zone we are very safe, but as soon as we use the power of speech or the power of action we have assumed responsibility of the thought or action or both.

Words have tremendous power. When you utter words by giving them the power of your bio-energy, they become nuclear devices on a very subtle level. In many countries threatening another human being is considered a criminal offense in the eyes of the law, whether it is in the form of written words or spoken.

The power of words is so intense that it can heal a person or make the person sick. In many countries the art of black magic is still practiced, which is nothing but using the power of words to hurt someone. Just as we have frequencies in the electronics world we have frequencies in the subtle world, and people who have mastered the access to these frequencies can use them positively or negatively based on the state of their individual consciousness.

Whether it be white magic or black magic, the power of sound is used in both systems to heal or harm the other. The day is not far when the doctor will not inject medicine in you but will inject a micro receiver and transmitter that will be remotely guided to the diseased area and then sound waves will be transmitted to that particular area, vibrating that particular area of the body at a certain frequency that will make the area heal in no time. Until then, we can use the traditional methods to heal our bodies.

You might not be aware but there are three groups of words, positive, negative and neutral. Neutral words exist in between the positive and the negative and they also become the source for the thoughts to travel forming complete sentences as well as relaying the exact message. I am not trying to teach English grammar here but I am trying to teach you a very subtle grammar, which will help you live this life in harmony.

Here is an example: Let's take few words and work with them. We take the following words for the example: the, Bob, sick, is, healing. Now if we just take "is" and "the" we cannot form a sentence, and even if we add "Bob" to the list, still no sentence is formed and no message is relayed, but if we add sick and healing we can start relaying messages.

1. Bob is sick (Negative)
2. Bob is healing the sick (Positive)

As you see "Bob" is neutral by itself but changeable into Positive or Negative using words, whereas "is" and "the" act as a bridge between the positive and the negative.

Since words have the power to be negative and positive, each moment we are making or breaking our future as well as the future of others, even the future of our planet by using words, as, once spoken, our words have been recorded in the universal databank and will influence us as well as others for times to come. The more positive words we use the healthier we get on all levels and the more we use negative words about our bodies the sicker we get and make our surroundings sickening.

Bob is in his fifties; he does not have the same swiftness as a 20-year-old, and neither does his memory function like a 10-year-old's. Poor Bob forgets his wallet at home and his wife remarks, "Bob! You are getting old." Do you know that Bob has been hit with thousands of negative words connected with the word "old" because the bio-computer has scanned all of its database for similar words connected with the word "OLD" and created a new software whose heading is "Bob is getting old," and the bio-computer will go on adding related words to this newly-created software, i.e., old, dead, rotten, gone, grave, fragile, sick, hospital, medicine, burial, trash, garbage, discard, past, history—one can go on depending upon one's vocabulary.

So next time someone tells Bob that: "Oh, Bob! You seem to be getting old," the software that was created by his wife's remarks will kick in and become stronger. Any time and every time someone will comment on Bob's weaknesses, the software gathers more and more power and every cell in his body will start believing that indeed the body is getting old and it is time to wrap up.

Someone was praying to God: "God! Just save me from my friends and relatives and I will take care of my enemies." People close to you can cause you more harm than even your enemies because you have given your trust to your close ones who are not enlightened masters.

You can see this principle working in all walks of life; rich, poor, educated or uneducated—it does not matter. You can find a person who is in his 30s but looks to be in his 50s and you can find a person in his 50s who looks to be in his 30s; it all depends on the people around you and your capacity to filter the negatives. If you are strong and aware, you can resist and filter the negative thoughts, words, events or circumstances instantly. If you are weak and unaware, you become a dumping ground.

The other day while I was at my daughter's school waiting in the office, a mother walked in and jokingly asked the clerk: "Where is my son? I'm sorry I'm late—by now he must be having a heart attack, the poor thing!" She must have gotten a kick out of trying to imitate one of those stand-up comedians on the comedy channel. Even though I would rate her an excellent mother for the way she showers love on her son, unknowingly she has added to the universal databank the possibility for her son to have a heart attack in the future.

Someone's wife has a headache and she has complained to her husband quite a few times about her problem; once, twice, three times, the fourth time the husband would comment: "You are always sick, what's wrong with you." We have become very cruel and sarcastic with our language, with the words we use, and even though the feelings are friendly the words we use are very unfriendly. Someone wins the lottery and his friend will say jokingly: "Are you including me in your will?" Now when is one supposed to write a will? When one knows that death is close.

Kids will often say this to another kid: "I will kill you." The body is young and the mind fresh and has not been exposed to the experience of being killed but the collective consciousness of that little soul knows what it is like to being killed because he might have been killed in many lives. So the fear, which is already there, starts hosting the mind. Another kid blasts: "I wish you would die." Again the kid does not know what death is all about but his collective consciousness does know. Swearing, cursing and using profane language is considered cool among the younger generation.

Can't we teach our young ones to use the right language? For instance, "I am feeling very happy this very moment, can I hug everyone?" All the other kids in range would then pick up the echo and start feeling blessed, and no one would ever think of killing his fellow humans when he or she grows up.

Most take verbalization for granted and very few among us are really careful while using language, and because of this improper use of language the whole society has become sick at its core. We talk about health and healing on a daily basis, but how can the healing happen? The fight for perfect health is undermined when you go to a doctor and he tells you that he feels that you may have cancer although he will have to confirm it by doing some tests. Whether you have cancer or not is immaterial, but he has given power to your fear as you went to him thinking he is an authority on the subject.

Do you know that to become a licensed pilot one has to answer hundreds of questions pertaining to psychology? And if one fails, the license is denied because the lives of hundreds of people depend on his mental stability. A smart pilot will never tell his passengers they are all going to die as the landing gear has malfunctioned, or as there is a short circuit in the electrical system, or as one of the engines has failed.

It seems the medical doctors are given a degree, which is no more than a "license to kill." This might shock you but you are no more than a prey for the insurance, medical and the pharmaceutical industry. The purpose of the insurance companies is to trap you using fear. Next comes the medical profession who hits you, and lastly the pharmaceutical companies who kill you. The other day I was reading on the Internet that some 850 people die every day in hospitals in the United States because of negligence, and doctors continue to go on strike to condemn the rising costs of malpractice insurance. In September of 2002 the House passed a medical malpractice bill that sets caps on damages awarded to patients harmed by doctors and limits fees collected by lawyers in malpractice cases. In most states, the House-passed bill would limit malpractice plaintiff awards for pain and suffering (also called non-economic damages) to $250,000. If the trend continues perhaps criminals will start using the medical profession to kill their victims and enemies since it will be cheaper and safer for them to do so.

How can you be in a positive state of health when the insurance agent tries to sell you a health policy by saying, "You will feel very lucky and thank me for writing this health policy for you, if tomorrow you come to know that your wife has cancer, or you have a heart attack." I was taken aback when I heard these words from an insurance agent who wanted to sell me a health policy for my family.

We need a revolution on this planet, where it should become a crime to use negative words. When a kid or an adult says "I will kill you," do you ever think who this "YOU" is? For me, both you and the whole world are this "YOU." When you use such negative words with a "YOU" in it, you have in fact abused the entire life form on this planet.

You seem to be sick, I am sick, I am old, you are getting old, today is a very unlucky day, and the list goes on.

If you are a very aware person—what I mean by being very aware is that any thought which pops on the screen of your conscious mind is not allowed to quietly slip away back into your unconscious mind or gets a chance to feed on your bio-energies or emotions without being analyzed by your awareness.—if you can stay aware about each and every thought without letting the thought replicate itself in many forms, you have taken a big jump towards healing yourself. The secret to man's freedom from all diseases lies with his ability to channel his thoughts towards health. Unless and until man understands this law of nature, all healing, all medicines have no value. The desire to heal oneself, combined with self-love, becomes a driving force towards being in an optimum state of health.

Next time you open your mouth to say something, wait for a split second and try to analyze the consequences of your words; try to focus on the emotions behind it and the motive behind those words because you might be saying, "I love you, you are an angel," to the other person, but in fact you are thanking him for the gifts he bought for you; a hug or a kiss should be enough instead of deceiving the other because until yesterday you hated this devil and today his gifts have made him into an angel. If you are not using the right words for the feelings you have, you are not only being unfair to the other but to yourself as well, because you are powering the lie or the negative within you.

Suggestions:
1. Slow down with words—do not try to pack the whole day into 60 minutes; life is not a TV show that you must become a perfectionist.
2. Talk as little as possible and be precise; one consumes the maximum amount of life force by thinking too much and by talking too much.
3. When it comes to words, learn to fast, then feast.
4. Speak your heart and not your mind.
5. Always review your day's words before you fall asleep.

6

Love and Relationships

Love is the need of every human who takes birth on this planet. Learn to differentiate between desire, need and love because desire is lust, while need is infatuation, but love is merging into the totality, just as the river merges into the ocean.

Besides God, love is another word that is widely abused in our society. If you are a man who has been in one of those barter relationships, you might have heard the woman saying: Buy me a diamond ring and I will love you a million times. As if she has a bucket full of love that she is going to unload on you and the so-called love is dependent on the diamond ring, as she cannot radiate love without the diamond.

Humans are very smart in fooling themselves as well as others. Man needs woman, woman needs man; the majority of relationships are based upon demand and need; woman is beautiful, man is rich, the two click. While women are looking for love and security, men are looking for looking for sex and ego satisfaction.

This might shock the females but the majority of men have one single goal in their minds and that is to have sex with women because men are egotistic by nature and it gives them a kick that they were able to achieve their goal in the shortest possible time. Since man's sexual center is active and powerful, it starts reacting just by the thought of a beautiful woman. In any relationship, man's position is very clear and his immediate and ultimate goal is to have sex. On the contrary, not all women are interested in sex and not all are interested in material benefits connected with the relationship. I would say the majority of women are very sincere and are in fact looking for the right person to shower their motherly energies on in exchange for security, stability and a chance to fulfill their promise of helping creation continue its creativity. Just as men have an abundant source of raw sexual energy, women have a source of love energy that is the higher form of creativity. A woman in search of a loving man will not sleep with the man she met a few hours ago, though the man would like that to happen instantaneously.

By nature women are not futuristic thinkers and rely on their instincts when trying to get a fuller picture, and these instincts get clouded by outside influences and the sweet talk, red roses, diamond rings, and perfumes offered by men. When young they are unable to understand the real motives behind men's sweet language, not realizing that by nature men are rarely sweet. When it comes to dealing with men, they easily fall in their trap, as they cannot hear the meaning behind the spoken words. A man walks to a woman and says: Hi, my name is Charlie! Would you like to have coffee with me, but in fact his mindset is saying: "Would you like to go to bed with me."

Very rarely men find themselves emotionally attracted towards women, and surprisingly these men never approach the women for sex, because they are emotionally involved, which is a higher state of their being, compared to sex. Even though they have been going out with this woman for quite some time, still they find themselves in a state of limbo in expressing their true feelings even though each breath they take revolves around this woman. They are unable to communicate their love towards the woman. They live and breathe the thought of being with their "dream girl" at all times, such is the fixation, just like a fish who is taken out of the water and desperately wants to rejoin with the water. The thirst is unbearable and unquenchable, a kind of obsession that cannot be explained by words.

But the sad part is, the majority ends up deserted and heartbroken, just because these poor men did not follow the traditional rule of dealing with women; the relationships ends with the woman finding another partner and our Mr. Crush falls into the category of her brother or a good friend only because his approach was non-sexual. Mr. Crush loses his dream girl to a playboy and the poor girl loses her virginity to someone who is looking to experience something different.

I would blame the fathers for not educating their daughters about the psychology of men and I would also blame the mothers who have not taught their young sons to respect the females, and I would also blame the west, which is shameless when it comes to the issue of sex and has become instrumental in removing the delicate veil of chastity of women's bodies. The majority takes sex as shaking hands in the western culture. On the contrary the east is very protective and controlling towards women.

The east is still protective when it comes to their growing sons and daughters but the west is psychotic. If a child of ten has not started dating, he or she is taken to a psychologist presuming that something is psychologically wrong with the child. No wonder the word love is more abused in the west than in the east and no wonder for the west "having sex" is taken as "making love." Young kids who have not been made aware of their own existence yet are made aware of the "birds and bees."

In the east, if a man loves his partner, he will never ever say: "I love you, honey" unless and until he feels a very strong need to say so and his way of showing love would be very passive, hugging or kissing the loved one, or she will make his head relax in her lap and start stroking his hair and the man will sing a poem or a song in her praise. The east is very romantic, the west thinks it is romantic: a dozen roses, greeting cards, love notes, but the west fails to realize that roses will die in few days and cards and love notes will collect dust in the attic but those moments of tenderness will be stored in the memory along with the emotions, and whenever this episode will flash in the conscious mind the emotions will tickle the heart and love will start flowing, re-coloring the present.

But the west is obsessed with sex and all roads lead to the bed. The east has started following the same track now and the east has started facing the same fate as the west. Women's lib, broken marriages, abused and deserted kids, sexually transmitted diseases, unwed mothers, and teenage pregnancies. The list of horrors will be longer than the west because the east will add its own spices to it.

What is a relationship? Companionship is the core of all relationships; you share what you have without thoughts of desire, possession, or control. You nurture each other, complement each other towards a fulfilling relationship. Man is in a bad mood—the woman changes his mood. The woman is feeling insecure—man makes her feel at ease. You complement the other as you balance your own self. When physically weak you take some vitamins; here you are emotionally weak and the other acts as an emotional supplement and the relationship starts blooming into love.

Just look at your own relationship and see where you stand today. Are you in love with your spouse or are you just hanging in there because you have no other choices available? Are you repenting the moment when you said yes to this man or woman? Maybe you were naïve when you opted for this person or you became the target of your family's foolishness or maybe a friend's when they introduced you to this person called hell in your life.

In companionship the interests are common, there are no contracts and no strings attached to their togetherness. When you are wed-locked, you are signing a contract that changes every day based on desires and needs. Your so-called freedom of choice is lost and you start losing your identity. In marriage, it always starts at mine and ends up at none. In friendship it is always "you choose" or what is more of an interest to both parties.

Do you lose yourself when you hug your wife or girlfriend or is your mind hovering around that sexy blonde you saw today? You are still trying to figure out the brand of perfume she was wearing so that you can buy that same perfume for your girlfriend and fantasize being with that blonde while in actuality you are with your brunette girlfriend.

Do you make sure that your husband or boyfriend is well cared for? Or is your mind contemplating your next purchase and trying to figure out when your husband or boyfriend will be getting his next paycheck as you look for the right moment to ask?

Has this ever crossed your mind? What if tomorrow your spouse dies—would you live the rest of your life in the memories of your spouse or wait until you get the life insurance money and go on a vacation with your new dream partner?

Be sincere because you are not fooling the other but your own self, as other is just an illusion and you are the only reality you have.

What is love? If you are one of those lucky kids who has experienced the tenderness of your mother's nurturing and the freedom and wisdom of your father, then you know what love is all about and the chances are you will not fall on the ground as far as love is concerned, but what if you were not one of those blessed ones?

Love is higher than companionship. You care for the person without asking anything in return and at the same time you give the freedom to the other person to be what they want to be, not trying to control or possess them. In mundane relationships people are trying to possess each other and their relationship never blooms into love as there is a constant fight going on to win over the other to control the other, to subdue the other.

Love is the language of the heart and not of the mind, and if you are merely using loving words in your language, then your love has not gone beyond body and mind and is very intellectual and physical. When two hearts join and as a result two bodies meet and merge into each other, then love flows and then you start singing just as birds sing early in the morning when the sun rises to welcome a new day; then there is no need to say to your spouse "I love you."

Love is the blossoming of the hearts and can only happen when you care for the other, when you nurture the other, when the other becomes a part of you, when you start accepting the pain and pleasure of the other as your own. Just as food is the need of the body, love is the food of God to nurture your being.

The majority falls into relationships for the wrong reasons. Even before you step into a relationship, know what you are looking for. Is it menopause? And you are in a hurry to bear a child. Is it financial security? Or you are getting old and you fear that unless you find someone soon your position will be just like the proverb "Beggars are not choosers." Do not fall for a man or woman for the wrong reasons—good looks, good car, good job and so on.

When you meet someone new you try to hide your real self and never tell the other that you have uncontrollable anger and at times you can be clumsy and weird. The other never discloses negative traits either, as there is a fear involved of losing each other on the issue of smelly socks. You always wait and wait until you are very secure and locked in the relationship or you have reached a stagnant point in your relationship and would not care if it is lost; only then you start showing your real self.

While men exaggerate their talents, their resources, their manliness, they try to portray a picture that they are the best: tough and gentle, just like James Bond. On the other hand, a woman creates a picture that she is the goddess of love and caring.

Each one of us has fetish dreams, and we react to those highly secretive mental videos. The moment a man sees a woman, his eyes go straight to the breast area and then move upwards. There is a deep psychology hidden in this behavior of man; it goes back to his relationship with his mother. Take it or leave it, but the truth is that all men are looking for a good mother, who will nurture them in the relationship, and once they are satisfied with the look of the breasts their eyes move to the head area to see if the face complements their imagination of a perfect woman. On the other hand, women never go on the physical body but go strictly by their senses and feelings. Women look for security in a man and then they move on to power. It all happens in a few seconds and the decisions are made by the unconscious mind and handed over to the "I" within you, and the preceding actions are based upon your logical abilities because your emotions have given you a green signal and it all depends upon your choice, your analytical abilities, whether you move ahead or you fall back.

Are you prepared to be with this person no matter if it rains or shines or will you be the first one to flee in case things don't work out as you had anticipated?

Looking for a relationship or the love of your life! Here are some tips that will help you develop a lasting and loving relationship:

1. Be patient, be caring and compassionate; love does not happen overnight and needs patience, caring, nurturing, support and understanding.
2. Try not to compare your partner with others, as it is a big detriment for the love to grow. Always look for the positive points in your partner while trying to help him/her overcome his/her negative traits.
3. Be open and understanding towards your partner; if you hide things, issues and your emotions, love will never grow. Be honest and truthful even if you have to suffer in the short term.
4. Learn to forgive and forget the negative past and always keep your focus on the good side of your partner.
5. Freedom is the key that opens the doors to love, but misuse of freedom will hamper love.
6. If you are feeling love for your partner, rather than wasting money on dinners, clothes, roses and other material objects, give your partner a massage, cook for him/her, make him/her relax, hug and kiss and show your true feelings to the other.
7. Do not try to create a false image; show your real self, what you are and who you are, trying to change only those habits in you and in your partner that would otherwise have a negative impact on the relationship.
8. Arguments are like snowballs and love and understanding are the only power that will melt an argument and dissolve it.
9. Finally, if there is an argument, always try to understand the other's point of view by putting yourself in the same position and then decide as to what is fair, and do not let any argument or issue prolong for more than one night. You will be better off if you go to sleep with a clean heart and mind. Once you take an argument to bed, the chances are your mind will become pregnant with a family of new arguments by next morning.

7

Man, Woman and Marriage

"Man should never get married but in case he is married, he should not leave his married wife." From a 3000-year-old ancient Hindu scripture

Ancients had the wisdom and the guts to come to certain conclusions while we are still toiling with the information. If we take world statistics, in the last 50 years the number of people have increased on the planet to some 6 billion. The technology has advanced as well, but if you look at the overall state of humanity, people's lives are in a greater mess than they were 50 years ago. Crime is high, the majority are physically, mentally and emotionally sick, poverty is on the rise; except for a few rich countries, the rest of the world is living in scarcity and unhygienic conditions where they do not even get their daily supply of fresh water, and their food is contaminated and not fit for human consumption. Unfortunately, while I finish this sentence and by the time this book is published, the world population would have increased by a few million.

Now who is responsible for the deteriorating state of our humanity and an increase in world population? Take a deep breath and think with me. Let's presume that you are an unmarried woman between the ages of 16-36; it does not matter whether you belong to a rich country or a poor one. What chances do you have of bearing a child? Zero percent, unless you are physically involved with a man. Even then you would be very careful because you are in an insecure relationship and might not be prepared to support a new being, but if you are married, now what chances have you of bearing a child? The answer is close to 100%. We have not even started yet and you can see that the concept of marriage has contributed to an increase in the world population, which in turn has depleted the resources and has contributed towards a downward trend in the quality of life people are living today.

This is just a big picture. Before we ponder the big question as to why the concept of marriage goes against having a healthy humanity, let me explain to you the inner psychology of man and woman, not what the psychologists have told you.

We exist in a world of duality: Male-Female, Positive-Negative, Sun and Moon, Day and Night, and so on. Our body consists of five "Tatvas" or elements that are the integral parts of the planet earth, i.e., air, fire, water, earth, and ether. Our physical body is a combination of these five basic elements. If we look at the human body, we will find five fingers on the left hand and feet connected to the right brain and five fingers on the right hand and feet connected to the left brain, each representing an element. Then we have the remembrance of our own selves, the feeling of "I AM." I am John, I am Rob, and so on. We are unable to function without the memory of "I AM" because in case the body goes into a coma, there is no one to claim that "I am so and so" even though the life energy is still vibrating within the body and medical science discards the person as mentally dead.

Based upon the five elements we have the five senses, i.e., hearing, seeing, smelling, feeling or touch and taste. All living forms live and nurture on the planet earth under the sky, which is vast and illusionary. Within our solar system we have the sun and the moon. The purpose of the sun is to give heat and the purpose of the moon is to balance that heat. The moon has no light of its own and reflects the light of the sun to the earth. In other words, we all exist between sky and earth and we get our hot and cold energy from the sun and the moon. Without the sun and the moon we would perish; the sun is the sole provider of our life energies. From an amoeba to large bodies in the universe, all are dependent on this duality of negative and positive. This is again a big picture.

Now let's look at the biology and physiology of the man and the woman. Whether man or woman, they both become a guest in the woman's body for nine months. Even at the time of intercourse, man enters the woman. The role of the woman is that of a host or mother. Since both men and women live and nurture on the planet earth, and just as a mother nurtures the baby for about one year by breast feeding, the whole of humanity depends upon the earth for its food supply right after the child stops taking mother's milk. Hence women and the earth are host and mother for all living forms on this planet. In India every woman whether 7 or 70 years old is taken as a mother and earth is also taken as mother. In a nutshell, woman belongs to the earth.

What is sky? Vast and illusionary, and so is man's ego. The way a woman loves and lives on her body, the same way man loves and lives on his ego. Man is subtle and woman is gross. Man is interested in "I" while the woman is interested in "Mine." Man belongs to the positive polarity.

What is the role of woman and who is woman? Woman belongs to the darkness or the negative polarity; that is the reason the natural flow of man's energies is always towards the woman. Man is the giver and woman is the taker; she refines it and gives it back to creation. In India woman is also represented by the goddess "KALI." She is the Goddess of Darkness and out of her everything is born and everything merges into her when dead. Woman belongs to the earth and earth belongs to the woman and both are integral elements in creation.

Woman or female energy is superior compared to existence. Man is superior compared to the woman and existence is superior compared to the man. In other words, no one is superior and the whole harmony of creation depends upon each other.

Man carries the blueprint or the seed to our life form and passes on to the woman and woman's purpose is to give it physical form and help the creation continue. Man to woman and woman back to the existence.

Woman belongs to the earth, as that is her home; man is a guest on the planet and his role is to provide and protect and enjoy the company of the woman and the children. Woman's role is to nourish the children and the man in return for security, as man is physically powerful.

On the surface, man's role is very limited and bland—just carry the sperm and pass it on to the woman. Woman, on the other hand, does the rest and enjoys those nine months of carrying a new life form, giving birth to existence itself. Her body is renewed and refreshed every 28 days and is connected with the cycle of the moon; on the other hand man goes through this period every 11 years and is connected with the cycle of the sun.

Instinctively man knows that his place is not earth, his home is not on this planet. The reason man is more unhappy than woman is that he feels out of place. Every man's inner desire is to find his freedom, as by nature, man is freedom loving, thus uprooted. By nature, woman is homely and grounded. Man and woman are opposite by nature. Man wants freedom and at the same time wants to enjoy the woman. Man is always in a state of limbo and yo-yos between the pull of creation and the pull of woman.

On the other hand, woman knows her purpose, but hankers for security and out of this insecurity is born the desire to possess. The inner thinking is very contradictory. So there is friction between man and woman.

If the above was not true, then the first person to make an airplane would have been a woman and the first person to land on the moon or reach Everest would have been a woman. Edison was not a female and neither was Newton. From Krishna to Buddha and from Jesus to Mohammed to Socrates—all were men. Whether it is science or spirituality, men are explorers, and that is their basic nature. Man has been blessed with intellect that is as vast as this cosmos and the ego that is again as illusionary as the sky.

As long as man is taking care of his duty of being a provider and the protector in return for love and freedom from the female, marriage goes smoothly, provided the female is intelligent and affectionate and understands the basic nature of the man; otherwise, it is no more than a hell for the poor man as he is locked in a relationship that is not giving him the basic happiness, not to speak of freedom which a man is robbed of as soon as he commits himself into wedlock, called marriage. This is the story of the majority of men as we enter the new millennium.

Agree or not, man is unhappy with his existence. History is the proof that man started all wars, and if ever woman had to jump in, it was just to protect the species. Out of frustration man has always chosen the path of destruction. As I wrote before, very few men have high cheekbones and the majority have flat cheekbones. If you look at the spiritual masters you will find protruding cheeks and/or high cheekbones just like those of happy toddlers. These men have found eternal happiness.

Unless humanity realizes that man is unhappy on the planet and something must be done to bring his happiness back, we will never be safe on this planet and we will always carry the risk of mass destruction. Every unhappy man on this planet carries the potential to be the next Hitler or Bin Laden.

In ancient civilizations men were happy just like women; the concept of marriage was unheard of and there was no pornography or rape. Couples used to live in a commune setup and while one man was gone in search for something more potent, his family was protected and well cared for and there was no trace of this so-called mirage. Oops! Marriage. Men would pass the seed on to the woman and while the woman was busy nourishing the young ones, man would go in search for truth that one day he will be able to release himself from this bondage called "Maya," or illusion of life, because what takes birth will die one day.

Whereas the challenge for the woman was to nurture the family, the challenge for the man was to unfold the secrets to this creation. History can affirm that men and women would not share the same bed at night and would live in separate rooms. Men would only mingle with men and women with women. Ancients were well aware of the male and female psychology and took extreme care in keeping the males and females away from each other. In ancient civilizations, men had full opportunity to dive deep within their consciousness and be creative. Do you think the Egyptian pyramids were created by some office-going married men? In ancient times men were not only creative—they were very powerful on the physical level as well. If you get a chance I suggest that you visit some of the ancient museums in South India; you will be shocked to look at the armory that was used in the wars just 3000 years ago. The strongest living weight lifter alive today would be unable to lift these pieces of armor that were used in wars just 3,000 years ago. In ancient times men knew the power of semen and would not waste it every day in a sex encounter with women, and masturbation was unheard of.

By nature man is a doer and fighter and if the need to protect is not there, the energy must be used to create; men need to be more creative than women, otherwise they become destructive. You must have heard the famous proverb "An idle man's brain is the devil's workshop." Since women have started imitating men we can create a new proverb to complement the old by replacing "men" with "women" and "devil" with "witch." No wonder witchcraft is becoming so popular in the west.

As we look around we find that majority of men are locked into cubicles and all they are creating is more numbers for their companies that can bring them a few pieces of paper or numbers to support their lives and the lives of their families.

Man by nature is freedom loving; bondage kills man from within and he turns into a heartless cruel creature and marriage is the most horrendous experience a man goes through. The concept of marriage has chopped off the only hope he had to free himself. Believe it or not, if every woman comes with a program to become pregnant and enjoy her motherhood, then every man comes with a program to be pregnant with God and enjoy the totality. Every man takes birth with two wings but marriage de-feathers him and he becomes unable to fly in a caged relationship called marriage.

If marriage proves to be such a misery, you will ask me: Why does the man get married in the first place? There are a couple of reasons to it. In the east, man marries due to social, family and physical reasons. A man without a wife is not accepted in social circles; in the majority of the cultures, a man without a wife is not even accepted within his family circle. Many cultures do not trust an unmarried man; as a result the family is constantly bombarding the poor man to get married. On the other hand, the woman is taken as a liability because of the responsibility connected with her. The east still believes in one relationship and in preservation of virginity and offering that flower of virginity to one man.

As a result, she is forced into marriage to relieve the family of this pressure of protecting her virginity. In the east, a girl's virginity is taken as a matter of respect for the family until she gets married to the man who is approved by the family.

In the east, getting married is more of a cultural issue than a need, and boys and girls are pressured into marriage using emotional blackmail.

In the east it is a man's world, as women do not have a choice; in the majority of cases their decisions pertaining to marriage are made by their family members and they have to accept it. In the east, marriage is an integral part of its stable family and social structure. Ever since the western culture has infested the east, the east has been fighting hard to protect its culture from disintegrating.

The ballgame is very different in the west because of the women's liberation movement. In the west, woman is free; she dates the man before she plans to get married. In the west, women are looking for security and will break the relationship after a few years of dating if the man is not talking of a wedding ring and are not willing to commit to marriage. The dilemma in the west is that as soon as the two individuals get married there is a turn in the soap opera because they have already enjoyed the fruits of marriage while dating, and the only thing left is to live together every day and know the hard realities about each other. While they are dating they create walls and show only the good stuff to each other—how compassionate, loving and caring they are—but right after marriage the walls drop and they come to know the real truth. In the east, we call it love-marriage and it is taken as a matter of shame for both families. I call it love-mirage because the love has ended and the couple is left with just a mirage—you may call it marriage.

Right after marriage a new struggle starts to take over the relationship. "Who's the boss" becomes a big issue. If both partners are working they are left with no time to communicate with each other, whereas before marriage they would find time to meet each other because of the insecurity of losing the other. Since they are now locked in a relationship, the insecurity ceases and they both take each other for granted. Before marriage they would find ways to please each other; after marriage they would expect the other to please them. Sacrificing their friends for their partner was a big challenge for them before and after marriage; sacrificing their partners over friends becomes an easy game.

While they were dating, if he forgot his way while driving, she would cutely brush it off by saying that it was a good ride and she needed that extra air, but right after marriage he turns stupid and it was a mistake for her to get married to him. Before marriage, if a woman acts bossy, the man says softly, I love the way you act, as I always wanted a challenging woman, but right after marriage she has turned into a bitch who wants to control and all men turn into dogs for women. Poor dogs and bitches get all the blame, even though they are more affectionate and loyal than humans.

The mind is the biggest culprit in this drama of marriage. Once married one turns into a yo-yo and starts jumping from one extreme to another. She is a goddess from hell. He is an angel from the land of idiots. Relationships turn sour as both start thinking that they are trapped in hell, and then the ways become separate and the marriage breaks.

In the majority of cases the greatest damage is done to the future of mankind as the couple have brought new beings into this world who are products of disharmony, and such an imbalanced product will have a tough time in life dealing with the opposite sex and can only create more disharmony on the planet and the rut continues.

Another reason for getting married for man is the availability of sex. Modern man has become so obsessed with sex that he must have it or his life is a waste. In western culture if a woman lets a man have sex with her, the man feels he is loved by the woman, not knowing that the majority of women in the west suffer from self-hate and have no respect for their bodies—letting a man dump his corrupted energies on the women is not a big deal for them.

On the other hand, in the cultures where sex before marriage is a taboo, men have no choice but to opt for marriage in order to satisfy their sexual hunger. Men get married and after a few years, while their woman cooks and takes care of the kids, the man is having an affair with some other woman. In the east, women are suffering whereas in the west men are the suffering party because of the women's lib.

In the west, woman has transformed herself into a product rather than a person; her image is more of a sex doll to seduce the man. She dresses up to market herself. As there is too much freedom for women, they go to bars, drink, smoke and change partners just like they would change their dresses. A real woman in the west is one who looks like a model and acts like a whore in bed. The reason for such behavior or upbringing in the western culture is that kids start knowing about the opposite sex through media and X-rated movies. The young ones are left alone to the grandfather of all miseries—television—and their role model becomes the actor in the show they are watching; no wonder the majority of females are material girls in the west. Thank God! Finally Mad-donna has been blessed with awareness and now she is into yoga and spirituality, as some of her fans will follow the same pattern.

In the west, kids are deprived of the love of parents and they grow in their loneliness. Young boys and girls are brought up on baby food, baby milk, day care centers and single parents. If that was all these poor kids needed, then we could have trained female animals as they would not mind feeding these innocent kids because motherly instincts are universal and it does not matter to animals whether it is one of their own or someone else's. At least we will have a brave and loyal species in few years, ready to be trained.

Overall in the west, men have no concept about the mother; their relationship with the female energy is very bland and scarce and they are brought up with no respect for the females, and the same goes for the females as when they watch that their mother is "liberated," they grow up the same way. No wonder we have babies giving birth to babies and 6-7-year-olds involved in senseless killings. In the west, while mothers are enjoying their friends in a club, their young ones are being sexually abused by their stepfather or the neighbor.

A real man in the west is one who looks like a hunk, drives a sports car and lives in a mansion. The west has created a bigger hell in the name of marriage than the east. The east has still survived, but recently with the influence of the western culture, the eastern system of marriage is doomed, and then we will have real chaos in this little world of ours as we do not know any other system except marriage to keep the males and females together.

Until men and women are at the same level of consciousness, and woman treats her man like she would treat her father, and the man starts taking woman as the creation itself and finds his mother (creation) within his woman, there is no way the two can stay together.

In the east, the system of marriage has survived just because of one little secret. The woman is taught to respect all men who are elder to her in age or in relationship; whether it is her father, brother or husband, she is taught to take her husband as a supreme figure, and as a gesture of respect a woman touches the feet of her husband every morning as soon as she wakes up and never raises her voice in an argument. This secret has made the east continue on the path of marriage, without even the thought of a divorce crossing a couple's mind. In case the woman is causing a problem to her husband, all the husband has to do is let her family know, which is worse than going through a divorce proceeding for the woman, and the same goes for the man. The man would be scolded by his family to the point that he will not be able to look at his own face in the mirror. Such is the power of the family system in the east. Marriage is a sacred ceremony and the thought of a divorce is taken as no less than a thought of committing suicide.

The most successful marriages in the east are where this tradition is followed with great reverence and discipline.

I know some of you must be getting ready to beat your head against the wall, thinking about the abuse women have to go through in the east. Wife beating prevails all over the world and the so-called civilized countries are not "holier than thou" either. But back in the east, this little tradition of respecting the man has helped women save themselves from the uncontrollable anger of men as well as keep the institution of marriage under control.

Man has ego and woman has a sharp tongue and any time it is used to hurt the man's ego, he is bound to hit back, and we are left with millions of abused women every year all over the world. Once a woman's body is hit, the relationship is doomed. The majority of women fail to realize that ego is vast and illusionary and there is no way she can win over the man's ego with sharp words. Her tool to control the man is not her sharp tongue but her loving smile which is so puissant that it has the power to bring the whole existence at her feet.

Overall the whole concept of marriage is ailing and rotting. In order to bring happiness on our planet, marriage must be abolished, as it is the cancer of society. The man and woman should not have legal binding to be together; the law should not be allowed to interfere in the relationships of man and woman. The marriage law was created to save both parties from material deprivation but in the process we have destroyed the bond.

There are tons of horror-filled divorce stories, millions of deserted children who will grow with a sense of abandonment and their lives will never be balanced—do you want to become part of this hell?

If you are a bachelor you really do not know what you have. You will only realize when you will lose this beautiful state called freedom. Oh! I see you feel lonely and need company and you want to share your life with someone who will return all those gifts to you what you have planned for the other. You must be living in fantasy. When the reality hits you, it will hit you so hard that you will cry for the angel of death to come and take you, or you will end up in some therapy clinic with depression and live the next couple of years or the rest of your life on Prozac trying to understand where things went wrong, not realizing that the whole concept of marriage is against living in harmony. Haven't you heard the famous joke: Unmarried men live longer than married men because married men are more eager to die.

Dating is more risky for women than for men, as man has nothing to lose before marriage and woman has already lost her virginity in a hope that she will get married with the man and settle, but in case the man drops the relationship she is devastated. She feels worthless in life and has a hard time coping with the devastation.

The story is quite different in the men's world. If a woman leaves them after marriage, they are left in the middle of the crowd just like a small child without a mother, as women are good at pampering and all men are looking for one thing, and that is the feeling of being in the womb and entering a woman reminds them of being in the womb. This is the story of every man who is sincere in his relationship, because a man who is fooling with other women outside of his marriage does not have a vested interest in the woman at home and it will not make any difference to him if his marriage ends into a divorce.

But for a man who is honest in his relationship, his marriage can put him in such a situation where he is hanging onto the cliff feeling helpless. Hanging onto the cliff is his only security, as he can still talk to his children and if he leaves that chance to divorce, he will fall to his death of separation, dejection, hurt, because in any divorce case, laws favor the woman. The fire of women's lib has taken over many countries—the east too besides the west where it originated.

This is a common-day story in the west, whether the men and women are white, black, Asians, Hispanics or other. The man has an argument with his wife in the morning and leaves for work; when he returns he finds a cop at his door who hands him a court order that he cannot enter his house. Shocking! Isn't it? The poor man baffled at the episode goes to a phone booth, starts calling his friends in a panic and ends up staying in a motel or at a friend's house. He goes through a hell of a time for about a week and gets another notice in his hand the next Friday, this time from his employer that his services are no longer needed and his job is being terminated. In a few days the so-called cultured western system has brought this man on the road with no resources and nowhere to go because before getting the court order the woman has already taken control of the bank accounts, credit cards, jewelry and other assets.

A few years back in downtown San Francisco, a beggar walked up to me with his cup asking for money. I looked at him from top to bottom and remarked, "You are not the kind who is fit for begging." You know what he said? He was a civil engineer by profession who was working for the city of Oakland and lost his kids, house, as well as his job in a divorce, and after that he had no will power to stand on his feet and was left with no choice but to beg. I feel sorry for the western man and the eastern woman, as the same percentage of women suffer in the east as men in the west.

You have more chances of hitting a jackpot in a casino compared to getting happiness in a marriage relationship. What guarantee do you have whether the man you are marrying is caring, loving and mentally stable? You could end up finding blue marks on your body every day while picking up the broken bottles of alcohol. Or it could be the other way round. The woman you got married to suffers from diarrhea of the mouth and the nails of insult are hitting your mind and emotions every single moment making your life into a hell. A nasty woman has enough power to make you cry for your mama. She has enough talent to barbecue your manliness with her fiery words.

East or west, cruel is the concept of marriage. Think 100 times even before you commit to a man or woman for marriage, as this is not a stereo you are buying from "Good Guys" that if you do not like the treble sound you will return it in 30 days. Once you are in this wedlock, you might not have enough brains and physical power left to find that lost key to open the so-called wedlock. No wonder society has made jokes about marriage: Why does a man laugh on his marriage and the woman cries? Because man is having his last laugh and the woman is crying for the last time.

If mankind would just abolish the word marriage and dissolve all contracts of marriage whether legal or religious, no doubt there would be chaos for a while and unhappy men and women would leave each other for a while in search of something better, but the chances are that they will find that their previous partners were more compatible and will return to them as there is no binding any more and no risk factor of their marriages ending in a divorce.

My experience says that 90% of the divorces happen just because the relationship has reached a stagnant point and they both want some air to breathe. Their marriage has become more of an obligation than a celebration, and then the marriage starts rotting and reaches a point where freedom becomes an issue and leads towards a divorce, but strangely their hearts are still together; it's only the mind that is looking for freedom and making them go through this horrible experience. The day the divorce is finalized, it breaks their hearts, but by then the damage has been done and finalized. Mentally they were already separated because of stagnancy; all the legal system is doing is breaking their hearts, their emotional and physical bond by breaking the legal contract. Look at the foolishness of our social structure; a piece of paper has more power than the values and emotions of a living man and woman.

I can bet that nine times out of ten couples regret their foolishness, but since their egos are involved and their bond has been destroyed by the legal system, they are unable to return to their relationship because of fear of society, because of the ridicule they will have to go through, the harsh words, the fun society will make of them. But if there was no legality involved here, whether it was religious or social, they had the choice to walk out of the relationship, and the door to return is still open and there would be no ego involved as both will get a chance to evaluate their positive and negative points and improve upon their relationship. Once we opt for this kind of system there is bound to be chaos, but right after the chaos a locust garden of a new era will erupt out of this slush of marriage. As people become more understanding of the new system, instead of walking out of the relationship they will become more responsible and will tell their partners with love and understanding that they need some air and will be back soon, and they will make sure that, before they leave, their families are taken care of while they are gone.

Remember, Confucius said that because of the law people have become criminals. I say to you marriage is destroying the sensitive bond between the males and females on our planet and the day is not far when men and women will be bitter enemies on this planet; they already are, but at present it is not very visible.

If a man and woman were living in harmony behind their four walls, there is no reason that we have nothing but dissonance on this planet. A woman and a man are alone before marriage but after marriage they end up being lonely.

The future of this institution called marriage is already doomed and will not last more than 10 years as the new generation is quite fast to get in and out of situations; they have more understanding at four years than we had at 30. Within our lifetime, we will see a change in the social structure.

I have talked to hundreds of people who have gone through this torture—some experience living in disharmony and the majority ended up in a divorce, heartbroken, helpless, confused, suffering from ill health.

Why do the majority of marriages end up in chaos and lead to divorce? Lack of compatibility, negative influences from the outside, impatient behavior, and the hidden secret even the scientist or the psychologist do not know is that, as I said, a female is like a bowl: empty! She belongs to the negative polarity and the flow of energy is always from positive to negative. In a physical relationship she absorbs all the energies from the man. In other words, man being the positive polarity and the woman being negative the flow of energy always starts from man to woman. So in a physical relationship the good and the bad of the man is absorbed by the woman as well, and after she has lived for a couple of years with the man she has absorbed all the traits of the man and acts as a sort of mirror to the man, baffling the man. If a man is angry his anger is absorbed by the woman in few years and reflected back to him.

The body of the woman is the most sophisticated biological machine the creators ever produced. She is not only capable of producing new life but is also able to recycle the energies of the man, just like the planet earth. No matter how much pollution man is creating, mother earth is always fighting its best to compensate. We release carbon dioxide, and trees that are part of mother earth release oxygen. I agree that all women are not fertile lands and some have the mentality of a marshland; some are as dry as the desert and some are as cold as Antarctica. On the other side, all men are not monsoons; some are hurricanes and some are tornadoes and some are just fluke clouds. If you look deeply we are no different than the creation around us but some of us are made to feel "holier than thou" and some are made to feel "the crap on this planet." In the process we have lost ourselves and the purpose of living this life.

If you look at the male population, the majority of men are foolish, childish and naïve by nature, but whose fault is it? The mother whose upbringing turned these young kids to foolish men. If Hitler's mother was affectionate, loving, caring, honest, spiritually minded, do you think he could have become instrumental in killing all those humans? I tell you the future of this humanity; this planet, lies in the hands of the women. Unless they take charge of the situation in a loving way, our future is not safe.

The process has to start at home, not outside of the home. If a woman is strong, intelligent, grounded and focused, she can filter the man's energy and return it back to the man in the form of love; otherwise, the energy creates a havoc within her body and mind disturbing her sensitive physical, emotional and mental chemistry.

I can prove my theory to the scientists. Take the most beautiful woman who is no less than an angel from within, get her married with a man who is ugly from inside and outside; in a few years you will see that the man has become less ugly from inside-out and the woman has lost her angelic charm and has turned nasty, which she never was, and also her beauty will start carrying a tint of ugliness. This is the hard truth of life and very few people know and understand this secret. By absorbing the negativity of the man she becomes a mirror to the man, and because of ego man does not see himself in that mirror and reacts to the changed behavior of his wife, which in reality, is his.

That is why we have the famous proverb that behind every successful man there is a woman, just because the woman has absorbed the drawbacks of her partner and the man is refined in the process as his negative traits are sucked out. His anger, his hate, his cruelty has been absorbed by the woman. It is one of the most sophisticated processes, which the scientists will take hundreds of years to understand.

For most men, their lives revolve around sex, anger, greed, attachment, and ego. Because of these weaknesses within their basic nature, they are unable to cope with the smart woman. The reason I say "smart woman" is because the majority of women are very mature, whereas the majority of men are very naïve and childish. Togetherness with a quality female refines them to the point that they start realizing their purpose of life—the freedom that is the basic instinct of every man who come on this planet to free himself from the bondage of these "five elements." And as soon as a man becomes aware, his dilemma starts because he is already wedlocked. Right there his fight starts, to be free, and the first thing that comes to his mind is marriage, and he starts finding fault in the woman. And if a woman is very smart she will let go of the man, let him loose with a faith that one day he will be back, just like Buddha, if not enlightened, then at least lightened.

Don't you see that in toddler boys, as long as they need the mother they are always close to her but when they realize that they have grown up they just want to go out and explore. The same happens in a relationship: as soon as man grows up, wakes up from his desires and fantasies, and realizes that there is much more in life than running after sex, power and money, his miseries start because he finds himself in a situation which is not easy to change. The very love of the woman, who has helped him reach this realization, which has helped him get free of his disillusion, becomes his new fetter.

The women of the 21st century have lost the wisdom of the ages and have turned themselves into Barbie dolls—they are fragile and crazy after fashion, perfection, and possession, burning themselves every moment with desire and jealousy. Just look back—our mothers, who are in their late 50s, 60s, or 70s now, are still down to earth and can still take big blows in life, whether they are physical, emotional, or mental. On the other hand, today's woman starts crying if one of her nails breaks.

You might laugh, but we have a very famous saying in India that the biggest enemy of a woman is another woman. Just as the saying goes that behind every successful man there is a smart woman, I can say with confidence that behind every divorce there is a stupid and envious woman, whether it be your mother, sister, friend, or even your divorce attorney. Modern woman is insecure because she has the fear of being left in the middle without a choice and she opts for the legal choice called divorce. As a result the modern woman wants to possess, control and manage her relationship. Women have changed according to the present times but man is where he was hundreds of years ago. This has brought a greater imbalance between the two sexes. Instead of helping each other in a relationship, it has become the me, myself, and I world.

The dilemma is that the institution of marriage hampers the growth of two individuals. If it was not so, then why did Gautam the Buddha leave his newly wedded wife and his child in the middle of the night, in search for something more potent. He was not poor; he had all the luxuries of life; he was the prince and was the only heir to his father's throne. He did not even tell his wife that he was leaving; otherwise, she would have made every effort to stop him.

Rich or poor, marriage treats them equally. It seems hundreds of years ago man was not free in marriage and had to escape to the jungle in search of truth, and his fight continues even today, but the search for truth has been lost and he does not know why he is fighting. Since men have lost the inner purpose of the true meaning of freedom, they are fighting outside of them, with their woman, with their boss, with their society, with their government, and now, many have started fighting with their maleness.

Man has become uprooted and has lost the emotional balance and started living in a world of fantasy, his mind wandering from one place to another. On the other hand, woman is earthly; she wants to enjoy all the fruits of the physical world: love, caring, security, closeness, creativity, which can only be accomplished through money and the dilemma is that she wants to enjoy all these at the same time.

Man cannot provide all at once because he will have to work hard to provide all of the above and then he will be left with no time to care for his woman, nor will he be left with the time to be in his aloneness in order to recharge himself. Marriage gives the power to demand, and if the demand is not fulfilled, then there is desperation and frustration.

With a change in the social structure and the advancement in technology, the state of the human mind has become expansive. Just a few years back there was no need for the Internet but now one must have e-mail and one needs hundreds of dollars to bring e-mail to one's home. Just 20 years ago TV was free; today we must pay the cable or the dish company—more channels, more work, more pressure. The list goes on as more and more toys come on the market and humans are made to believe that they need them in order to live in harmony. Man has burdened his mind so much in the last few decades that he has now started depending on gadgets to remind him of what he is supposed to do next.

The root cause of all problems is our social structure; there are too many choices out there, more than the mind can handle, and the man's ability to attain and acquire everything out there has decreased. On the other hand, desires have skyrocketed and a desire whether fulfilled or not is bound to end in frustration and every marriage is based upon wishes and desires.

The only way the institution of marriage can survive is through living in a commune situation, where there is a guide or guru full of wisdom and the resources are pooled, or in families where the parents are full of wisdom and no less than a guru figure, and all the kids and their families live under one roof where the man has the freedom to explore his avenues for growth. Only in those conditions can the institution of marriage survive.

Despite all the love you can get from a woman, the caring, the nurturing, the heaven-like feeling, I would still say that the concept of marriage is the most cruel invention of society and man is better off without getting married as it does more harm to both men and women and gives birth to kids who are products of disharmony on the planet, spoiling the future of mankind. The concept of marriage is doing nothing but giving an identity to the couple, a social standing. Married! They are socially accepted. The contract of marriage becomes a wall between the two individuals, not letting them merge into each other, transforming their lives into land of miseries, in their own little worlds.

Still want to get married? Well! Here are some ways to make the marriage successful if you are married and having problems or want to improve your married life. Here are some tips:

Tips for women:
1. Men hate nagging and the majority of men are touchy as well. Nagging and using hurtful words can break a relationship faster than any other issue; thus you must control your tongue. Love and sweetness should be your way to communicate with your man.
2. Men are very egotistical and hate to take orders, especially from women, as it hurts their ego. But if you can rearrange your language and make it polite, you can achieve your goal. Like women, men like to be appreciated. Be thankful to him from the bottom of your heart; he will get those vibes from you and will respond with more love and caring for you in return.
3. Do not try to correct your man directly as he is bound to attack you back. Men always try to learn from their own experience and do not like someone trying to correct them. If you want your word to

penetrate their egotistic mind, you will have to use the strength of your love.

4. Do not concentrate too much on outer looks and balance yourself between looking good and having the sweetness in your tongue and love and compassion in your heart.

5. It is better for the relationship if you are not too demanding; the majority of men are calculating and hence miserly by nature and do not like to waste money.

6. Men need charging just like a battery and they need to be alone in order to recharge; give them the freedom they need so that you keep on getting clean supplies of energies for you. Let them loose, let them go into the woods, be around their friends; it all depends on the personality of the man, but they all need charging, that is for sure, and they all love the wilderness. If you want to keep a marriage healthy and lasting, do not sleep in the same bed. I would even suggest that men and women should sleep in their own rooms.

7. In order to keep your man flowing with life, you must change your modes from time to time. Be a mother at times to your husband— men miss their mothers after marriage, and if they did not get a mother's love, they desperately want it even though they will not express it openly. If you can be a better mother, there is no reason that this man will ever look for someone else in his life. This is the ancient wisdom passed on to daughters by their mothers.

8. Men break under pressure, so try to take control of your desires and only demand what is necessary and your husband can afford within his budget. Even if you are making money and the finances are pooled together, still give him the respect of making that decision for you. It keeps their egos in shape and also the finances. Of course there are exceptions to the above rule.

9. Men need crying just like women to clean themselves; otherwise, they become vulnerable to cardiac arrest; it is not always the cholesterol which kills the men, so make sure at times you make him very emotional and help him release his emotions; otherwise, you will have to release his emotions for him. When next time you have sex with him that corrupted emotional energy will be passed on to you—no wonder women are more sick in the western countries.

Tips For Men:
1. Do not fight with women as you would be the losing party; there is no way a man can win with a woman in arguments as she can cry, hit and argue at the same time.

2. If your woman is in a nasty mood, be compassionate with her instead of retaliating with nasty words, as women are very sensitive by nature and are greatly influenced by the vibes around them. Instead of arguing, try to take charge of her mood by changing the vibes around her. The best way will be to let her clean herself with tears. Since women go through a changing period every 28 days, give them love and understanding just before they have their periods as it gives that extra energy to their bodies to cleanse itself properly.

3. Women need lots of security and caring; make sure you hold your woman in your arms for long times and kiss them all over and make them feel very important and wanted. When it comes to kissing, her body is not part of one unity but each area is unique and acts on its own, so do not neglect the left cheek or right ear; you must cover as much as you can. Normally what men think is that pumping really hard while making love is all that women need, which is a very wrong notion.

4. Listen more and talk less should be your motto with your wife. The more you talk the less weight your words will have.

5. Do not follow them as their tail or neglect them. Keep your distance while maintaining the closeness.

6. If you think that commenting on a situation is going to create tension, leave the decision to the woman; let her make her own mistakes if she is the kind who learns from her own experiences.

7. If you have children, it is very important that you give them more love, understanding and caring than your wife. The best way to keep your wife balanced is to have the kids love you equally if not more. Men think that taking care of the kids is a woman's job, but they pay for it with losing their families in the long run.

8. Try not to discuss issues about her family and parents as women remain inclined towards their families all their lives and hate the man if the man says anything against the woman's family. Also try not to be too friendly with her family; otherwise, they will start interfering in your family life. The reasons marriages are more successful in the eastern cultures is that men follow the above rules very strictly.

9. Finally, be a father figure when you see the need and take charge of the situation. Women may not like it in the moment but they definitely need it, and internally they will thank you and respect you in the long run. A man and woman can never be friends and you will have to change the roles from being a father to a lover and a provider to the protector.

Golden Rule for Men and Women: No argument or fight should be left unfinished for more than a few hours, and once you are done with it, just dump the whole experience forever and start fresh with a smile and a hug where not just the two bodies or identities are meeting but two beautiful creations of one existence are meeting.

8

Sex

Humanity will never experience eternal bliss until they understand the real meaning of sex. Sex is the ultimate union of two beings and not just a game that you play on the bed.

Man's sexual center is very active, as active as a car's temperature meter. As soon as one starts imagining the kind of woman one likes, the penis starts showing activity, and within a few seconds that piece of hanging flesh has tripled in length as well as in diameter.

Man is ever ready, just like the bunny in the commercial, unless his bio-batteries have become weak or he drops dead. On the other hand, a woman is never ready and needs her time to prepare for the guest to come in as her whole physical construction is that of a host—first she hosts the men's penis and then she hosts the new life.

For a man who has not reached a higher state of consciousness, sex is more of a release than a celebration. He comes home from work, is mentally exhausted, gulps a few cans of beer, gets into bed with the woman, gives her a few kisses here and there, and even before she realizes it, he is already inside of her, pumping and pushing just like a woodpecker. Within a few seconds or minutes—depending on his ability to hold—the gun shoots, releasing the nectar that has hidden in itself the seeds of mankind.

Poor woman? She is left with the feeling of being trespassed upon by her lover, but just because she has no choice, she becomes a cheerleader in the final moments and fakes an orgasm. Her frustration comes out the next day and baffles the man because as far as he knew she was having fun too and the vicious circle continues, creating a bigger gap between men and women with every sexual encounter.

We eat food and the food is converted into blood and the blood converts into bone marrow and from bone marrow we get the final product, which is semen. Do you think the creators of this human body were foolish to create such a long process of semen production, which takes about forty days, so that every night the man could waste it through ejaculation? The hardship the body must go through for forty days to make a few drops of this liquid is wasted in a mere ten seconds. The emission of this divine nectar gives the body such a shock that the mind blacks out for a few moments and the poor man thinks he is having an orgasm.

Humanity has been obsessed with sex for millennia, from the times when "Kamasutra" came into existence. Even though every living person knows the anatomy of man and woman, there is so much propaganda involved around the word sex or the world of sex. There are millions of web sites, books, videos available in the market, which promote nothing but sex, and the whole game has an ending moment which takes less than a few seconds.

If only man or woman could stay in that particular moment that we know as orgasm for just a minute, either the man or woman would lose their mind or would go beyond this life into the world what we call beyond death, because this experience we go through is no more than a death for the physical body which involves the mind. The only difference is that we do not know what happens after death but here we return into our unconscious awareness.

Man has always been misguided about sex, and, for ages, ambiguous knowledge has been passed on from one male to another. His obsession for sex has sickened him to the point where there is nothing left to fantasize about. Man has turned himself into a sexual slave. Man's consciousness has been auctioned in the sexual market and whenever his mind takes a break from survival, all he can think of is sex.

Billboards, radio, TV, fashion magazines—you name it—all are using sex as a tool to sell. The physical body of the woman is being used to sell material objects; the height of unawareness is that now cigarette companies are using the psychology of sex to attract young kids into smoking. And let us not mention the alcohol manufacturers who have long used women to promote their products.

What is next? Since California has legalized marijuana, I guess we will have billboards advertising a brand of marijuana next to a blonde.

The concept of sex surrounding the woman's body has been so overblown that now women dress not to cover their bodies but to show their nudity in a very selective way. They have made their bodies into a cover page of a fashion magazine; the day is not far when they will start advertising their bust size and other body measurements along with their fantasies on their dresses. Women today dress up to increase their market value as women have become aware of man's obsession towards their bodies.

If there was a way to record the times a common man thinks about sex in just 24 hours, it would exceed the number of times one will actually have sex in one year. No wonder we have hundreds of rapes every day; thousands of innocent victims of sexual abuse are reported every year and the victims are as young as a few days to a few years. It is all due to one reason, and that one reason is lack of knowledge and misconceptions passed on to men for ages.

It amazes me to see that from Buddha to the modern sages, all were scared to touch this issue, even though they were brought into this world by the same means, i.e., sexual union of a man and woman. I have yet to come across a holy book that focuses on the issue of sex. Interestingly, some seers and sages who did touch the subject had to take the wrath of the masses and were branded as sex gurus.

Even animals have more understanding of sex than humans. Have you ever looked at animals involved in a sex act? It happens only when the female is all ready to take the responsibility of giving it back to the creation. Even though the whole act might take only a few minutes, the wooing could take days before the female allows the male of her choice to enter her vagina. Look at humans—they do not even ask whether the other is ready or not. If one partner is feeling sexual, the other is pressured into sex. I feel extremely sorry for the newly-wedded virgin Indian brides who are impelled into a sexual encounter by some unknown person they have been married to by their parents' wishes only a few hours before. The whole experience leaves a lifelong scar on their minds and bodies. They may call it a marriage in India but I call it the socially accepted rape of a woman. On the other hand, the western woman is herself eager to jump in bed with some man she may have met at the disco only a few hours before. Is it not a shame for humans that these beings we call animals have more understanding about the game of sex and its rules?

The poor animals are not educated nor do they have any videos to watch or books to read. They just follow their instincts and it happens in a very natural way and only happens once or twice in one year depending on their individual species.

Have you ever seen an animal masturbating and wasting his precious nectar of life? Even monkeys and apes that are our ancestors as per Darwin's theory have no concept of masturbation.

Have you ever seen a bird breaking her eggs because she is not ready to take the responsibility of the young ones? I do not think there are any abortion clinics in the jungle managed by animals. If we compare humans and animals, we will find animals to be more honest and responsible than humans.

If you have ever seen a lion and lioness involved in a sex act, you will be shocked to see that such a powerful animal as a lion falls on the ground after he has ejaculated as if he lost all his energy. Do you think man is physically more powerful than the lion?

Amazingly, it is hard to find handicapped animals in the animal world; neither do they suffer from horrendous diseases as humans do, they do not have any hospitals either or psychologists. They live at the pinnacle and die when their energies have reached very low. Why? No animal wastes its semen unnecessarily as they are programmed into a certain pattern and they have no other choice but to abide by these laws of nature.

Do we ever teach our kids to preserve their semen power? On the contrary, we provide them with the means to waste their energies in a safe way and allow them to get the wrong message, which directs their lives towards destruction.

Animals do not suffer from heart attacks, insomnia, memory loss, weak eyesight, and so on. You will not find a dog who has become old in his mid-life but you will find many men who have started growing old in their mid-30s. Why? They were introduced to masturbation at a very young age.

Animals live their lives to the fullest; when they become old they die. Their lives are involved around perfection and survival of the fittest. Whereas man on the other hand lives his whole life not knowing the purpose and dies one day, not knowing what his purpose was. We could blame it on karma if we come from an eastern background or dump the blame on society if we come from a western background, but has anybody tried to look into the real meaning of life, which starts at sex?

People have explored Kamasutra, and most have given only more tools to mankind with which to waste this powerful nectar of life called semen, simply in more enchanting ways. In fact, all that Kamasutra did was to beautify the door with flags, balloons, bells and whistles, and just gave new ways of entering the door. One could enter from the right, the left, from the top, and so on, but he forgot all about the person who was supposed to enter and he also forgot to mention as to where one will reach, once one enters this door. Very few have really known the real meaning of sex.

A man was planning a trip in the wilderness and he went to a shop looking for a compass. The salesman gave him the compass; interestingly, the compass had a mirror on the back. The baffled man commented, "I understand that if one is lost one needs a compass but why do you have a mirror on the back of the compass?" The salesman responded, "So that one can look in the mirror and know who is lost."

We all come into existence through sex. Sex is the door for us to enter this physical world. A man has intercourse with a woman and the seed or sperm is planted into the woman. It fertilizes the egg and the egg develops into a baby and a child is born in nine months. This is what science has come up with. So in other words sex is a door for a new being to come into this life, but has anybody ever thought that the same door which has brought us into this world can also take us back?

Just as we come through this door, we have been given a chance by the existence to go back to the source and open the mysteries of this universe. And the reason it takes 40 days for food to convert into semen is because man needs all the power to open the doors to the universe using the power of his semen.

You do not have to be a rocket scientist to know that you need batteries to make the flashlight work. The flashlight needs batteries to run but do we use the mixture within the batteries to make it work or do we use them in the sealed form? Are you not using the current within batteries to run the flashlight? Don't you need to insert the batteries in a certain way so that the positive pole touches the base of the light bulb?

Man's penis is the divine battery blessed to him by the creator, and wasting that semen in the form of ejaculation is nothing but weakening his powers bit by bit, creating a void. A few seconds before, this powerful liquid was part of the body, and a few seconds later it has been wasted. The middle few seconds create a void, a space where the whole body goes through the shock of being robbed of its nuclear fuel and the mind goes blank, and in that blankness everything stops for a few moments, including thoughts. Being in that non-thinking state, one feels out of this world, just as one reboots one's computer and the memory is refreshed.

If orgasm is the goal of sex, then it can also be achieved with Kundalini Yoga, and one can have bursts of orgasms just like the Fourth of July fireworks. One can make them continue for hours and no semen is wasted, and after going through this meditative process, there is no need to hate the woman one is married to for robbing you of your vital energy. In fact, you do not even need a female to experience these orgasms.

Man has been misguided towards his destruction, bit by bit, day by day. No wonder man has created the nuclear bomb and Hitler, the Oklahoma city bombers, Bin Laden, and hundreds of serial killers. Why do we have men in the army? In the west man has become ruthless with his own body due to the half-cooked knowledge passed on by so-called MDs and PhDs on their radio talk shows.

If men are getting the ultimate enjoyment in sex, then why do we have chaos on the planet? Look at our jail population, it consists of 90% men and 10% women. If you take the statistics you will find an equal number of males and females on the planet. Should we not have an equal number of males and females in our jail population as well? If men were enjoying sex as women do, then we would have nothing but love and harmony around us. The truth is that the majority of women are happier compared to men and this can be easily seen from the structure of the face as I have explained before.

For a married man, wasting his energies becomes a routine and causes more frustration. The whole secret, the mystery, lies in that small pouch in which that nectar of life is stored. If we want to know the secret to our existence, this is one of the most visible doors available to us which can be opened with just a little patience and practice, and that practice is nothing but to involve ourselves in sex play with awareness and hold the semen, concentrating just on the enjoyment of the woman.

Why do you think women are frustrated with men? The clear reason is that even before a woman can reach the peak, the man's ladder has already slipped and so does the woman who has depended upon the man to reach a peak, and being able to peek into the mysterious window of life so that she can open the doors to her love energy for the man to taste the divine.

As a man you might feel sad, but the fact is that you have been created for the enjoyment of the woman. Some PhD (potentially harmful dictator) has given this idea to the man that women are made for man's enjoyment and he can have sex and enjoy an orgasm through ejaculation. Ejaculation is only meant for reproduction and nothing else. If semen were meant to be wasted every night in a sexual encounter, then monkeys and apes would have been the source of our sex education rather than the birds and the bees or Kamasutra or PhDs.

The position of man is no more than a bug who is attracted towards light and then dies in the light. Man is attracted towards the woman and not the other way around. In the last few decades, woman has come to understand this secret and they have started capitalizing on it. Never in the history of mankind is there is a mention about women dressing to expose her nudity.

As we enter the Aquarian age it is difficult to distinguish between a prostitute standing on a street to sell her body or a secretary working in an office. From housewives to CEOs, the majority dress up to expose their nudity rather than cover it. This might shock you, but in big business deals, women play a very important role in securing contracts that are worth millions of dollars.

Have you ever thought why those fleshy domes that hang from the women's chest known as breasts have been the center point of the fashion and the advertising industry? It is the first contact point of every human who comes on this planet, a place where a young baby nurtures for many months to get his daily supply of food, the emotional center of the woman, the driving force of all actions which take place on our planet and a door to the divine. Has the fashion industry used a woman's vagina or a man's penis to sell? No! Why not? Just because love energy has more power than the sex energy. Sex energy has just the potential to open the door to this mystery called life and a lot of practice and patience is involved. On the other hand, love energy is like a window—you can have a glimpse any time you are ready to open the door to your heart.

If ever you had the good luck of being with a loving partner, haven't you thought of dying in her arms under the shadow of her hair; did you not get the feeling of being in the womb when she had pressed your head against her bosom? Did you not forget in that moment that you were the CEO of a large organization who was in control of thousands of employees? Or you were the Commander in Chief of an army on whose order thousand of lives can be sacrificed? From Presidents to paupers, all become puppies in the arms of a loving woman.

Losing yourself in the embrace of a woman who has opened her door of love to you is like getting a glimpse into the unknown. You should be thankful to her because she is the host and you are the guest and she has welcomed you, but sadly that door has a fee now and is not a window to the unknown any more, but has dropped to a mere toy of pleasure for those who can afford to buy the woman jewelry, good clothes, fancy cars, etc. Woman's lust for the material objects has blocked the doors to her love energy. As a result women have started losing their bust size and breast cancer is on the rise.

For the poor it is a release of energy and for the rich it is a game of money. There are very few women left on the planet who have the power to look and transmit motherly love; otherwise, men and women are transmitting hate, anger and sexual diseases.

It's all a game of the quality of the woman one has, as the most beautiful woman can make you feel worthless in life and one who is not attractive at all can make you feel at home. It all depends upon how active her love center is or the heart chakra is and how balanced her mind is.

Now just look around and look at men and women around you—90% of the women will have raised cheekbones, with an exception in the western countries because western women have started competing with men and in the process they have lost their inner happiness. You will find only 10% of men on an average have round, fleshy and raised cheeks. Again we have exceptions; in some countries, men are very happy because of the social structure, but I am taking the big picture and the big picture is that men are unhappy on this planet just because they are not educated properly about sex, which plays the primary role in their lives.

The west has grossly contributed in destroying the male and female image. In the west a woman should look sexy and act sexy and a man should look and act like a playboy.

The anatomy of all women is the same—how can the shape of her body make her sexier? Do you know fat women are considered very sexy in some of the eastern and African countries and a slim woman is taken as a squeezed lemon? Yet in the west a very slim woman is taken as sexy. So does being sexy lie in the fat woman or the skinny? The real answer is that different men are programmed differently based on their cultures. It boils down to one thing: it is all in the mindset because of being misled.

The secret of Kundalini Yoga is nothing but using one's sex energy, and one can only use this energy if one has preserved one's semen; otherwise, one is only trying to enroll in the "school of lunatics." In order to practice Kundalini Yoga one must eat healthy, stay clean, keep one's thoughts pure and practice celibacy so that the same energy one dumps in a sexual encounter can be used into opening up the higher chakras.

Man has been given the choice—either give it to the woman or use it to reach the highest state of consciousness. Man's function is dual—carry the seed and pass it on to the woman and then use the energy to open the doors to the mystery and also help woman achieve that state.

The flow of all energy is towards and into the Earth, whether it is a man or woman. Now look at the mystery. For man, woman is the earth and the flow of the energy is towards the woman from man. The flow of the energy of the woman is also towards the earth, and since woman is the representative of the earth, her part is to help the creation create, so she is an offshoot of the earth. The reason her energy center is located at the breast area is because the flow of energy is downwards so that all energy passes through the womb nurturing the baby, helping the baby grow. You might not know this, but in the east, sex is forbidden once the woman has conceived because the flow of energy is disrupted in intercourse and can cause damage to the fetus.

Easterners were not fools when they said man is God and woman his creation. You can see the principle working in a 3-year-old girl—she wants to be the mother of her doll. Have you ever seen a boy who wants to be the father of his toys?

The fault lies with the man, because man has mistreated the woman in the past and has opened the doors to its own destruction. I strongly feel that women have enough power to bring this humanity back on its feet provided they open their doors to love, which can only happen if they stop competing with men. It's time that woman should stop crying about their broken nails or smudged lipstick and realize their true potential.

Love is the only power available to mankind that can liberate humans and take them to the source. Unfortunately, women have lost the ancient wisdom that the power of love is stronger than the power of sex, and they have started using the power of sex to control men. Both will lose in the end because grounding will be lost due to lack of love, and humanity will be lost in the world of intellect which is self-destructive without love.

Try to understand this and you will understand what I am trying to say. Man belongs to the sky and he is a stranger on this planet—a guest. His connection is with the sky; he gets all the energy from the sky. Man is full of sexual energy. That is one reason why, if he cannot recycle that energy or get rid of it, he does it through masturbation or by raping a woman. Have you ever heard or read in the history books that a woman raped a man? I do not think that is even biologically possible.

Since man belongs to the sky he has ego, which is very false just like the sky, but the wisdom of the universe is hidden behind this fog called ego. Man is not concerned with his body, which is gross. He is more concerned with the intellect, which is again illusionary, and void just like the stars—they are all dead planets and have gone through their own experiences. Intellect is man's toy, which creates a new experience for him every moment, and these experiences rot in his bio-computer in the form of memory, just like dead stars, and one cannot re-experience that experience again. So man is not worried about his body but he is very worried about his intellect or ego. Tell a man that he is stupid; he will be all ready to kill the person. Calling a man stupid is just like telling a small child that his toy is bad. Tell a man that his nose is weird and he will say, "Yeah! But that is okay." On the other hand, woman is very earthly and is not much interested in the intellect. This might hurt the men again but women have more brainpower than a man because their energy center is closer to the brain—95% of women can be artistic and logical at the same time using both sides of their brain. On the other hand, the same percentage of men can only use one side of their brain and it is out of jealousy and frustration that man has suppressed woman for ages using his physical power, not realizing that he has taken birth out of this woman.

In the modern world women have lost the ability to use both sides of the brain in harmony and they constantly jump from one side to the other, confusing themselves as well as the man. Whereas the majority of men can only use one side of their brain and stay one-sided all their lives. Only men who are emotional and logical cross the boundaries of creativity and are able to peek into the universe. Singers, actors, painters, writers reach a point where they use both sides of their minds in harmony, thus creating masterpieces.

So, woman is very earthy and is more interested in her body. Tell a woman that she is crazy she will give you a smile, but tell a woman that she needs to lose weight and you have not only lost the relationship with her but have added another name to her enemy list.

The reason man and woman have become dire enemies on the planet is that a woman knows now that hurting a man's ego is a silent killer and she can use intellect to hurt and destroy men, as a man's confidence equals his ego. The only reason woman is abused physically on this planet is that the man's ego has been shaken by the woman.

Women do not have sex energy; a woman can live without sex all her life if she wants to, whereas a man cannot—he must utilize that energy, whether it is meditation, manifestation, or he will use it in unhealthy ways, i.e., masturbation! This is the worst kind of experience a man can give to his body as his own positive poles and negative poles are connected for a moment giving him that spark, exactly the same way as one accidentally joins the two opposite poles of a car battery and there is a sudden spark, but it can ruin the battery as the cells overheat.

Sex has long been used to enter the realms of divinity but one must follow its principles. Since a woman has been given the ability to reproduce, her ways to reach the divine are very different than men. When she is pregnant, she not only carries the baby but existence itself, and during that period she is connected with the divine. Other times, her way is of devotion, "Bhakti," or during a sex act she could go beyond. She cannot meditate or use meditation towards liberation. Since she is living the life of a host she has to wait for the guest to come whether it is her man in this life or it is God, hence devotion is her only way. She cannot achieve God through meditation and history can affirm my statement that there have always been enlightened men and very rarely enlightened women.

Whenever I made the above statement in front of liberated women I was hit back with the remarks that women are already enlightened. OK! Let's presume for a moment that women are enlightened. In that case, we would not have kids on this planet who are abused every day by their own mothers and we would not have mothers who are killing or abusing their kids due to disharmony in their relationships with their sexual partners; moreover, enlightened people do not produce religious fanatics and serial killers. History can affirm that we have had more "Hitler" types than "Mother Teresa" types on this planet.

For meditation one needs a one-pointed mind, and due to biological reasons, every woman has to go through a cycle of change every 28 days in which her whole body is renewed and there is no way she can be one-pointed. Meditation is very dangerous for women as it will imbalance their mental and biological state. Their way is devotion, and only through devotion can they stay balanced. Only after they reach menopause should they venture into meditation.

On the other hand, man has been given three ways to solve this mystery

1. Sex
2. Meditation
3. Devotion or Bhakti.

Sex and Spirituality are so close that dividing the two is like trying to separate thirst from water.

Another problem in the west is that men and women keep changing their partners. Just like one changes one's car every few years, it is more of a fashion to change partners. Another sad point is that for the majority of men and women, having sex has boiled down to shaking hands now. Man meets a girl in the bar and even before they know each other they are having sex in bed.

As I said before, in the east, we do not have this problem since the majority of women are virgins and they preserve their virginity for one man, but unfortunately man is allowed to have sex on the wedding night even before they have a chance to know each other. This is creating a lot of anger in the hearts of women on a deeper level and the majority of women hate men, and when they hate men, they cannot love their kids, especially boys, because boys are the symbols of their fathers. Again there is more hate in the minds of western women than in the eastern, the reason being that women in the west change too many partners, failing to realize that in the first few sessions of their union with men, all they are getting is negative, corrupted energy full of mental, emotional and karmic waste. It all depends upon the power of the woman as to how she handles and discards the corrupted energy into the earth and transforms it to pure energy which we call love; otherwise, changing partners every few weeks, months or years, she is making herself into a garbage dump of corrupted mental, emotional and karmic energies, which is bound to imbalance her chemistry, causing a change in her blood synthesis and causing her to suffer from incurable physical problems like cancer of the breasts, something very common in the west. The reason for this is that the breast area is connected with the heart chakra, or the emotional center, and by changing too many partners, women have disrupted the sensitive balance of this chakra.

Unconsciously, men know this secret that if they have sex with a new woman they are cleaning their minds and bodies of imbalanced electromagnetic energy. Look at history—the Hindu mythology or Islam, where men are allowed to have many wives. Kings were allowed to have as many wives as they wanted and history is the proof that some kings had a hundred wives or even more and all those hundred women were only in a relationship with one man, the king.

Another reason for breast cancer among women is self-hate—poor eating habits. Eating too much meat goes against woman's basic nature of compassion and creativity. As a result, women have started developing hate for their own bodies.

The male and female bodies have been so beautifully designed that it will take centuries for scientists to know the hidden secrets connected with the body as their approach is working with the gross or physical. You have a pain—the medical doctor will give you a pain killer medicine and the purpose of that medicine is to numb the sensitive nerves that are taking that important message to the brain to work on the problem. Go to a healer or acupuncturist and he will release the stagnant energy if the pain area is overloaded, or bring in new energies to nourish the depleted area, thus relieving the patient of pain.

A man should not have intercourse with a woman unless and until the woman's body has become attuned with the man's body and her body has started swaying towards the man's body. Unless and until there is love and emotional attachment, they should not jump into bed; otherwise, they are nurturing hate and nothing else, which is bound to widen their search for a better one and the rut continues.

Another problem is mismatching on the planet. Man is looking for an attractive woman who is sexy and the woman is looking for a wealthy man with a fancy car, good education and a secure financial status. The reasons for liking each other are very material and superfluous. Even before the two individuals get a chance to know each other, they are already in bed having sex. Woman are in a hurry to find out if this is the right man and man is in a hurry to have sex. Man is more impatient than the woman. Women fail to realize that the majority of men have one goal—to enter the woman—and the faster they can achieve it the more boost their egos get. Women are more interested in the wedding ring and men are more interested in widening the ring, and in the majority of cases the woman is the losing party, as she ends up losing her virginity as well as the man.

Sex is not a game of tennis that you hit the balls, sweat, and make some points. Just as too much fast food is bad and spoils your physical health, the same way too much fast sex is bad and will spoil your emotional and physical health in the long run. If you want to enjoy the depths of sex, you need hours of preparation. Patience and practice are the keys that will unlock the doors to the mysterious world of sex. You need to move slowly and gently, as if there is no hurry, and make it into a festivity and not a fast activity. Be creative, use your imagination, be in touch with yourself, and open up and let the other join your energies, because if you hold and your focus is on the orgasm, then you are no more than an organism.

Here are some suggestions that will help you have a better sex life:

Rules for Women:
1. Do not involve yourself in a sex act during full moon and dark moon nights and also during your monthly cycles. Sex in early morning hours, afternoon, at sunset and during eclipses is also forbidden in the ancient Vedic scriptures.
2. Play some relaxing music and also try not to have sex right after a heavy meal; wait at least three hours; also do not have red meat or hot and spicy food as it tends to aggravate the bio-energies.
3. Respect your man as you would respect your father. Give him love as your mother loved you and understand him and guide him as you would try to understand your brother. If you can be all of the above, the man's energies will flow towards you in harmony and you will enjoy him from his center. Never use your sexuality as a tool to win over man or to control him because you will end up losing him to some other woman.
4. When in bed, make sure the man is on your right and you are on his left. Relax him by giving him a massage—the calmer he is the more enjoyable your sex will be. The best position is when a woman is above a man, the reason being that earth is negative pole and a man is positive and the woman is negative and the sky is positive. This position aligns the poles correctly and the energy can flow easily. In

this position man is able to hold his ejaculation for a longer period. Help the man to retain the erection and not ejaculate because as soon as he ejaculates the play is over. Just feel him inside of you and relax yourself on his body. If either of you is not emotionally involved with the other there would be a need to hurry and patience would be missing or one partner will feel bored and lose interest in the sex play and would want to end it. This is a good test to know how close you are with your partner. There should not be any hurry. Mind it, you are not in an aerobic studio.

5. If you can have an orgasm without making him ejaculate, I can promise you will be very happy in your sex life. Men hate women after ejaculation, as deep inside they know that they have been robbed of their vital power. You will both feel very nourished and will like to shower your love energies on your partner. You can feel the power of lovemaking for days to come. Throw this notion out of your mind that he has to ejaculate. If the man can help you reach a climax without ejaculation, he might not enjoy at the moment but the next 24 hours he will be enjoying life just as a small child, as if some hidden fountain opened up within him.

Rules for Men:
1. Preserve your semen, as your semen is the nectar of your life. The more power you have within you the less you will be bothered by diseases in old age and also you will live longer.
2. Do not mistreat your woman; be friendly with her as you would be with your mother. Love her and understand her as you would love and care for your sister. The majority of women are very attached to their fathers and if you can try being one at times they will love you forever, as women need security.
3. Protect your woman from negative company, whether it is your friends or her friends; drinking and smoking are extremely harmful to her sensitive body.
4. Do not change your partner unless and until it becomes a life and death issue; try to match your energies with love and harmony using your intellect. Changing partners is not going to make much difference; chances are that you will end up being with the same kind in a different body.
5. The best time to have sex with your partner is when her menses are over, as that is the right time to be in the sex play and the safest one where there is no need to use contraceptives. Contraceptives of any kind alter her sensitive chemistry.

6. Make sure the squeezing of the breasts is inwards towards the center of the chest; otherwise you can cause the magnetic energies in the breast area to become imbalanced, causing lumps that can contribute to breast cancer.
7. Pumping in and out frantically will not only damage her vagina but can also harm your penis. Enter and relax and be in that position for as long as you can or until she is ready to reach a climax.

9

Children

Children are our future and we are their past. Future is an outcome of the past. If we want a better future we must start this very moment because by the time I finish writing this sentence it will have gone into the past.

Whether we will die in peace in the company of our kids or we will end up being miserable and lonely in a 10 x 10 room for the old, it depends upon the way we have brought up our kids. Will my child be a prodigy? Will he use his mind for the benefit of the mankind or will he end up as a jailbird, hooked on drugs, sex and violence? It depends upon what you have taught them.

Kids are our future and we will always be their past, and if the past was rotten, cruel, dirty and dark, how can the future be bright, happy and clean?

Today, parents are more worried about their children staying away from sex, violence, and drugs; just 50 years ago, parents were more concerned about their kids failing to get good grades at school.

When it comes to kids, the western culture has created more problems for mankind than the eastern culture. Look deeply and you will find the truth. Let's take an example. The place is somewhere in a third-world country. Mr. P just came to know that his son is hooked on drugs: What is he going to do? He will lock his son in a room, take a big stick and bust his ass, until he falls on his feet and vows that he will never touch drugs in his life. Mr. P will make sure that he comes to know right away if ever his son is seen with friends who are drug addicts and have no future, he is not going to stop there and will make sure that similar action is taken by the parents of other kids who are on drugs. If it does not work, he will involve other parents and force the kids who are on drugs and their families out of the area, and he will also eliminate the source of the drugs. This is the story of every family belonging to the so-called underdeveloped countries. In the east, parents have been hard on their kids to the point of cruelty at times, but in the long run this cruelty has saved their kids from wasting their lives on drugs, sex, and violence.

Take Mr. S—he is a westerner living in a developed country like the USA, and he finds out that his son is on drugs. Good chances are he will throw his son out of the house and get rid of the problem once for all. In case he loves his child dearly, he will let him stay at home with a warning that if he finds out that he has not stopped using drugs he will have to go to drug rehabilitation camp. If the father is not well educated, he will think: Well, that's his age to have fun; as a growing teenager he had experimented with some drugs back in the '60s. One day my son will find on his own that drugs are bad; moreover, he cannot take any strict measures. Otherwise he will end up in jail in a child abuse case.

Look at the state the west is in by following the above principle. Just the other day I read in the "Arizona Republic" that students in Arizona have topped the list in drug use in the whole of the USA. A very high percentage of kids are using drugs and alcohol; they smoke cigarettes; gang violence is very common in the west, and the government is spending billions of dollars to control the problem and it seems to be rising and getting out of control. Do you think these kids will listen to the requests of their parents: "Oh, please, honey! Do not use drugs—they are bad for you." The young mind is going to laugh within because drugs control their life now. The best way to deal with these kids is by using lot of hot and cold treatment; they need lot of love as well as lot of hard discipline.

Believe it or not, it starts at a very young age, when the child is left alone at home at the mercy of the babysitter and the TV and is made to watch what the babysitter likes or what the child wants. Just scan the channels at any time of the day and you will find that at least half of the channels are showing material not appropriate or healthy for young minds. The height of foolishness is that the panel of judges who have years of experience in child psychology do not censor the cartoons made for the kids because they are bribed into approving the undesirable clips from these shows. In the name of cartoons and movies, the media is dumping pornography and male bashing, hate, anger, and racism, which promotes sexual abuse towards women in the long run.

Lack of discipline and reckless behavior starts at a very young age. I feel sorry for the kids who watch Rug-Rats, Butthead and many other undesirable shows and violent movies.

Cartoons filled with guns are shown every hour—no wonder we have news channels to update us every hour as to who was killed or is being killed, and it is not surprising at all that 20-year-olds are making pipe bombs and dumping them in mailboxes. Take a trip to any toy store and you will find more toy guns and toys of destruction than educational toys. I guess they should rename the toy store to "Guns R Us" or "Violence R Us." If you are looking for an educational toy that will enhance the future of your kid, the chances are that you will not find many options, and even if you find some, either they will be boring for the child or too expensive. I wish the toy industry would hire more people with common sense who are educated in making toys that can create the image of a better future in the minds of our kids.

Wake up, people, where do you think you are heading? You might be taking all this lightly, but in the future you will have more chances of getting killed by your own son or daughter than by a criminal. The trend has already started; it has happened in America and England many times. Kids have started butchering other kids in schools and at home and it will spread like wildfire unless and until something is done about it.

Partly the media is to be blamed and partly it is the fault of the parents, as they are the decision makers for their kids, who are the end users of the information, technology and products.

If they start rejecting what is shown on TV and what is sold in the market as toys and video games, there is no way the producers of these shows will produce these violent movies and shows. Neither will the manufacturers dump toys or video games on the market that can program the young minds into being violent. What can you expect from a child who is fed red meat for breakfast, lunch and dinner, watches cartoons which are full of violence, plays on the video games that are action-packed with violence and destructive weapons, is kept aloof from the love of his parents and made to sleep in his own room? Are you raising children or a product that can serve the army? It might shock you but Bin Laden has become the role model for many American kids and we already have the first American juvenile who has wasted his life following the principles of Bin Laden. Charles Bishop of Florida deliberately flew the single-engine Cessna 172R into the 42-story Bank of America Plaza in downtown Tampa, killing himself, and a note was found in his pocket that he was supporting Osama Bin Laden.

The number of juveniles who have been involved in federal crimes is on the rise. If the trend continues, the day is not far off when the law will be passing on the death penalties or life in prison to six- and seven-year-olds. The other day I read the following on a bumper sticker: "My child was inmate of the month at San Quentin." These sorts of statements will no longer be a joke but a reality and we will have to replace the lethal injection with a lethal candy bar and the electric chair with a video game that ends with the kid being electrocuted.

The root cause of all problems is based on our own upbringing. In the underdeveloped countries, parents are strict and so are the teachers at school. If a child does something nasty no matter where the mischief occurred, his parents and teachers come to know about it even before the child has reached home from school; such is the social network. It is just like what they have started in the west, the so called "neighborhood watch" to protect communities from crime. The west needs to implement "watch your buddy" system, as it will help the west to protect its future and the future of mankind. The reason I say the future of mankind is because the west has created more sophisticated weapons of mass destruction and the young generation who is growing up around toy guns and laser guns will not have the wisdom to understand what destruction is, and they will be in control of these arsenals in the coming future and one idiot is enough to destroy the whole civilization.

You must have heard this statement "Babies having Babies." Instead of teaching the young girls to protect their virginity for the man of their dreams, they are being supplied with condoms in the schools to protect them from getting pregnant. People who are making these decisions have the mind of a blind man who is left with no choice but to use his stick to find his way. It all boils down to "Blind directing Blind." "Pro-abortion" or "Anti-abortion"—what difference does it make? Why not follow the golden rule and start educating them to "abstain from sex" unless they have reached a particular age and are prepared to bring a new life on this planet.

Do you think it is a joke to bring up a child? A child needs all the caring, the love, the nourishing of two responsible adults who have contributed their minds and bodies into the creation of this new being. If we do not stop here, "Cabbage Patch kids" will become outdated and every girl will have her real cabbage patch kid, and the schools will have to be transformed into day care centers as well, where the young kids can go to school with their own young ones and young girls would be found nursing their babies during their snack times and lunch breaks.

Lack of understanding and sacrificing the interest of the young ones for the sake of fulfilling one's own interests and desires are the real cause of our deteriorating social structure, which is becoming cancerous, day by day. The majority do not know what responsibility is. An infant who is a few days old is left to sleep in his own bed, and in a few months the poor baby is left to sleep in its own room. Kids are not breast fed because the woman is afraid that her breasts will sag, and instead of getting nurtured by their mother's love and caring, they are brought up on baby food and teddy bears. It is becoming more of a fashion to separate the kids at a very young age. No wonder when the kids grow up they have no love for their parents and they are just waiting for the right moment to leave the old ones, and the long-term effect on their psyche is that they grow up to be uncaring adults.

Father is sick in the hospital and he receives a get-well card from his son. There is no family system left in the west; people do not know who their real father or mother is, as more and more unmarried women are becoming mothers, and when they have changed quite a few partners in one night or in a week's time, how can they even determine who the real father is? Every day newborns are found dead or alive in dumpsters, being left by teenage girls.

Western women are as eager to get in bed as the eastern men. This might come as a shock to western women but eastern men have a notion in their minds that western women crave good sex and material objects. As a result, these women are offered material objects for sex by men when they are visiting the eastern countries. I do not blame the eastern men because there is sexual repression in the east, and also western women visiting these eastern countries do not hesitate to sleep with a rich attractive hunk as it adds to their adventure. The east was never nude but east has started following the west and is overtaking the west in the race for nudity in the name of fashion. The east is becoming morally polluted as well due to the western influence.

I would blame the west because the west starts everything and the east follows it. The west is the role model for the east as far as day-to-day life, technology or fashion goes. The west has been very smart and talented and innovative, making life easier and attractive on the physical level. Cosmetic surgery, breast implants, artificial makeup, hair dyes, and stunning hairstyles and clothes have transformed the lives of people towards perfection, but in the process, the west has lost its peace of mind and its connection with the divine and the inner self. The outer has become beautiful, but the state of the inner being is at its ugliest.

The west has no control over its family system, as it is discipline and control that make any system work. The family system is still a reality in the east—grandparents, sons and daughter-in-laws, and their kids all living under one roof, eating together, crying together, laughing together. In the east, one's family is always there to help, whether for an emotional, physical, or material problem.

A few months back I read in the newspaper that a 10-year-old has filed bankruptcy, which makes him the youngest person to file bankruptcy in the history of America, because he and his brothers and sisters were orphaned a few months ago and in order to save their house from being repossessed by the mortgage company, this measure was taken by their attorney. Don't you think it is a matter of shame for the richest country in the world? Where people are spending millions on their mansions, the financial and the real estate giants have billions of dollars lying in their accounts; on the other hand, these 10-year-olds are struggling to save their shelter. Is this capitalism or cruelism?

On the other hand, the east is far behind in technology but has maintained its relationship with its ancient culture, the family system, its peace of mind. The biggest positive point the east has is its spiritual stability—its faith in the higher force. Go to any part of India, 24 hours, 365 days a year, and someone, somewhere, is meditating or chanting the name of God. There are hundreds and thousands of temples belonging to different sects and religions in India. Kids in the east grow up around respect, compassion, spirituality, and love, while the kids in the west grow up around uncaring or overworked single parents or in foster homes, in a logically-obsessed environment that lacks emotion or compassion.

In the east, people are still living in joint family systems, where a child wakes up in the arms of his/her grandfather or grandmother, unlike the western child who has been deprived of love, whose sun rises around stuffed animals. In the east, communities live like families where neighbors care for their neighbors.

A poor man sitting under the shade of a tree in a third world country has more patience and peace of mind compared to a stockbroker sitting in front of his computer in his posh New York City penthouse—his happiness rises and falls based on the stock prices. What is the reason behind all this? A four-year-old is taught to sell lemonade on the street corner. Kids are taught capitalism from a very early age—this is yours, this is mine; you do not touch my things. The word "share" should be scratched off of the English dictionary as no one uses that word in real life; everyone uses what they pay for. Maybe we should redefine the word "share" as a capitalistic means of exchange.

It is very common for kids to tell their friends: "Get out of my house, this is my house." If a child says this in the east the parents will punish their child by making him or her stand outside the house until the child feels sorry for his or her uncaring attitude towards others. But you cannot correct your child's behavior in the west as your neighbor might complain and you would then run the risk of losing your child to the care of social services.

Here in the United States, every year thousands of kids have to go through the horrendous experience of watching their parents go through a divorce proceeding and hundreds of families are broken every year. Men and the kids are the suffering party in the west because the kids go to the woman and the child is deprived of the love of father and grows around a confused mother who thinks like a man but acts as a woman. No wonder the population of men who have started thinking and acting like women is on the rise.

If western laws which favor the woman in case of a divorce are not going to change, then it will be better that before the couple is wed-locked, the ownership of the yet-to-be-born is predetermined and put on a piece of legal paper so that the man can also have a say in the matter who is the sole owner of his seed, so that the poor man is not left without kids in a woman's world. Men love their offspring equally but are unable to show their emotions because of their physical chemistry and a woman can cry in court and win over the judge and the kids. If, in a divorce proceeding, the items which have been gifts between husband and wife are asked to be returned to each other, then why not kids, as the husband has given a gift to his wife in the form of his sperm and should have equal right to the ownership of the kids unless it is proven beyond doubt that the man is not a loving father and is unable to take care of the kids. In my opinion the final decision should be left to the kids to decide with whom they want to spend their teenage years.

Kids need both the female energy and the male. Mothers are their only source for compassion, love, understanding, caring, communication, emotional stability, sharing, grounding, whereas men give them a sense of security, knowledge, wisdom, confidence, responsibility, freedom, direction, the ability to fight in the outside world, and also judgment, which is one's ability to know between right and wrong, and how can we omit spirituality? Surprisingly, what is taught by the mother and father are complementary and two sides of the same coin. When one side is lost and the child is left to a single parent, he or she is unable to balance and trips in life choosing the opposites of compassion and judgment. The reverse is absorbed which is cruelty and disrespect for honesty, justice and fairness. Confidence transforms into recklessness and egoism, where love transforms into hate and so on.

Schools contribute their own share of horrors where teachers bring their personal problems in the school and shower their frustrations on the poor kids. The majority of teachers come to the teaching profession because of money; they have no interest in contributing to the healthy growth of society. I suggest you pay a visit to one of the public schools and day care centers and you will be shocked to find that many teachers lack the normal smile, are rude and uncaring, and some even look as if they just walked out of a mental asylum.

At the end of the school day, if your child walks out seeming happy, that could mean two things: either the teacher is very good, or the child is happy that another bad day has come to an end with a teacher who is unloving, uncaring, rude, takes out her frustrations in the name of discipline, and is promoting favoritism/racism while paying more attention to the kids of her choice or race.

If we want the world to be happy, we must start with caring for our kids as one cares for a rose plant in his garden, protecting it from wild animals and waiting for the bud to bloom into a rose, but sadly with gang violence on the increase and 7-8-year-olds becoming serial killers, we are left with no choice but to offer roses to the buds who are buried in their graves.

A better world will be where the east and west join hands and the west and the east learn from each other and we can have a universal system of bringing up our kids, which is based upon love, freedom and caring, a system that is clean and safe so that we can have a better society in the future. It is time to bring a revolutionary change in the upbringing of the young generation in order to save the kids who are the future of mankind.

Since each child is unique, there can be no hard and fast rules for dealing with them, but here are some tips that will help you achieve a good rapport with your kids.

1. Love is the only language your kids will respond to. Give as much love as you can to your kids and that will be returned to you in many forms.
2. Discipline is an extremely important ingredient for the upbringing of your kids; make sure you use the power of "No" when you do not want to say yes, and stick to your no. And the no should come from both parents. Do not chant the mantra of no-no and no with kids all the time or your "no" will lose its value. Use "no" only when it will have an impact on the future of your kid—your one "no" will carry the strength of the "yes" mantra and your kid will willingly accept your "no."
3. Finally, do not give kids access to your wealth until they have understood the laws of money; you will be spoiling their future if you buy them expensive material objects. Give them your culture, your values, your understanding, your caring, and your wisdom coated with love.

10

Food

We have landed on the moon and sent probes in the skies to explore the universe, reached Everest a number of times, explored the depths of the ocean. On the other hand, humans do not know what to send to the stomach, which is a few feet away from the mouth. There are hundreds of books available on the market on what to eat and how to eat. Thousands of pages to go through and they leave the reader more confused.

When it comes to food, man is a slave to his taste buds, temptations and desires. Food is the number one weakness of man; even sex is not that big a problem, but food is. The first sex happens within the mouth, and unless and until you have known how to enjoy food you cannot enjoy sex.

With more food choices becoming available to us, the majority has started living to eat rather than eating to live. Obesity has become a major concern for the scientists as human bodies are constantly being dumped with food from the time we wake up to the time we go to sleep. Food has become our obsession. More variety, more confusion, and our taste buds rule what we are going to send to the stomach. We do not even care about the needs of the body in term of quantity and/or quality.

Non-vegetarians are crueler towards their bodies than vegetarians as they have more choices than vegetarians. This is a typical eating schedule for a non-vegetarian. One wakes up and starts his day by visiting one of the fast food chains. The day is started with an egg and sausage sandwich with bacon along with some French fries. In order to push all that heavy stuff down the food-pipe, a glass of orange juice made from concentrate is gulped. The poor stomach is slammed with hundreds of calories after working hard all night long to discard the waste. After eating all that junk one is bound to feel tired and sleepy. Presently fast food stores do not provide a bed, but they are honestly working hard to provide you with a coffin where you can rest for the rest of your life and not be disturbed. So after this heavy breakfast, you need something that will boost your body and you gulp a few cups of strong coffee, and in just few hours you will be hungry again because the body had to work even harder to digest those extra calories and toxins and is now feeling depleted.

Very soon it is lunchtime, and you grab another sandwich—this time chicken along with some salad and a soft drink to neutralize the gases, which the body has been producing from the digestion of last night's dinner and this morning's breakfast. Of course, everyone loves sweets and you need something sweet as your blood sugar has also dropped due to the rough time the body had to go through: candies, chocolate or pies. Again your body is tired and you have another cup of coffee. A few hours pass and dinner time comes closer and you have already started imagining the juicy steak or a big hamburger. By the time you are finished eating the cow's meat, the TV cries out loud: "Got Milk?" Before you retire for the day, you gulp a glass of cold milk, which is going to act as a cold-blooded murderer for your stomach's furnace.

Do you think after having all that food you will have the desire to eat any fruits or even have your daily minimum water intake? No wonder two-thirds of humanity is suffering from stomach-related diseases and the health care industry, drug companies and the insurance companies are booming, and so is the fast food industry. It seems they are all very good partners as they know your weaknesses. The day is not far when the hospitals will start advertising that 100% cure is guaranteed or your coffin is free.

If we close the fast food industry and educate people on eating healthy, within ten years hospitals will start packing up and the medical profession will no longer be the most wanted profession. Doctors will be left with no choice but to find jobs at the New Age food stores working as grocery clerks. Don't you think it will be a big achievement for us?

Man's consciousness has reached so low that he has left nothing that is not being eaten in the world today. From monkey brains to snakes, dogs and rats, from frogs to fishes, even their eggs. Humans have created a mess on this planet. No wonder humans today think like a monkey, are more dangerous than snakes, have egos like cats, bark like dogs, and smell like rats; they jump like frogs when intimidated, and kill like lions; their thinking is wishy-washy and their talk is fishy.

What you eat today will influence the way you think, which in turn will influence the way you look, which in turn will influence your future. Eat lovingly and you will be loved, eat mercilessly and existence will not be compassionate towards you.

We are losing compassion on the planet, as the majority hates their existence; we do not love ourselves, not to speak of loving others. What can you expect from a man who eats meat day in and day out; for him everything is blood and meat, which can be consumed. The way one eats different varieties of non-vegetarian food with a sense of mercilessness, how can one be merciful towards fellow humans when no mercy is shown towards the fellow animals who are butchered in thousands every day to be consumed by man? Show me one holy book that promotes meat eating. Don't the animals have an equal right to share this planet with us and enjoy it without the fear of being butchered for food?

The law of eating is very simple—look at the food people eat in any country and you can know the state of their minds. I am not trying to promote vegetarianism. Vegetarianism is good but all bodies are not designed for vegetables; it all depends upon the shape of your teeth, but eating too much red meat, particularly cow's meat, will not only pollute you mentally, but will disturb your electromagnetic energy, giving you diseases like cancer, allergies, Alzheimer's disease, pollution of the blood, stress and depression. The cow is a spiritually elevated animal. Vedic seers had the vision to realize this. If you crave meat, stay with lower-consciousness animals till your consciousness grows, where you start respecting life.

Do you think animals do not suffer when killed or they have no brains to realize that death is very close? Just imagine this—you are a meat eater and are enjoying your safari in Africa; all of a sudden an African tribe whose delicacy is human flesh attacks you. From the time you are captured to the time when the sword has chopped your head from your body, you will go through an experience that will be worse than hell, because if you had died in your sleep, you would have been the most lucky human as you would not have experienced death in this horrible way. The fear you will go through, the helplessness, the agony, it will make your electromagnetic energy go haywire and make your body go into chaos. If you are a weak human you will have a heart attack and die even before you are butchered. Do you think the poor animals that are very instinctive by nature really enjoy the experience of dying such a horrible death in the slaughterhouse?

If you love meat, take my challenge and take a trip to the slaughterhouse and look at the animals being butchered; look into their eyes when the sharp metal is dropped on their necks. If you do not feel their helplessness, pain and agony, then it is perfectly all right to eat meat because your consciousness has not developed to a state where you respect the creation and your being wants to experience the taste of death and dead flesh.

At the time when animals are being killed, they go through a situation which is horrendous. Fear, helplessness and unwillingness to die create havoc within their body chemistry. Since the five elements are going to be disintegrated in a short while and the dark energies have taken over the process of extermination, their body chemistry becomes chaotic; their glands start releasing chemicals which react with each other and become poisonous and are distributed into each cell of the body because of the accelerated blood flow, and guess what happens: their body's electromagnetic energy becomes highly disturbed and each and every cell in their body has become a storehouse of poisonous electromagnetic energy at the time of their death. When you eat that meat, your protective web that protects and filters the incoming thought waves and saves you from negative forces becomes weak, and your blood chemistry changes and turns more acidic. No wonder cancer is the number one killer today.

Another big mistake we make when eating is to eat the wrong combinations of food items. Humans do not know what to combine, and western countries are very backward when it comes to food combinations. In India, most of the mothers know this ancient secret and they will not allow their families to eat certain food items in combination with other foods. Certain food items are forbidden to enter the kitchen during certain months. There is a definite science behind eating that has been practiced for ages in the east.

Westerners are very poor when it comes to food combinations: Eating ice cream with coffee is more of a fashion in the west and some add spice to it by combining it with smoking. What a way to live life. In the west, people do not know what to eat, when to eat, how to eat, where to eat, and with whom to share their food.

The other day I saw this man driving in his convertible on University Avenue in Berkeley, his Irish setter sitting in the back seat. The man was eating an ice cream cone and after a few licks, he would turn the cone to his dog that was sharing the ice cream with him. Wake up! Your genetic coding is very different than the dog's and saliva has enough elements that can alter your body chemistry and genetic coding.

There are many books available in the market that can teach you about proper food combinations. I will not go into details but would like to give you the basics of food combinations. One of the books I have loved and found useful is *Fit for Life* by Marilyn Diamond. It will help you live a better life if you want to stay healthy.

As we have three groups of people, the same way we have three groups of food available to us:

1. Acidic
2. Alkaline
3. Neutral

When we combine acidic foods with alkaline, we confuse our bodies. One good example of the wrong combinations is meat and potatoes. Meat is protein and acidic by nature and potatoes are carbohydrates and alkaline by nature. When we eat the above, the body is going to release two kinds of juices—one to digest the acidic food and the other to digest the alkaline food—and both juices will get neutralized in the process and the food will start rotting in the stomach giving you bloating, gas, indigestion, nausea, lack of energy, constipation, and on you go. Besides that, you have added another shipment of toxins to your body's storehouse of toxins.

Day in and day out you are adding more and more toxins, because if you do not know what food items to combine and you are a lover of junk food and you crave meat, the chances are you have no awareness about your body and your knowledge about toxins is only limited to "Industrial Toxic Waste" because you saw the news on TV about chemical industries illegally dumping their toxic waste.

Since the majority is living a very fast-paced life—10-14 hours of work schedule with a few minutes of break to eat food—one is left with no choice but to eat whatever is available at the time. If the above fits your lifestyle, you need to give a good look at your life and think whether you are here for yourself or for others. How long will you carry on like this before your cells are overflowing with toxins and your whole body goes into a mayday situation?

The wisdom of eating is very simple—if you are very much in touch with your heart, you will always crave the right food at the right time. The ultimate goal is to satisfy the body and nourish it to get the most out of it. Your bowel movements are the best indicator of your food intake. If your stool is well formed and floats on the water, does not smell horrible and you do not feel any pain while passing your stool, if urine and the stool are not released at the same time, you are eating healthily. Also, the shine and clarity of your skin is the best indicator of whether or not you are eating healthily. Other indicators are the color, clarity and the smell of your urine, the natural smell of your body besides the quality of your breath and the condition of your gums and teeth.

If you are having at least one bowel movement every day within two hours of your waking up in the morning and you seldom feel constipated or bloated, do not suffer from mood swings or fits of anger and repulsiveness (leave-me-alone kind of thoughts), your breath smells normal without the use of any mouth fresheners and your urine is clear, transparent in color and does not give a pungent smell, your body is in good shape. You are eating the food that your body likes.

On the other hand, if your face is filled with acne, your skin looks dirty and lacks shine and clarity, and you do not get bowel movements for days, your mood changes as you change channels on the TV. You must have a mouth freshener in order to talk to people face to face. You need to re-evaluate what you are eating, as you are not eating right. The food you are eating is not the kind of food your body wants and lacks the proper balance of acids and juices to digest it properly, making it rot in your stomach for days before your body succeeds in throwing it out. You are increasing the toxin level in your body and the day is not far when you will join the list of people waiting to see a medical specialist who drives a top-of-the-line BMW with personalized license plates saying "UR GLBLDR."

My way is very simple. The food you eat should be as freshly cooked as possible without using many different and large amounts of species, should not be a canned product, should not be overcooked, should smell aromatic. After eating that food, you should feel satisfied, yet light and energetic.

Unless you are in the military or in the business of passing the death sentence on people, you should stay away from meat items, especially red meat. Research has shown that the human body is not designed for meat products, and, moreover, meat products belong to the lower frequencies. As a result you will have a hard time accessing the higher frequencies from the universal consciousness.

In order to explore the inner world and live a blissful life, you will need to remember the following:

1. Aromatic foods nourish the higher chakras. Lightly cooked vegetables are the best, along with grains in any form. They are easily digested by the body and nourish the body instead of adding another load of toxins to the body.
2. Pungent and old foods nourish the lower chakras as well as the past memories. Food that has been sitting in the refrigerator for many days will keep you trapped in the past memories and will nourish the emotional blocks from the past and are extremely detrimental to a balanced state of mind and also spiritual progress.
3. Ghee (clarified butter), sugar, milk, yogurt, almonds (you might not have realized this but the shape of the almonds matches the shape of the eyes). Walnuts (the shape of the walnuts matches the shape of the

brain). Coconuts (the shape of the coconut matches the shape of the head and human face and has two eyes and one mouth and the mouth is the only hole that can be punctured to get the water out; the other two holes which represent eyes are solid. Cashews match the shape of your kidneys. Saffron, cardamom (big and small), cinnamon, and many other fruits and spices nourish the bio-energies within us. The above food items also make our protective web stronger, which saves us from harmful energies trying to access our bio-energies through our thoughts.

Food items you should avoid
1. Red meat of all kinds
2. Chemically processed sugar and any consumable product made with it.
3. Too much coffee or tea can cause high blood pressure, nervousness and arthritis; it also makes the blood hot and acidic.
4. Pound cakes cause stagnation of the digestive system; if you must eat cake, make sure it has a lot of nuts and fiber.
5. Try not to mix proteins and carbohydrates.
6. Cold drinks and sodas rob the body of vital heat.
7. Canned food, frozen foods and processed foods.

Always remember! Our connection with the earth is through food. Earth is a storehouse of all kinds of energies. The food we eat helps us to tap the negative or positive forces from the earth. If you are happy, you must be eating healthily. If you are sad and lifeless, change the foods you eat and the way you eat. Eat healthily and live long and happy, eat junk and your body will end up in the human junkyard. The choice is yours.

11

Health and Healing of Your Body

Your body is your temple where the supreme light resides; it is a gift from existence to you. Live with reverence and enjoy the existence around you. That is your sole purpose

A healthy body is the first sign of happiness. Unfortunately, we are going through a period on this planet that is extremely negative and has been mentioned in the ancient texts as "Kaliyug," or the Dark Age—global warming, erratic change of weather patterns, extremely hot and cold days, pollution, toxins within our food. It seems we are eating, drinking and breathing poison every single moment.

To top it all, humans have no understanding that in the name of growth and technology we have created an environmental mess. Just 100 years ago our planet was not like this, and we are responsible for the state we are in. Every time we throw paper, plastic or any other waste into the garbage that is not biodegradable, we are throwing away our future bit-by-bit, adding to our devastation. Unless stricter ecological laws are created in every country to recycle the waste and stop producing chemicals that can damage the ozone layer or cause drastic changes within the atmosphere, the future of this planet is at risk.

We have more diseases on this planet than systems of medicine, diseases like AIDS, cancer, TB, Alzheimer's, arthritis, and the list goes on and on. Living on this planet has become more like we have been punished by some higher force into being here, to go through this suffering in this jail called the rib cage.

If we take statistics it will be very hard to find even a few hundred people out of billions who are in perfect health. The majority suffers from one sort of disease or the other and chanting the mantra "I am happy, healthy and prosperous" is not going to take us too far, though it might help us to look for avenues towards having good health.

There are various systems of healing available to us, to protect our bodies from diseases, and to bring it to an optimum level of health. To name a few, we have the medical science that is based upon suppression of the symptoms, or if you cannot heal an organ, cut it or replace it. For every disease medical science has a medicine to suppress it.

You might not be aware, but if you or someone you know suffers from migraine, you will be surprised to know that migraine is not a disease, but a symptom of a disease, even though medical science takes it as a disease and suppresses it with medicines. You have a pain in the stomach and you go to the doctor and the chances are your gall bladder will be removed if the doctors are unable to find the root cause of your problem. Having trouble with your tonsils? Well, you will be treated with antibiotics first, and if you still are having problems, your tonsils will be surgically thrown out as waste and you will never come to know that the function of tonsils is to indicate the level of toxins in the body.

A three-month-old has an earache, give him amoxicillin; a 14-year-old has an earache, give him amoxicycline, and if it cannot be cured, operate on the ear. Infant to adult, the remedy is the same. A few years back one of my clients mentioned to me that her son's ears were going to be operated on the following week as he had an inner ear infection. Her son's doctor had tried antibiotics with no success. I suggested that she give her son these German remedies called "Kali Muir & Nat Muir." These are bio-chemical salts found within our bodies and are readily available for less than five dollars a bottle from the local health food store. Call it faith or desperation, but she started giving him these bio-chemical remedies and on her next visit to the doctor she was told that the infection was gone and there was no need for an operation.

Let's presume that the enemy has attacked a country and the defense forces of that country are unable to beat the enemy and win the war. So the head of state decides to get outside help, but the outside help says that in order to win over the enemy, we will have to destroy all your soldiers first. Having no choice, the head says, "Fine, go ahead." Exactly the same logic is used behind these antibiotic drugs.

Next time you have an infection try increasing your Vitamin C intake to boost your immune system before you run to your doctor. Give your body a chance to heal itself.

Do you realize how much harm these antibiotics cause to the sensitive balance of our stomachs? Our stomachs are very sophisticated chemical factories and a medical center where the remedies to correct the body are created and distributed to the rest of the body.

The approach of medical science has always been in the wrong direction and only recently they have started exploring the cause of diseases rather than suppressing the symptoms.

Besides the widely known medical science we have acupuncture, which comes from China. Acupuncture is a very powerful system but there are not many good acupuncturists available in the west, as Chinese are very traditional people and they have no interest in the pomp and show of the western life and they are happy in the mainland. As a result the acupuncture treatment that is available in the west is mundane and it is not easy to find a good acupuncturist in the U.S., and not many have the resources to go to China for treatment.

Then we have Ayurveda, which has started spreading its wings in the west but has the same fate as Acupuncture. Ayurveda has its own pitfalls, as these herbal medicines are ingested in crude form and can cause considerable harm to the sensitive organs of the body if not suggested by an experienced Ayurvedic doctor who has spent years learning the system under the discipleship of an experienced Ayurvedic doctor. The system of Ayurveda is based upon knowing the constitution and type of the patient by examining the pulse, tongue, food habits, family history, date of birth, etc., which cannot be learned from books, as one needs years of practice. In the long run Ayurveda will prove to be very dangerous in the hands of novices who can start suggesting medicines after a crash course of a few months, compared to getting a degree from an Ayurvedic college in India where it takes five years to become an Ayurvedic doctor, the same amount of time to become a medical doctor.

Then come the herbal medicines available in the health food store; these herbs are in crude form and carry the same risk factor of messing with people's health.

Yoga is another way to heal the body, and again it is not easy to follow the correct yogic positions, and moreover, it takes a long time for the body to heal using different poses that have been made available to the west. The traditional Yogic techniques of healing which are faster and safer are still not seen in the west.

Then we have Homeopathy, which is quite popular in all countries except the United States because of strong lobbying from the medical community, as they are well aware of the fact that if this form of healing is allowed to penetrate the U.S. market, no longer will they be able to wash their hands under their gold-plated faucets, no more private jets, mansions or expensive vacations.

I do not blame the medical community but I would blame the system, which is focused on making more money rather than helping people. Why do people go for the medical profession? I would say three-fourths of people opt for the medical profession just because there is an abundance of money in it and only one-third have a desire to heal.

Coming back to Homeopathy, it is such a powerful system of medicine that it gives me goose bumps when I refresh my memories about this particular episode besides many other miracles I have experienced using Homeopathy.

Back in 1978, my father was very sick, as he had been suffering from prostate problems. He was taken to a major hospital in New Delhi whose head of the urology department went to medical school in London, England. So this England-returned doctor ran some tests on my father and my father started bleeding profusely because of the carelessness of the doctor, and my father was transferred to the intensive care unit. His condition worsened in the next 24 hours. At this stage the doctor said, "I am sorry, and it is all in God's hands." When my father came to know about these so-called words of wisdom of the head of the urology department, he insisted that he must go home because if he has to die, he would like to die in his home. So we took him home and his condition went from worse to critical by evening.

In those times I used to hang around with a young Homeopathic doctor who had become a good friend of mine. So I rushed to him and explained to him the situation. He gave me just one dose of this Homeopathic remedy called "Cantharis" which stopped my father's internal bleeding in less than an hour and he was back on his feet within the next few days. He lived in perfect health for another 10 years and died at the age of 75. Such is the power of homeopathy. This is one of the experiences I went through but it opened my doors to trusting homeopathy and I became a staunch follower of this healing system. I have seen miracles taking place in people's health just because of this science. You will be shocked to know that people who are suffering from diseases like cancer, AIDS and TB, who were given a few months to live by medical science, have stretched their lives to many years, even decades, just because of this one system which took birth in Germany. The only problem with this system is that there are hundreds of medicines and thousands of symptoms associated with these medicines and the doctor has to be educated enough to find the root cause based on the symptoms and prescribe the right kind of remedy in order to have remarkable results in a short time; otherwise, the remedy will act as a placebo.

In chronic cases where the disease has started camping in the body, it could take months and years using this system for the body to clean itself from that particular disease as the problem is brought under control bit by bit, even though it is a very slow system of medicine but amazingly safe and reliable provided the patient is not counting his last breaths.

There is a branch of Homeopathy known as "12 tissue salts." There are twelve salts found within our tissues and any imbalance of these salts causes diseases. You do not have to be a genius to figure out which tissue salt is causing that problem, as the book that prescribes these salts is only 50 pages thick. The remedy I suggested to my client for her son's ear infection was among these tissue salts. There is no way, and I emphasize "NO WAY" one can make one's physical situation worsen using these salts because:

1. They are in extremely low potency, as low as 600 times dilution of a grain of your kitchen salt.
2. If the body does not need it, it will throw it out of the system as the body takes it as food and these salts are part of the body chemistry. There are absolutely no side effects and I have not heard of someone dying by taking these salt tissue remedies.

Do you know what happens in cases where people die because a wrong medicine is given to them? Our body is very smart and is very familiar with all the chemicals, nutrients, their composition, all kinds of bacteria, which is friendly to the body and its hosts. Now, these medicines, which modern science has produced, are mere chemicals designed to kill the bacteria within our bodies, which are causing the symptoms of those diseases. As far as the body is concerned, these drugs are taken as poison within our system. Since the body has a protective system that knows what is good and what is bad, it suddenly goes into chaos and starts to rebel and has started reacting to the chemical. It starts protecting itself so strongly that it can exhaust itself—as a result, people die.

So these tissue salts are the safest remedies on the face of the planet. Even if a child or an infant gulps the whole bottle of 100 pills, the maximum effect he or she could have is minor diarrhea.

We are all born with a healing system, but as we step into adulthood we lose this power to heal ourselves. As kids we are clear as a calm lake, but as we grow older, we are being constantly dumped with social toxins in the form of negative language and messages and lose our ability to look at ourselves from a distance and heal our bodies. As we grow older, the "I" within us is taken over by the identity we are given by society, i.e., Bob, Charlie, Sara, or whatever your name is, and Bob or Charlie have their own role models, and these role models can be anyone: a favorite teacher, actor, singer etc. Let's assume that Sara grew up around music and her favorite singer is Whitney, who has become her unconscious role model. Thus the image of Whitney is controlling the "I" which is Sara, and the poor awareness—the watcher within Sara—watches the drama, unable to do anything. The only way Sara is going to respond to her healing system is if Whitney comes and blesses her, since the focus of Sara's psyche has been on Whitney from the moment Sara started hosting Whitney within her psyche and feeding her with her emotional energies.

Kids are very smart when it comes to healing and they respond very quickly to the therapist (not to the medicine) provided the therapist is more of a healer than a doctor. As a child I used to suffer from headaches and fever and my mother used to take me to this doctor who looked like the goddess of sweetness. She really liked me and every time she would look at me, she would smile, which was 100 times more powerful than any antibiotics available. All she had to say was: "What happened to you, why do you have to get sick," and my fever would drop, baffling my mother, because just before we would start for the clinic, she would take my temperature and the thermometer would show 103 degrees and my condition would look pathetic, and when the doctor would check, it would have dropped to 99 and I would look fine and happy. She would send me home with some B and C complex vitamins. In India, doctors are not paid good salaries; even now a medical doctor who works for a government hospital and has years of experience will have a salary of equivalent to $300-$500 a month. But the desire and wisdom to heal people, the caring for people, exceeds the greed of a western doctor who craves for material wealth and prescribes expensive CAT scans and surgeries to make big bucks. Eventually medical science will lose trust and people will be left with no choice but to explore other forms of therapies.

Did you know that there are people on this planet—normal people like you and me—who can heal you of your problems permanently or who can give you relief for days to come? They can heal you in person or by talking to you over the phone or they can hold your picture in their hands thousands of miles away and you will start feeling healthy.

I have been with many healers and have watched them very closely and I can write with confidence that their work is as honest as your disease. Some healers who are a step ahead and carry the ability to look into your past lives and understand the root cause of the disease are able to delete it from your subconscious memory and then you are not bothered by that problem ever. But these types of healers are very few and not accessible to the common man.

All humans are created equally and have access to the same powers as these healers do but we have lost the faith in our own selves and also we do not have the distance between us like the kids have. A small kid who has just started learning the language will not use the word "I" but will use his name instead. "Mom! John is hungry." "Dad! John is having a pain in the stomach."

Take a deep breath and dive deep into these sentences: John is having a pain in the stomach. For a kid, John is a body that is having the pain only in the stomach area; they will never even say John is sick, as they do not have the understanding of what sickness is. There is no "I" but the duality is still there—John and the awareness, but the awareness of John has been untouched and is very much available to start the healing process because the gap is there.

Poor John will grow up one day and say, "Dad! I am sick." The whole psychology has changed; "I" has taken over John and his awareness of being separate from the body. They are both in total control of this "I." The sensitive distance between John and the awareness has been lost, gone forever. Now who is sick? "I" am sick; the whole body of that "I" is sick, and since John and the awareness have become mere slaves to this "I," the awareness stands there helpless as who is going to cure the "I" as "I" is a mere illusion. Before the "I," this body was identified as John.

Let's presume the body is a car and the awareness or the watcher within John is the driver. When John's car (body) has a flat tire (stomach ache), the driver could fix it but now the car and the driver have both become "I" and this "I" cannot come out of the car and fix the tire because there is no driver anymore as the car is the "I" and so is the driver, and now the tire is not flat but the totality of the car has a problem. A gap is very necessary to heal one's self.

If you live with the spiritual masters you will be amazed to see that they act very much like three-year-olds. They will not use the word "I" and will always use their names while talking about themselves, "Baba has to go there," "Baba is hungry," "Baba needs to go to sleep now" and in case they have a physical problem they will refer to their bodies as "this body" or "Baba's body."

The first step towards the healing process is to create a gap between your awareness and the body. The body is not you and you are not John because before birth there was no John and after death there will be no John. The body has been given its identity by society, and this body is known by the name "John" because the watcher within you cannot be named.

Another area where humans are lacking is self-love. We have not only lost self-love but the majority hate their existence. If we do not love ourselves, what else will we do? We will hate ourselves because of the duality. If we do not have faith in the creator, what will we have? Fear! If we are not happy, we will be unhappy. The reason the majority of humans are sick today is because people are bored with their lives because contentment is missing. The mind is obsessed with having more and more, which is nothing but moving away and breaking off from your being. The focus of the mind has been on the outward and to accumulate more and more.

You must practice self-love in order to heal yourself. You must not hate yourself or the people you meet or see because if you practice hate, you cannot love. Hate is a very powerful energy and sends a lot of heat to the blood causing the blood to overheat and turn acidic, causing cancer and other inflammatory diseases. On the other hand, anger robs the body of vital heat.

Let's come back to diseases. Not all diseases are the outcome of your actions or outside influences; some are karmic, connected with your past lives, and some are contributed by your parents and some are the outcome of your wrong actions, i.e., drinking water while exercising or right after an exercise routine, taking the wrong kinds of foods, taking food which is contaminated, rotten and old, eating too much processed food, not following proper hygiene, taking alcohol, smoking, eating food that is not in harmony with the body, and so on. Our body is so remarkable that it can take care of the above up to a point, provided we are in tune with ourselves and helping ourselves in the healing process.

The creators of this human body were extremely smart people, but the psychologists and the software programmers who wrote the operating software for the mind goofed up because they could not foresee that one day man would become so negative that he could destroy the sensitive balance of the body just by giving power to negative thoughts. While the hardware within us is very brawny, the software needs an upgrade because humanity has reached a point where our window to existence has bugs and will not open up for us to see our true selves. As a result, we are constantly performing illegal functions in the outer and inner world. No wonder many among us are locked into depression and are no longer able to reboot ourselves in our sleep. Our dreaming states are doing nothing but acting as screen savers so that the screens of our conscious awareness does not get burnt.

The scientists need to look into the bio-computer instead of looking into the diseases and their causes, as the problem lies within us, not outside of us. I can prove my point to the medical community.

Take a man who has been given a few months or a few days to live by the medical community and I will check his longevity and resistance power with my methods. If in his destiny he has a few years to live, I will select just five people of my choice and make this man live with them for just six months, and every day these people will give him love, caring, nurturing, and a positive attitude about life. I can guarantee you he will come out of his most horrible disease and in less than six months he will be on his way to final recovery, provided he is not sent back to the same old society where every moment negativity is being tossed at him.

The science of body features is a fascinating science and the more we know about the hidden secrets pertaining to our bodies the faster we will be able to eradicate disease from the planet.

As I mentioned before there are three areas from where diseases are born:
1. Karmic or hereditary diseases
2. Mental and emotional diseases
3. Physical diseases

Karmic or Hereditary Diseases: Karmic diseases are ones where the person is born with a birth defect or a hereditary disease; this can include physical deformities as well as mental problems. Some of these incurable diseases can be healed with mantra repetition or with the grace of a spiritual healer, but the majority of these problems are hard to cure. All we can do is pray for the person because the person has taken this body, just to go through the suffering because of their past karma, and the best we can do is to help the person go through the suffering and help them clear their negative past with prayers and affirmations. In case the suffering person cannot speak or hear, the parents or a person who has tremendous kindness within their psyche should do the above.

Mental and Emotional Diseases: The diseases that occur due to our improper actions start at the mind level first and then move towards different parts of the body when they get charged with negative emotional energy. All diseases pertaining to one's mind start due to an imbalance between the male and the female energies. Man or woman are both combinations of male and female energies. The left side of a man or woman is the female side and the right side of the man or woman is the male side. Above the navel, the area belongs to the male energies, ether and father, and below the navel, the area belongs to the female energies, mother and earth, all different forms of "Shakti" or divine mother.

Emotions are the source of all actions. The energy which runs the mind and body rises from your heart chakra and spreads into the left and the right nipples and then rises up to the third eye which is called the "Agya Chakra" or the action center, which is our link to the universal consciousness; all thoughts are processed here. I will not discuss the deeper insights in this book as it will confuse the reader and defeat the purpose of the book.

The left side of our body is our past and the right side of our body is the future. If we live too much in our past we will be taxing our left side or the emotional side, and if we live too much in the future, we will be taxing our right side or the immune system. An imbalance between the two causes stress in our bodies, which contributes to weakness in different body parts and organs.

Here is an example. Someone cheated you five years ago and that put you in a financial mess that is still haunting you and you feel terrible; you are constantly brooding and thinking about this past foolishness. This kind of thinking creates all the stress. But if you are a balanced being, you will say FINE! I learned my lesson, now I will plan for the future based on my past and get over this messy situation. Here you are in perfect alignment with the laws of nature. You are using both energies in harmony.

Let's presume that a lion is hungry in the jungle and looking for an animal for his next meal. He spots a deer and starts running towards his prey. In the meantime, the deer who has become aware of the danger has started running towards safety. Call it luck or survival instincts, the deer is able to jump a high fence and save himself. Do you think the lion is going to sit there and cry and grumble? What is going on, Mr. Lion? Are you getting old? Have you lost your ability to run? This is the second time in two months that you have lost your meal. Remember the other day you could not catch this monkey as he climbed up a tall tree. Do you want to die of hunger? The moment the deer escaped, the lion's eyes will start searching for the next catch, but his limited mind has learned from the experience and it has improved upon its system.

Wake up, people, we are humans and carry bodies and brains that have abilities a million times superior to a lion. Animals live in perfect harmony and each and every product is an outcome of perfection and harmony. In their case, the condom never breaks, they do not abort their babies, nor do they waste their semen or fake orgasms. They are always interested in supporting their species as it is part of their basic instincts; their reproduction process is pre-planned and well planned. When they are in a sexual union, the sole purpose is reproduction of their species. Animals live in perfect harmony and balance and seldom get sick.

If the toes on both feet are in perfect shape and straight, you are a balanced person, but if they have started bending away from each other, you have started losing the sensitive balance between your male side and the female side.

Even if your toes are straight but the nails on the big toes have lost their natural color and carry any shade of black you are living a stressful life and are sitting on a depressive volcano.

In both cases, you are not in harmony and are creating an imbalance, causing stress to happen which will take the shape of depression one day, which further develops into insomnia, memory loss, emotional imbalance. At this point, the whole body has gone into a turmoil and the effects start showing up within the body, as the individual's body stays fatigued most of the time, blood pressure goes up or down, indigestion and constipation become a common scene. Palpitations, blackouts, body pains—these are all symptoms of the body being imbalanced and not the actual disease, but sadly the poor doctor is going to give medicine for blood pressure or vitamins for fatigue which are going to overload the system even more, worsening the situation. Complete rest for a few days, fasting and eating the right foods, nurturing yourself by spending time in the wilderness, listening to healing music can do miracles for you at this stage.

As I mentioned before, our connection to the earth is through feet and our connection to the sky is through our head. The normal pattern of energy is to flow downwards, from sky to the ground, unless we reach a higher state of consciousness where the energy starts moving upwards through "sushumana Nadi," which happens in the case of a Kundalini awakening. So we exist in between the sky and the earth and our body is a vehicle for energy to flow through us. As far as our body and mind is concerned, our well-being is based upon the free movement of energies, which pass through us, nourishing our bodies. Our relationship with our body is through our feet and our relationship with the existence is through our head. Our relationship with the outside world is through our hands.

In order to live happily we need to stay in balance where we have the ability to resist any abuse and also release any overload on our heart center or the emotional side. Say if someone loved his/her father and the father dies, the shock will be too much to handle and one's mind is locked in a state where one loses the ability to release the shock by letting tears clean the heart chakra. The shock has blocked the flow of energy to the earth as the electrical circuits have been disrupted and the flow of energy has been cut. In case the suffering party is weak, the result can be as severe as the body going through a cardiac arrest followed by going into a coma. On a lesser note, one will go through severe depression, and if one has enough control over one's mind, one will be able to handle the situation very calmly.

Since the roots of all mind-oriented diseases start with depression, if not taken care of, they can spread to other areas of the body by weakening the immune system.

Here is a very simple remedy which will be easy to follow and will show its positive effects in as little as four weeks. The remedies I am offering here are very simple to follow but the results will astonish you.

In order to remove depression at its roots, you will need a few things that you can buy from any New Age, Indian, or health food store, and your local department store or drugstore.

Therapy for Eradicating Depression:

You will need the following:

Water-Based Foot Massager (You can buy it from any drug store or department store)

"Ghee"—Clarified Butter: Any Indian Grocery store or New Age food store carries it. Ghee can also be made at home by boiling sweet butter on medium heat until it turns golden yellow and you can see residue in the form of granules at the bottom of the pot. At this point you can take it off the heat, strain and save the liquid ghee, and throw away the residue (granules and hard matter).

A clean pair of 100% cotton socks

A clean hand towel

Maximum benefit will be experienced if you do this treatment two hours before going to bed.

MUST BE REPEATED EVERY DAY FOR AT LEAST SIX WEEKS

Instructions:

Fill the foot massager with warm water and turn the heat and massager on. (Follow instructions and take suggested precautions that come with the foot massager.)

Place your feet in the foot massager as instructed in the manual.

Massage your feet in the foot massager for about 15 minutes.

Wipe your feet clean and dry with a soft towel.

Rub the palms of your hands for 2 minutes to make them warm. Now take a small spoonful of ghee in your palms and massage it into your feet (tops and soles) concentrating on the toes and nails. Pull on your toes while you massage them. Let the skin and nails absorb the oil. Make sure you devote 10-15 minutes to each foot. If the skin on your feet is very dry, please use more ghee as needed.

After the massage put on a pair of cotton socks and relax in a chair and listen to some calming music (please do not watch TV). You may go to sleep after the massage but do not take the socks off or wash your feet. **Optional:** While relaxing in a chair or on the bed do the following exercise: Bring the thumb of your hands under the base of your little finger and close your fist as if you are holding your thumb in the grip of your 4 fingers. Breathe in and out in a deep and relaxed way for about 15 minutes while holding your thumb in the grip of your fingers (do not hold it too tightly or too loosely).

You can wash your feet after two hours (but avoid doing so if you can). If you want the maximum results in the shortest possible time, you need to go to sleep with the socks on and wash your feet with lukewarm water the next morning.

Try complementing the above with eating raw fruits and vegetables and drinking 6-8 glasses of water every day.

Avoid the following for the next 6-8 weeks:

Avoid watching negative shows on TV.

Stop eating red meat, canned food, sodas, ice cream, and cold, old, and leftover food.

Stay away from coffee, smoking, and alcohol.

Be conscious of your thought patterns and do not jump into the past or the future—try to stay in the present moment.

Gossiping and negative talk about yourself and others.

The results you can expect in a few weeks:

In a few weeks your rotten or black-colored nails will be replaced with new nails or the old ones will start turning pink, bright, and shiny. **IMPORTANT: If your old nails come off, make sure you protect the sensitive skin with extreme care by covering them with a thick cotton pad all day long, which you may remove when you go to bed.**

You will start sleeping better within a week.

You will start experiencing better health, better memory, less fatigue, and numerous other benefits.

No matter how deep your problem is, you will notice a change in your consciousness, and you will not feel stuck within your thoughts.

Please take a picture of your feet before starting this therapy and take a fresh picture every week to record your progress.

Contemplate the following a few times a day:

This life is a gift to you from God and when someone gives you a gift you cannot demand the type of gift you want. Be happy with what you have and stay contented.

Always Remember: All desires (fulfilled or unfulfilled) will end in frustration.

All is beautiful—just live and love this life.

The above therapy will not only treat your depression but will eliminate many other diseases and will also give you calmness of mind, good memory, and a sound sleep. I have experienced astonishing results with people who were on chemotherapy—their lives have changed to being in a perfect state of health by following the above therapy.

Physical Diseases:

The circulation, pressure and the quality of the blood within our bodies determine the state of our health. If our blood is weak and lacks the right pressure, all the organs will be in a state of work-slow attitude. If you want your body to act like a sports car, you should examine your gums every week as gums are the indicators of the state of blood in the body. If your gums are healthy and pinkish, then your blood is in very good condition, but if your gums have turned black or have lost their real color and bleed while brushing the teeth, you should get your blood tested.

One very important area of the human body is its heat system. What will happen if one day the sun starts cooling down? Our planet will freeze to death and there will be nothing left but ice. In exactly the same way, we have in our bodies a place called the "solar center," which is located directly behind the belly button. Your solar center must stay centered at all times. Extreme stress, worry, or too much physical work can knock it off balance and lead to constipation or diarrhea. If the body starts losing its heat, the body becomes sick. The state of the heat system within our bodies can be seen very clearly from the feet. Just look at the Sun toe, which is the fourth toe if counted from the big toe and the second if counted from the small one. Look to see if this toe is bent or crooked on both feet as shown in the figure below.

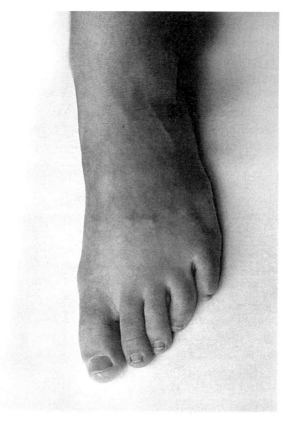

If it looks bent or crooked, the heat system is disturbed within your body (check your solar center) and you do not know what food combining is. The chances are you are mixing the wrong kinds of foods or eating foods that are not in harmony with your body, or your diet consists of cold cuts, sodas, beer, ice cream and cold water, etc. Re-evaluate your diet and bring changes to make your body happy.

Teeth are the best indicators of your stomach. It is an ancient wisdom that 90% of the diseases are born due to stomach disorders. If your teeth are getting loose or holes are forming in your teeth, then the problem is within your stomach. You must get a checkup done immediately and also keep your stomach clean by detoxifying your body. Eat healthy by eliminating concentrated foods and try to eat fresh fruits and vegetables that have been boiled, and make sure you drink filtered water.

Constipation is man's biggest enemy as too much pressure at the anus weakens the heart muscle. The following remedy will eradicate constipation:

Take 1 to 2 spoons of castor oil every day along with milk or warm water which will help your body clean itself and it will also lubricate your elimination system and you will not suffer from constipation. Follow the above for a few days until your bowel movements have become regular.

Since our body is composed of five elements, i.e., air, fire, water, earth and ether, you must include all tastes in your diet—Bitter, Astringent, Pungent, Sweet, Salty, and Sour. Besides breathing deeply from your stomach, you need one large glass of water every 1-2 hours. If you are not going to the bathroom to pee every two-three hours, you are taxing your system and your kidneys.

Another way to keep track of your health is to know about the pressure points on the body. By regularly checking and massaging the major points, you can keep track of your inner state; if a point is disturbed, you will have pain by pressing that point.

If you have been diagnosed with dangerous diseases like cancer, AIDS, leukemia, etc., I would suggest that you take the help of homeopathy instead of allowing yourself to be killed with radiation. I have come across many people who have expanded their life span to many years after the doctors gave them a few months to live. There are many alternative therapies out there that can heal cancer and many other dangerous diseases.

Here are some suggestions to keep your body in an optimum state of health:

1. Have protein during the daytime and carbohydrates in the evening and try not to mix them.
2. Do not drink liquids while taking solid foods or during meals. Always keep a gap of two hours.
3. Follow an exercise routine.
4. Stay away from ice-cold foods or drinks and always take lukewarm water or water at room temperature.
5. Eat lots of fresh fruits and vegetables and eliminate canned, packed, processed or frozen foods that carry a lot of chemicals in the form of preservatives.
6. Personal hygiene is very important because if the pores in your body can breathe properly, you are not taxing the body and saving yourself from skin diseases.
7. It is always a good idea to start your day with citrus fruits and then jump to concentrated food towards the afternoon. You must form a

habit to eat your supper at least 2-3 hours before retiring, but in case it is not possible, make sure you walk at least 200 steps before retiring.

8. If your finances permit, you should get a full body massage every two weeks. Alternate it between a certified acupressurist and a certified massage therapist, but make sure the nails of the massage therapist are not discolored at all and are in good health and there is calmness on his or her face.

9. Finally keep your thoughts clean; do not involve in idle gossiping to hurt others or get hurt. Whatever you say, your body vibrates with the sound waves of those words, so stay very aware and be very careful when using words. Never ever use negative words about your body, mind or existence or the existence of others.

Always remember Prevention is better than Cure.

12

Money and Politics: Our Future

Unless we reform politics and the politicians, unless we redefine the way money is distributed, we will always carry the risk of civil wars and mass annihilation.

I remember an old proverb, which does not seem to be valid in today's society: It goes: "If wealth is lost, nothing is lost. If health is lost, something is lost, and if character is lost, everything is lost."

Our ancestors used to put character on the top, but today we can rephrase the above proverb so that it fits with the present day social structure: "If character is lost, nothing is lost; if health is lost, something is lost; and if wealth is lost, everything is lost."

If we consider character and wealth, east and west are both morally bankrupt. Whereas the east is sexually repressed, the west is shameless. When it comes to money, east and west are both corrupt. The east is visibly corrupt while the west has coated the corruption with logic; hence it is invisible. The east is hungry after wealth and will go to any length to achieve it, so we have corruption, vandalism; people kill for money. Even the politicians who run these countries are corrupt and their reason to join the political trade is for one reason, and that is money. They know very well that power can attract money as power is above money; on the other hand, the west has deviously improved its system of achieving the money goals so no longer is the corruption visible or people are kidnapped and killed for money.

In the east, everyone is corrupt, from a peon to judges, and from politicians to government officials—all are corrupt, the whole system is corrupt. In the east, even if you are 100% honest, you will be forced into corruption or your life will be made into a living hell—such is the power of corruption. Money can buy anything and the power of money is used to snatch anything from anyone, even another person's life.

On the other hand, the west has improved its system of cheating people. People are logically ripped off every day: by businesses, crooks and the government. Politicians depend upon the businesses to fund their election campaigns. Businesses depend upon the politicians to make money. The justice system is blind anyway and is controlled and manipulated by the lawyers. Whether it is framing someone in a criminal case or traffic citations or a parking violation, police officers have quotas to meet. The DA's job depends upon how many cases have been won and people put behind bars. Judges cannot be bought by individuals, but they are lavishly rewarded by the attorneys for making judgments in their favor or are politically pressured into making decisions that will help the politicians. Have you ever fought a court case without an attorney? You could be 100% right but if you go to the court without an attorney, you can be 100% assured that injustice will be served upon you. Want to fight a traffic ticket on your own, you will lose because the police officer who issued the citation and the judge who is deciding the case both are paid by the same branch of the government.

The hard work you do to make few bucks is being snatched from you at every turn. You pay the taxes to support these individuals to run the government and then you are cited by the same individuals to pay the fines. If you are one of those honest people who get paid by the hour, you might not have realized that you pay taxes on the money you have already paid the taxes on in the first place. You are robbed bit by bit, here and there. You are made to lose every moment and whatever is left is taken away from you in the form of state lotteries. Why do you think the governments control the lotteries? It is the most easy and legal way to rob people of their hard-earned monies. Money has become the devil of the dark world.

Money is one of the cruelest inventions of man, which has eaten the social structure from its core. Humans are frantically running here and there in the longing for money. People are losing their health, happiness and peace just for a few numbers which are printed on a piece of paper. People are gambling with their lives each and every moment. Bit by bit they are throwing their life energies into the system that has been designed to rob them instead of rewarding them. Very few get rewarded at the top levels and the majority are being robbed on multiple levels: Their bio-energies, their talents, their precious time, and finally the few papers they earn or the few numbers they gather are snatched logically and sucked back into the system, leaving the future of the masses in a deeper mess with every rising sun.

What is money? A means to exchange products and services in order to ease our lives and make our lives more beautiful, safe, and hassle-free. But are we living up to its purpose? Tomorrow, if Wall Street crashes by 33% in one day and another decline follows with no recovery in sight, I can bet hundreds of people will commit suicide and thousands will end up in hospitals with depression and heart attacks, or end up in mental institutions—all just because a few digits were restructured, which in reality should not have any impact on the functions of the human body. But the mere thought that one has lost in the financial game will impact the mind so much that all functions of the body will be disturbed to the point that in many individuals there will be chaos on the physical level. So one thing is proven: that thought powered by belief has enough power even to kill.

Let's take an example: A poor man can say that he is a millionaire but it is not backed by the power of belief, whereas a millionaire has the power to back his thought with belief. So if you tell the poor man that he has lost millions, he will laugh, but the same sentence can make the millionaire's heartbeat stop. We humans have been blessed with the power of thought. If used positively along with faith, we can use this power to create a heaven on this planet. The sad part is that instead of using this power for the elevation of mankind we have used it to destroy the masses and ourselves. The whole concept of money and its offshoots is slowly eating away our lives. Money has degraded the state of humans to the point that man has become selfish, rude, uncaring and cruel.

From the slums of Bombay to the streets of the Bronx, the story is the same. For the common man, money is primarily used for satisfying his hunger of the material for the illusionary, i.e., automobiles, home, clothes, sex, alcohol, gambling—the list can be as long as your desires. Every day many kids go to sleep sick and hungry while their fathers waste their day's income in alcohol and gambling. This is the everyday story in every part of the world, whether rich or poor. Somehow poverty has always been associated with the east. In the west people always point towards the east and say: the east is poor, but here in the USA, the richest country in the whole world, where a great number of wealthy live in million dollar mansions, their own brethren pass their nights shivering in cold on streets all over the country. A visit to the San Francisco Bay Area will show that the homeless population is on the rise, and on every block of downtown San Francisco you will find at least one person begging for food.

Despite America being abundantly rich, why is the homeless population on the rise? An imbalance in the distribution of money is the cause of rising poverty among Americans. Every year thousands of families file bankruptcies; credit card debt is on the rise, jobs are being cut so that the CEOs can afford their mansions and private jets. The few who are smart at the numbers game are successful in robbing the numbers from others, adding them to their booty. The only difference between a millionaire and a homeless man is that one was able to win the rat race and the other lost it.

The concept of money was created for the benefit of mankind and there is nothing wrong with the concept because it brings a certain discipline, but it has taken the shape of rheumatoid arthritis where the pillars of the system are becoming deformed. The concept needs to be changed before the masses are left with nothing to eat while these money-gulping greedy people who own the giant industries—i.e., banking, finance, oil, real estate, electronic, medical, insurance etc.—are overflowing with money. Very soon you will see that in poor countries civil wars will become a common scene, as the poor countries are getting so poor that their economic structure is in a mess. With every rising sun a greater part of the world's population is losing points in the survival game and the numbers grow every day.

The day the poor man is going to be denied food, his survival instincts are bound to kick in and he will be left with no choice but to kill the affluent for food, as for him it would be death either way.

If the rich countries do not straighten their acts now, very soon the lives of people in these rich countries will be held at stake by the poor ones who have denied their people good lives but have procured nuclear arms. Then the "Jihad" will not be against America but against capitalism, and if you look closely at world affairs the virus of anti-capitalism has taken birth and is spreading. The September 11, 2001, attack on the World Trade Center is a clear indication that we are heading towards anarchy on a mass level.

There is a dire need to bring equilibrium to the social and political structure in the world, as we cannot continue this game for long. The only way we can achieve this is by bringing in more awareness within ourselves towards money. You might not have realized this, but in today's world, the most powerful religion is not Christianity or Islam but capitalism, and the son of this capitalistic God is: Money. From Popes to preachers, presidents to paupers—all need money. In reality, the majority of religious institutions have become more a source of income than places of worship. All over the world people are fighting left and right to control these institutions because they are a good source of income for many, as well as a podium for the power-hungry people to control the masses or amass wealth.

We must realize that money is a mere tool to exchange services and not an evil that controls the masses. The dilemma is that for the majority, this tool has become a driving force to live this life. Just a few hundred years ago, there was no money; people would share their resources with each other, but then the sharing was lost to the barter system and then came the concept of money and this concept has taken the shape of a social termite. The person who works the hardest gets the least and vice versa. Money controls the lives of the masses and a few greedy and uncompassionate people on the planet control money. It does not matter if you live in India or America, China or Chile, Africa or Australia, you will never be able to control your life if someone else has control over your income. As money becomes the supreme God on this planet, no longer is a man known by his character but a man is known by the amount of money he makes.

Money is no longer a means to exchange services but it has reached a point where it has become a tool to control others. Money has become more of a drug for us as we must have money in order to live; it's more of an addiction. Do you know that in America we call credit cards a bigger addiction than drugs?

Recession, a weak economy and a slowdown are the creations of capitalistic cartels. This is the way of the rich man to stay rich and keep the "poor" poor. Do we see that in nature? No! Does the earth ever say: Oh! I am not going to allow the seeds to sprout because there is a slowdown in the movement of the earth particles? Has the sun ever denied heat to the earth because there was a slowdown in the fusion of elements within the sun's atmosphere? Does the ice ever stop melting in the mountains because it snowed less than normal? No, it can never happen, and the day it starts happening, we will cease to exist. Then why does the economy slow down? Why are people hired when needed and fired when not needed? Can we stop the cycle of hunger by telling the body that we are jobless and cannot afford to feed you and we will resume feeding you when we get a new job? No, it is not possible. There is a strong need for the masses to learn that they in fact are responsible for their downfall and making a few greedy people control their lives. The majority are so foolish that they are made to believe the opposite way. If every worker quits his work in every country, there is bound to be chaos for some time, but a new world will appear out of this chaos that will be based more upon sharing than exploiting. We must bring a change in the distribution of money: How can we do it? One suggestion would be that it should become mandatory for every business to equally distribute 33% of the gross profit among all employees, as they are the ones who are contributing towards the growth of the company.

If we want harmony on the planet, we must change the concepts of capitalism. Think deeply and you will realize that capitalism is the fool who is using the ax of greed and chopping the branch he is standing on, not realizing that when the branch is completely chopped off, he will fall to the ground as well.

If we want to change the present system we must educate the masses. People need to be made aware that they should not fall into the trap of advancement/upgrade on the outer level and should stay within their limited resources and focus on self-sufficiency.

In the east, money is still a need, but the east is catching up with the west and in few years the east will be addicted, too. The east has also started spreading the virus of credit within its economic structure.

Your whole life revolves and depends on money even though every dollar bill says "In God we trust." I guess we should change the line to "in capitalistic God we trust," because if this one dollar bill is not available to you, your life will be in a mess and your trust in God will drop like a dead leaf. May be we are misleading ourselves and the real meaning of God on the dollar bill is "Good Old Dollar."

Every single moment people are rushing in search of this capitalistic God, and I agree it is easier to understand than the real God, who is illusionary to start with. One needs to meditate for months, years and maybe lifetimes to have a mere glimpse of him. Still there is no guarantee, because just meditation alone is not good enough; you need humbleness, compassion, love, sharing, and the list goes on. Whereas to become enlightened with the capitalistic God, all you need is greed and cruelty. Chant the mantra of cruelty for a few months and you will become a capitalistic guru. Every day more and more are joining the list of people who have been obsessed with numbers. More numbers, more power, more control.

The other day I read the following on the Internet:

SOCIALISM

You have two cows. The government takes one to give to someone else.

COMMUNISM

You have two cows. The government takes both and gives you the milk.

FASCISM

You have two cows. The government takes both and sells you the milk.

NAZISM
You have two cows. The government takes both and shoots you.
BUREAUCRACY
You have two cows. The government takes both, shoots one and pours the milk down the drain.
CAPITALISM
You have two cows. You sell one and buy a bull.
ANARCHY
Steal neighbor's bull, shoot the government.

We have experienced everything up to capitalism in the past 200 years and we have come to the last point where we have stepped into anarchy, because anarchy has already started spreading towards the west from these poverty-stricken, third-world countries where people's lives are in a mess because of economic sanctions and political instability. When people are not making enough to survive, then it becomes easy for a few power-hungry people to exploit these people. How do you think terrorist organizations are formed? One power-hungry person like Bin Laden, who has the resources, exploits a few angry, poor, and unemployed men by giving them money to support their families, and they feel indebted towards this person, and when this person backs his ideas with the power of religion, the people in the group start taking this person as their "messiah," Son of God, and they are ready to sacrifice their lives at his beck and call.

If we look at the present day political scenario, we have three kinds of politicians ruling different parts of the world.
1. Mill Politicians
2. Military Politicians
3. Militant Politicians

Mill Politicians are the products of political mills; they are thoroughbred from childhood and their sole purpose is to serve/govern the country in some way or the other. The majority of these politicians are honest, sincere, and carry strong desires and abilities to serve their countries. Politics is their life, their passion and their power to live this life. It does not matter whether they belong to the left or the right, Republicans or Democrats, or if they belong to the communist or social party, their sole purpose is to be in charge. We can call these types of politicians the Mill Politicians. From Washington to Kennedy, Nehru to Gandhi to Gorbachev and Clinton to the Bushes, they all fall in this category.

Military Politicians are heads of the armed forces that have always resented taking orders from Mill Politicians and they develop a strong desire to rule the countries. They are always on the lookout for a weak government so that they can fulfill their devious motives of ruling the country. The first chance they get, they overthrow the government and take over as the heads of the countries. These types of politicians are the neutral type, and after gaining power either they work for the people or against the people. Pakistan's Musharaf, Cuba's Fidel Castro, and many others belong to the Military Politicians group.

Militant Politicians are an emerging breed of politicians who are either very poor or very wealthy; these kinds of politicians want power, fame and control. They jump into politics with a cause, and they would go to any length in order to fulfill their passion, even if it means sacrificing their lives or the lives of others. Since they have a motive, a target, they seldom care for other humans. These are the most dangerous forms of politicians who have started popping up all over the world, including the United States. If you look deeply you will not find much difference between the Oklahoma City bombers or the World Trade Center destroyers. They shared many common values and goals even though one belonged to the Christian group and the other to Islam. Both were angry with the U.S. government, both were backed by religious fanaticism, both wanted to make a point with mass destruction killing of hundreds and thousands.

If we scan the world we will find many groups working all over the world. Many such groups have been responsible for creating chaos in Kashmir and other parts of India. The IRA is another example, the Hamas group in Palestine, and we can go on and on. Hitler and Bin Laden types are products of these types of politicians.

As we progress into a more sophisticated and advanced world, we find that the political system has not progressed much and needs a major overhauling. There is a dire need to bring equilibrium to the social and political structure in the world if we want to protect the human species from mass destruction at the hands of these Militant Politicians.

Here are my suggestions that can help the masses live better and safer lives in this chaotic world, which is progressing towards its extinction quite rapidly.

1. A group of people is formed based on their state of consciousness. These people should have power above the President and above the Congress or over the Government and they should have the ability to fire anybody from the government including the head of the country. Their purpose should be to watch over the affairs of the government. Currently, one government takes over and they know that they are on

a joy ride for the next couple of years; some take good interest in order to continue and some are just there to enjoy the perks which come with their political positions. Since the rich have money and money brings in power, the only people to take advantage of the government are the rich and the poor and the middle class never ever get a chance to make their voices heard. The suffering party is not even in the big picture. This watch group should keep an eye on all politicians and all affairs of the country and should be able to change any concept, laws, rules that are detrimental to the progress of society.

2. The industries, which are extremely profitable, should be partly run by the government and partly by the private sector. The management should be taken care of by the private sector because government employees know that their jobs are secure. They do not care if the job is done right or not, and if the private sector has control over operations, then everybody will work at their best. The money generated from the above industries should be used towards the welfare of the masses, educate people towards what they love to do and not to make them into machines to be of use to the economy because economy is for people and not the other way around.

3. The concept of nine to five should be abolished and there should be two shifts—one for early risers and one for late risers—but no one should work for more than 6 hours a day. This way more people could be employed and also productivity will increase as there will be less pressure on the people, and also offices will be open for 12 hours a day. This way people will be able to spend more time with their families, and while the parents work, their kids will be in school and they can all be together at the same time. Families will be much closer to each other and also the kids will not get a chance to be on their own unless they are mature enough to understand life.

4. Every employee should have a two-week vacation after every six months, which should be mandatory and should be paid for by the company. We can have two benefits from this. One, the vacation will refresh the employee and he will work with full dedication. Two, the travel industry and its subsidiaries will do well, thus making the economy flourish; moreover, the distribution of the money will be much better.

5. It should be the responsibility of the government that anybody who is working full time will have basic amenities—food, clothes, and shelter, as well as full health coverage. People are busting their buns out there just for their daily bread and butter, whereas these money-

hungry multinational companies have money to throw away. You can call it capitalism but I call it imbalance. Humans have had enough of this unfair system. Communism and democracy have both failed. I do not know much about politics but I do know that it is time that we change the system in order to save this world from the chaos that is imminent.

6. A new world body should be formed or the United Nations should be rearranged and this new body should bring all countries under its umbrella. This new organization should have an army, navy and air force under their control, which should be formed by taking the best cadets from all the military, navy and air force organizations from every country. Each country's national security system should be dissolved so that there is no threat left for the world about a nuclear crisis. And if any country's government refuses to follow the instructions, their governments should be removed forcibly and a new government be formed with the help of the UN or this new body and law and order restored. It should be the responsibility of this new body that every person in that country has a place to sleep at night, food to eat and a doctor to take care of their health. Once all countries abolish their national security systems we will have more harmony on the planet as these patriotic men and women can be absorbed into the justice system, which is becoming corrupt day by day. Then Russia, China, and America will not be a threat to each other or to the rest of the world.

7. Anyone who is found and proven to be an enemy of mankind beyond any doubt should be removed from the face of the planet— we do not need any more Hitler types on this planet. One fish spoils the whole pond and in order to save the rest of the fish, it is very fair to exterminate that one fish. If only someone could have killed Hitler, we would not have had so much bad karma around Germans. For ages to come each Jew will curse the Germans.

8. The president or the head of state should select one citizen every week, randomly chosen from a state, who will get a chance to be the guest of the head of state or the president for just two days. For these two days this person should get a chance to stay by the side of the head of state from the time he wakes up to the time he goes to sleep—this way the president will get a chance to know what is happening in the lives of his citizens. Currently the President has no contact with the common man and whatever information reaches him is well polished by all the president's men, who in turn are greatly influenced by the lobbying of rich industrialists. A few

hundred years ago, in the times of kings and kingdoms, a good king was one who would dress up in different costumes every night and would roam in the streets disguised as a common man just to see what was going on in the real world.

9. Education should be free for all. At present, there are people who are very intelligent but will never get a chance to explore their talents because of the money issue. For them, the big question is how to break the vicious cycle of survival, and persist in their quest for knowledge.

10. Chemical industries that are known to cause an imbalance in the ecological cycle should be shut down forever to save the planet from harmful gasses, and research should be done into finding new ways of generating energy. Otherwise, in just a few years, the weather will change for the worse, destroying all habitat.

11. The population of the planet should be brought under control and new ways should be found using the ancient sciences to match couples in order to produce high-quality kids.

There is a strong need to change the course of humanity because we are very close to our extinction as the destructive trend has already started, economically speaking. Except for a few countries, the world is in a mess; crime is becoming high tech as criminals find new ways of mass destruction. Natural disasters are on the increase and so are man's desires, which are causing devastation in people's lives. The majority are suffering and are in pain and anger and a feeling of helplessness and hopelessness prevails. If you are very sensitive to the vibrations around you, just take a drive in an affluent neighborhood and then pass through a economically depressed area and you will know the difference.

The future of humanity as well as the future of these politicians lies in the hands of these Mill Politicians. People vote for a candidate based upon face value and they are not made aware of the pasts of these candidates in the election campaigns.

Many of these politicians are smart crooks who are there to take care of their interests as well as the interests of their own kind. Some are hardworking and have a genuine interest in the progress of the nation, but these people are brought down by the opposition parties or are made to suffer with negative propaganda and false scandals by the people who control the media.

Once we decide that such and such a person is going to be the head of a country, his past life relating to his personal matters should not be brought up in public as it would hamper his morale to serve his country or mankind, unless he was a criminal and became an instrument directly or indirectly in killing or destroying someone's life or property.

Politics is the man and money is woman. We cannot separate them but there is a strong need to reshape these two bodies in order to have a healthy, sane, educated, and happy baby called society.

13

The Game of Misery

Misery is a state of mind experienced by you, within you. It is your choice to allow yourself to be in a state of misery or to laugh at the moment and learn from it.

I would like to tell you an episode that took place thousand of years ago in India. There lived a pundit who was very famous for his knowledge and he was the favorite of the king. The king's name was Janak. This pundit had a child who was deformed in eight places and his name was "Astakavakra." "Astaka" means eight and "vakra" means deformed. Even though this child was deformed, he was one step ahead of his father in knowledge and wisdom as he was a young sage. So one day there was a contest going on in the palace and the theme was, "What is truth or reality." The arguments continued all day long.

The sun was setting and the decision time was coming closer; this young child knew that his father was losing the contest to another pundit. So he decided to go to the palace. As he reached the hall where the king and the other pundits were sitting, everybody started laughing as he walked into the meeting. Since he was handicapped in eight places, his walk was very funny and whosoever saw him could not resist laughing, including the king himself. So the child started laughing, too. The king was taken aback and asked the child, "I understand if others are laughing, but why are you laughing?" So the child responded that I laugh because these "Chamaars" (in India, people who make shoes or make products from leather or dead skin are known as Chamaars and they are treated as the lowest of the lowest castes in India—even now they are not allowed to drink water from the wells belonging to higher caste people, just because of their profession which relates to dead skin) are deciding about the truth, about the reality who cannot even see beyond my skin; they can only see my deformities and not what I am from within.

The king felt very guilty but did not say anything. The next morning when the king was enjoying his morning ride outside his palace and he saw "Astakavakra" coming, he got off the horse and fell at the feet of this young boy and said "Master, forgive me for yesterday and please come to my palace and explain what the real truth is."

Our misery starts the moment we open our eyes to look, the moment we tune our ears to hear, the moment we touch, smell or taste, because we have only two choices—take it or leave it, accept it or reject it, love it or hate it. The judge within us is blind, just like the picture of the woman in the courtroom, who has covered her eyes and is holding a balance. We might be able to look at this world but we are blind as far as other dimensions go. Even animals carry more sense as well as abilities to hear, smell, and see far beyond human abilities. We only see what we want to see; we only hear what we want to hear.

We are constantly judging, accepting or rejecting. The majority of our time is lost in judgments; we seldom experience, but we are always ready to make a judgment in a hurry. Even though Jesus' message was "Judge ye not," we love to judge others and we never look at our own thoughts, words and actions, because we do not have the awareness to look at our own selves. Awareness creates that gap within us to look at ourselves from a distance. It is easy to judge others and form opinions because we are not concerned with the well-being of the other, even though we create the fog of caring for the other, but in reality, our motives, our selfishness is working as an undercurrent. The clear reason Jesus said not to judge others was because on the final judgment day, we will not be able to look at ourselves since all our lives we had been judging others. You enjoy judging others as it makes you feel better. For many, ridiculing others, being sarcastic, putting them down, and being a heart breaker is a fun way to live this life, but remember—what you do to others will be returned to you.

The justice system seems puny if you look at the functioning of the mind. In 24 hours we have thousands of thoughts and we keep on comparing and judging every moment, first inside of us, and then outside. I am black, he is white; I am more qualified than others, I have more money, a better car, a better house, a better job, a better wife, a better husband, and so on. We have created a judgmental mess all around us.

The reason we have so much hate on the planet is because of judgment. The east has the caste system and hundreds are killed every year just because someone passed judgment that these people belonged to a lower caste and have no right to be alive.

The west is more civilized and a little polished and does not use the caste system but uses a similar word called "racism." A non-white or a black person goes looking for a job, a house or a loan from the bank, and he is told that he is not eligible even though he is more qualified than a white man or has a better credit rating. Instead of using "racism," we can use "not eligible." Man is cruel when it comes to using words; if ever words could kill, we would not be alive here today. By constantly judging ourselves and others we are chopping the roots to our survival, bit by bit, by fragmenting our fellow humans. It seems we have fallen below the level of animals because even animals do not ridicule or judge other animals.

What is misery and why do we become miserable?

Ponder on the following and you will understand the basics of misery. Presently the electronics industry is not so advanced, especially the communication industry, even though we have cellular phones, talk radios and telephones, but for a telephone to communicate with another telephone, two wires or circuits are needed, the same goes for the cellular phones. We need cell sites to receive the signals and transmit them back to the wanted frequency, or the satellites in orbit function as a catalyst.

This is my vision about the future of the electronics industry: The day will come when the underground wires or cables will not be needed nor will we have to cramp space with useless communication satellites because the communication equipment will become standard and each equipment will act as a cell site or a satellite and there will be a web of network around the world. Each person will have his own communication device that will act as a channel for other frequencies to receive and transmit data and then we will have a web of these channels.

Then we will not have to send hundreds of communication satellites into space or lay miles and miles of underground cables—we will have to send just a few satellites into orbit to cover the very remote areas on the planet and to link the continents.

My vision is based upon the functioning of our minds. Our minds are the most sophisticated communication device ever created on this planet and the scientists will take hundreds of years to even come close to what we have called the mind. We are constantly communicating with other minds and exchanging thoughts. Not only this, our minds also act as a vehicle to channel the thoughts of the minds of others. If we nurture love and happiness, we are exchanging harmony. If we nurture anger, hate, resentment, and criticism, we are exchanging and spreading misery using the thought frequencies.

Let's get back to racism. Mr. Black hates Mr. White or vice versa, and one of them thinks of killing the other because of their race or color; the thought waves are transmitted to every human on the planet who nurtures hate and is stored in the unconscious mind and would be readily available when a demand is created in the external world.

What exactly is there in skin color? Do you know that in the mother's womb it is pitch dark and we are born out of this darkness and will dissolve into this darkness. White or black, all will rot in their graves or turn into ashes one day, but here judgment is the real culprit and racism, hate, violence are its byproducts.

This is exactly what happened in the 1984 riots in India in which thousands of Sikhs were killed; a similar episode was repeated in California after the Rodney King beating. The frequency used was hate, and whosoever nurtured hate within them was able to access the frequencies and get so much power that they could tune them into killing other humans.

The same power was used by Hitler and the same power was used when India and Pakistan were divided in 1947; Hindus were butchering Muslims and Muslims were butchering Hindus even though they had a history of living together as families for hundreds of years.

Not long ago three white men in Texas tied a black man to their pickup and dragged him to his death. What happens? The negative thought energy is transmitted and received by the humans who nurture hate. It might sound cruel, but if a white man who breeds racism within his heart and mind hears this episode, he will laugh and say, "One more gone. Let's kill all of them." On the other hand a black man will think that the day he gets his chance, he will clean the white race from the face of the planet. Hate is the frequency and racism is being communicated.

In group meditations, the same principle works on a positive note. One person who has a clean mind and heart and has the ability to access the higher frequencies can trigger similar effects in people around him. Everyone gets influenced and the cycle gets stronger and stronger. Since we live in a world of positive and negative frequencies we get affected by these frequencies especially when we are in close proximity of another life force, whether they are animals or humans. Spiritual masters have known this secret for ages and they do not allow any "Tom, Dick or Harry" to come near their physical bodies; they keep their distance. You might think that they are being racist but they are just protecting their aura from being polluted by negativity. A few drops of lemon juice can spoil gallons of milk in an instant.

Next comes desire. Once we agree to play the game of misery, we must have a judge and desire to play the game. As soon as we jump into the world of desires we start hurting ourselves as desire creates wanting and wanting creates impatience and impatience creates stress and stress transforms into depression and then over to insanity where we become functionless and lose the sensitive equilibrium within our psyche.

If one visits the remote areas in the Himalayas, people have more happiness on their faces, there is a glow to their skin and a shine on their face and they do not have access to any beauty products, nor do they have electricity; they have to walk a mile every day to fetch drinking water and they have to walk a few miles to the nearest grocery store. On the other hand, someone who lives in Bombay in his posh apartment on Marine Drive is living a scared-to-death existence. Crime is high, economy is unstable, government changes every few months, his driver did not show up, his maid is on vacation, telephone is not working, life is a mess for him. It seems the more we try to ease our lives the worse they become.

We have needs, and where our needs end, desire takes birth. In order to live our lives peacefully, all we need is food to eat, clothes to wear, and a shelter to live, but technology has advanced so much that we need to have electricity, appliances, automobiles to move around, telephone, now computers and the Internet, and the list goes on and on, as there is no limit to increasing one's wants, and man is so smart that he has changed his desire into needs. One has a VCR but you know how hard it is to store all those bulky videos and the VCR is such an old concept, you have to play with the tracking button if the picture is fuzzy and it takes ages for the video to rewind and you can justify the need to upgrade to a DVD. It goes for computers as well, more power—less time spent on the job. Man goes on upgrading in the external world and internally he is becoming more and more outdated and disabled.

With logic, one can bend any rules, because with logic one can play with words. Attorneys follow the same principle in court; a killer turns into a defendant. There are many instances where the cop shot and killed someone holding a 3-inch knife and the case against the cop has been dropped because he killed defending his life.

No game has fun unless it has competition.

It is another of man's cruel inventions and we start teaching it at a very young age. "Look, Johnny, you are behind your sister; Sara has already finished her breakfast." Johnny must be enjoying his breakfast or he has taken birth with wisdom to chew his food a hundred times before he swallows it. The same mother is going to tell Johnny after few years, that he must chew his food properly because the doctor has said so and the reason he has poor health is because he does not chew his food properly and is always in a hurry to finish his food, causing him ill health. Competition has become such an obsession that the majority are ready to lose their lives for the sake of winning a competition. The winners become the losers in the end.

When the other is playing better than you, your jealousy kicks in.

We have so much jealousy on the planet. He has more than I do. There is a famous proverb used among men in India, "It always seems bigger in someone else's underpants."

You must have heard the famous story about two cats fighting for a piece of bread and they could not decide which piece was bigger. This monkey comes along and acts as a mediator and he eats a small portion from the bigger piece and then the other piece looks bigger and he eats another piece from the bigger one and finally he ends up eating all of it. And the cats are left with nothing.

In this world of competition and jealousy, we are eating our own lives away piece by piece. Look at the old people—the majority are living hopeless and helpless lives, rotting in old homes, unhappy, looking for someone to talk to, scared because anytime there can be a knock on the door and the angel of death can show up. They are in no hurry now, whereas all their lives they have pushed others and themselves into hurrying up, being fast and quick. How can you relax when all your life you have been rushing?

If you are losing the game of life you start blaming others for your pitfalls. When a child is growing up, often he is told to be responsible, but in any family structure the most powerful blames the less powerful and the chain continues. We even lie and put the blame on others because we are scared of the repercussions. We always look for someone, something, some issue to dump the blame on as it hurts us to say: "I goofed up"; why not throw the blame on others and get it over with. Blaming the other is nothing but being a coward running away from taking the responsibility.

If you are one of those lucky people who are always in a win-win situation, you are so stimulated that you start feeling "holier than thou" and the ego takes over you. Because of this ego, you tell others "I know you." But have you known yourself, who you are, what your purpose is on this planet? It seems just before you get pushed into the world from your mother's womb, someone whispers into your ears the sacred mantra of ego: "You are the best and no one can beat you."

Man is the only greedy living form on this planet. A lion does not kill more than his need and store it in his cave, nor do elephants break some extra branches and carry them on their backs in order to save them for tomorrow. Man goes on holding more and more. The rich have food to waste as they have too much, more than they can handle; most of the food prepared in their kitchen goes to the dump while others go hungry in this world. One is living in a mansion, which has 20 rooms, while another sleeps on the side of the road. Insecurity is the force, which works behind greed. Greed is one of the root causes of disharmony on the planet that will make the majority perish one day. In the third world countries where people are uneducated, they go on producing more and more kids, increasing the world population. The clear reason is greed; more kids, more people to bring in the resources. Greed for power, greed for money, greed for sex, greed for information, and the list is long. If we divide the world's resources equally I am sure everyone will start living a comfortable life. No wonder in America 10% of the people own 90% of the wealth and the other 90% own the 10%. So just because of this imbalance, the ten percent who are successful in their greed are making the rest of the ninety percent struggle for food, clothes and shelter.

When people get attached to their greed and their winning streak, it becomes their obsession, and in the process the freedom to grow is lost. Because you are the best, who is going to compete with you? Attachment can be another meaning for lack of freedom. You have a bird at home, and the bird is caged. You are attached to the bird, as every morning the bird starts singing and you love that sound, not realizing that the bird might be singing about the times when he was free and hopes that the day will come when he will fly free in the sky. Capturing or caging someone in your emotions is nothing but attachment. We beautify the word attachment. We say, "I am very attached to you," but in reality, we mean that I have attached you to me and you are my living force. I depend on you as I do not have my own strength to live this life in my aloneness. People who are lonely, weak and emotionally unstable, people who are negative and lack the guts to live this life with a force called "current of life," use this vice called attachment to suck the life force of other humans, just like a leech. Attachment is the foundation of all miseries.

The fear of losing this game of life forces one to win and win. What is this fear all about? All fears are products of one single fear known as "death." Man's only fear is death, which is definite. Man kills out of fear, destroys out of fear, loves out of fear, speaks out of fear—where is this fear coming from? Fear comes from our ancestors who had to hunt for food and save themselves from the ferocious animals, but as the world became more civilized, the criminals took the place of animals and the fear continues. Fear is the barrier to man's spiritual growth. If you were taken to a place where you are told to do whatever you want and you will not die or get hurt, you will come out of that place enlightened. Watch the movie "Groundhog Day" or "Defending Your Life."

Because of fear one goes for the power. The day you stop getting a kick out of amassing wealth, you jump to power.

Politicians are very smart people, smarter than the common man, because a common man's thinking is very limited. He thinks that one day he will be very wealthy and then he will have power over others, but the politicians think a step ahead. That is why they are able to rule the masses. They know this little secret—get the power and they will have everything available on this planet.

The famous old proverb that "power corrupts" is very true. A feeling of worthlessness attracts one to power; the majority of the politicians carry the feeling of self-contempt on their faces and you can see this very clearly. While they are in power everybody around them lifts them and as soon as they lose power they are thrown out of the system and no one acknowledges them.

Politicians, government officials, people in power, movie actors, actresses, and the majority are energy suckers. Even some of the singers are energy suckers and you can find a cult around their lyrics. Have you ever realized that many times when you meet a new person and start talking with the individual, within seconds you start feeling a lack of energy and get a feeling that your energy is being drained out of your body? If you are very perceptive, you will move away from that person on some pretext. If you do not have the awareness to know this little secret of bio-energy, you are in for a ride on the negative energy wheel because you are bound to feel lifeless after being with such a person who has drained your energy.

Learn to understand your own self, your body, what your body needs, and what it rejects. Know the kinds of people your unconscious is getting attracted to, compared to the kinds of people you like and get a kick out of. It is pure and simple. You like smoking and you love the company of other smokers, or you are an alcoholic and you love the company of alcoholics because non-drinkers are bound to reject you as soon as they know that you are addicted to alcohol.

Your unconscious is very aware of the situation and will attract people towards you who will try to pull you out of your addictions, but since your desires are stronger and man is nothing but a slave to his obsessions, you are bound to reject and push these people away from you. If these people are perceptive, even though your unconscious has sent a "mayday" message to other beings who are not living in the same frequency as a smoker, druggie or alcoholic, their unconscious minds have their own protective system to guard their bodies from negative energies, and they are bound to reject you, even though you could be the nicest person on the planet.

Guilt is man's No. 1 enemy, as guilt can take you to the graveyard faster than AIDS. Guilt only hits people who are weak and lack the understanding to cope with their mistakes. They do not know the golden secret of life—that to be a human is to err. Man learns from his own mistakes and it is perfectly all right to err provided your mistake does not cost someone his life and provided you do not start living your life by following the rule of trial and error.

The one who has lost the game of life starts resenting his own self as well as other's. Since we are good at calling our faults as human mistakes, when the other makes a mistake just as we do, we take it as an act of deliberation to hurt us. It seems we all have a stockpot within our minds in which we are always boiling the soup of resentment over the fire of anger. Even after years we keep on resenting the episode, the people involved, as we were never taught to forgive and forget. Everyone must have heard his parent saying, "If so and so had not done that to him, he would had been in a better position in life." We brood, resent, grumble, complain over and over again and sometimes we just love to do it. We are obsessed with our past.

The reason cancer is on the rise in the world is just because people are short-circuiting their own bio-energies. How? Say, we had a negative experience with someone that had a deep impact on our psyche. Ten years have passed and our body and mind are no longer in the situation and just the memory is there, along with the emotions. The state we are in at this very moment is positive and we start thinking about what happened ten years ago; we are connecting the present which is a positive polarity to something which was negative in nature and happened in the past. In other words we have pulled a negative polarity wire from our bio-energies and joined it with a positive polarity and have short-circuited this very moment, creating misery. When we continue the pattern of short-circuiting our bio-energies for many years it weakens our system and our bodies become a breeding ground for harmful bacteria contributing to physical and emotional problems.

Our life is very short and energies very limited. Our positive polarity is very sensitive and fragile because of the times we are going through and if we let these negative polarity frequencies suck away our positive energies, we will be creating a black hole for ourselves for the future. Since the flow of energy is always from positive to negative, higher to lower, in order to survive through these negative times, we must strengthen our awareness and must opt for the positive frequencies and have faith in the existence. Drop by drop we will be able to collect our powers which will help us take a jump into the realms of happiness and bliss.

Some tips to stay away from misery:
1. Next time you are thrown in a miserable experience, shake yourself out of the misery by breathing in and out vigorously. Now relax your breathing and think for a moment and ask yourself whether you want to experience this misery or continue with your happiness.
2. No matter how bad the situation is, your calmness equals your awareness which in turn is the deciding factor whether you will opt for misery, stay neutral or make the situation into a learning experience. The more aware you are the easier it will be for you to deal with the situation.
3. Anger, frustration and jealousy, etc., are passing clouds on the screen of your consciousness; they are harmless until you start feeding them with your emotions. Your emotions are the power they nurture on and then become powerful and make you miserable. Learn to channel your emotions towards the positive. The choice is yours.

14

Happiness to Bliss

Each one of us relates happiness based on our state of consciousness. For the majority happiness is a mere absence of misery since happiness and misery are the two sides of the same coin belonging to this world of duality. If we are not sick that does not mean that we are healthy. If we are not miserable that does not mean we are happy.

The majority have very wrong notions about happiness. While the poor think that driving a fancy car and living in a mansion is pure happiness, someone who has accumulated all the luxuries of materialism thinks being in power or being famous is where all the happiness is. Someone who is famous and powerful thinks this fame and power is robbing him of happiness and wishes that he was better off without this name and fame and thinks of the poor man sitting under the shade of a tree by a lake enjoying all the happiness of life.

There is an interesting Indian story. There lived a bum named Krishna in a small village. He would make enough to survive and enjoy the rest of his time playing with the village kids, helping the old, trekking in the wilderness. One day while he was enjoying the shade of the tree a rich farmer remarked:

Farmer: Krishna! Most of the time I see you wasting your life with kids and loitering, why don't you find a stable job and start enjoying your life?
Krishna: How will finding a job make me enjoy my life?
Farmer: You will have money!
Krishna: How will money make me enjoy my life?
Farmer: Then you can buy a house!
Krishna: How will buying a house make me enjoy my life?
Farmer: With money and a house you can get married and have a wife!
Krishna: How will money, house and wife make me enjoy my life?

Farmer: Then you can have kids and when they grow up they will work and you can relax and enjoy life as you wish.
Krishna: Oh! I am doing that right now!

Does buying a new car, new house or new clothes give you happiness? Do you consider fulfillment of your desires as happiness? Or is having a beer and watching a game on TV the real happiness for you? In case they are, you are missing life, as these are mundane toys which can only give you temporary excitement and as soon as you are done with them, you go back into your boredom, your void, your futility of life.

Mankind has reached a point where the flow of happiness has boiled down to a few bubbles, which you experience when there is no misery for you. You are suffering from a headache or from hemorrhoids and you take some painkiller and no longer you feel the pain but that does not mean that the painkillers have healed your problem. On the contrary, they have knocked out the friendly messengers who were trying to let you know that you have a problem within your body.

Let's do a test before we go any further: start laughing this very moment—just laugh, without any reason, without any thought, and make your whole body go in the laughter, let the tears roll. If you can be in a state of laughter without any cause, then I will give you an "A+" because you are carrying tremendous potential within you to enjoy happiness. But the truth is that many of you will start thinking that you have lost the balance of your mind. How can I laugh without hearing a good joke? We must have a good reason to laugh and cry. Most people need a reason to laugh or cry.

Salesmen laugh while making a good sales pitch or after closing a sale, doctors laugh when they are able to operate successfully on a patient, an office secretary laughs when her boss tells a stupid blonde joke. Have you ever laughed on your own? Or must you have a reason to laugh?

Anything that can be traded in material sense or you get benefited materially in some way or the other is not real happiness. A young lad wanted a VCR and never had the money to buy it. On his next birthday his favorite aunt gives him a VCR as a present and he says to her that he loves her so much as she has made him the happiest person in this world. But in the real sense he should be saying that he likes her very much as she has fulfilled his desires. The life goes on as the aunt is as foolish as her nephew because she is going to feel "holier than thou" and blessed, as she is going to feel that God has been so kind to her that she is able to bring happiness into someone's life. Poor aunt will never know whether her gift of happiness is being used to watch educational programs or her dear nephew is watching X-rated movies sitting next to his teenage girlfriend with a joint of marijuana between his lips. Now would you call that happiness? Sure, if your state of mind is limited to material objects then this is real happiness because of the kick one is getting out of the scenario. Parents not at home, so the fear is there that any moment they can walk in, and the excitement of the X-rated movie and the feeling of being in the company of his teenage girlfriend, the intoxication of a drug. Well, it is a cocktail of different states of mind. Have you ever tried pulling on the ends of a rubber band? It feels good for a while as your mind enjoys stretching it while hosting the fear of breaking it.

You might not have realized it, but combining the wrong foods creates the most delicious foods. Pizza is one example: 50% protein and 50% carbohydrates. Bean burrito is another. The taste buds are controlled by your mind, and if the mind can enjoy the opposites at the same time, it gets a kick out of it. Driving a car very fast is another example: You are secure inside as the car speeds at 100 miles an hour. The thrill is the speed and the challenge and fear of being caught by police radar.

So coming back to our young lad—no doubt it will give him a kick in that moment where his mind has stopped rationalizing and has entered into the hollow-deck where he can create his own fantasy. But is this so-called happiness going to last? His so called happiness will wither away when he finds out that he is about to become a father to a child through a child. His so-called happiness of enjoying a fresh bud has turned into a misery. Very soon he will be calling friends to get him out of this trouble by helping him with money so that his girlfriend can go to an abortion clinic. Don't think I am going too far. This is a true scenario of our young generation, our future, the future of the mankind, and the poor girl is left at the mercy of her boyfriend who is telling her: "I love you, honey, but I am not ready for a child or marriage." Or maybe he might dump the issue on his girlfriend and blame her for becoming pregnant. By the way, "love" is the most abused word on this planet. In the dating game, often the girl is seen saying to her boyfriend that I will love you a million times if you buy me that dress or piece of jewelry. Her happiness lies in the jewelry while her boyfriend's happiness lies in taking her to bed.

When our kids are growing up, we teach them to share, to be compassionate, to be kind, to trust and to have patience in life, as these are the traits that can make a man happy. So is compassion a form of happiness? The word compassion is an offshoot of compensate. You find a hurt dog on the road and you take him to the vet because he does not know where the hospital is, if there is any, he cannot walk and he cannot talk, he cannot think what to do in that moment. Mother Nature has given him one tool and that is to lick his wound. As a human you have more knowledge than the dog, more understanding, more wisdom and strength, so you are compensating. But the sad story is that no one compensates and there are few who are compassionate; otherwise, compensating should be part of every human psyche and there should be no use for the word compassionate. The word compassion is the distorted form of compensation, because if you look for the meaning of compassion, it will also give you pity, so why don't people say that I am a pitiable person instead of saying I am a compassionate person. I suggest someone should come forward and delete the words from the dictionary that do not fit in society and add new ones, which can give humanity new direction.

When you start walking on the road of compensation you have stepped into the world of spirituality. The first rule of compensation is to preserve the gifts of existence. Existence does its best to keep the planet clean by starting forest fires and by creating floods so that the earth and its plantation is able to recycle, but we pollute, so we are not even compassionate; we do not have pity for our planet, let alone the thought of compensating, helping nature where it is unable to protect and restore. We go on killing animals for food, for fancy fur coats and leather furniture. We go on cutting the trees, the rainforests, we go on dumping the toxic waste, and we have a number of oil spills every year polluting the ocean waters and killing the fish and the birds, destroying the ecological balance. Are we compassionate? We do not even compensate.

Is patience the real happiness? Patience has become a hard-to-find commodity. Technology has advanced so much that you can achieve more than you want in the shortest possible time: Drive-in banking, drive-in fast food, drive-in marriage cathedrals, drive-in movie theater, drive-in grocery, drive-in car wash, and very soon we will have drive-in hospitals, drive-in churches, no need to sit through the sermon, just go by the drive-through: Thanks for coming to Episcopal church, what can I get you today? I would like to have the sermon where Moses talks about bread and fish. And a window will pop out for donations and you will be handed over an audiotape to which you can listen in your car while ordering your fish filet sandwich at a drive-through fast food restaurant.

How can man develop patience when every moment the genie of technology is at his command. It takes less time for an e-mail to travel thousands of miles compared to the time it will take you to dial that location and talk to your buddy. So next time your Internet Service

Provider has a shutdown you panic because your email is not working and you have no patience to cope with the situation: You start yelling at the ISP people: "I am expecting an important e-mail and your system is down." By the way, was President Bush sending you the latest Monica Lewinsky joke? Next time your plane is delayed you start howling at the airline employees: I have a meeting to attend in New York, your service is bad, I want my ticket to be endorsed on some other carrier, and frantically you start punching numbers on your cell phone trying to reach your contact because you know very well that the other party has no patience either and you will lose this deal. Poor God! He must be crying his heart out because he was the one who became instrumental in delaying your plane so that your business deal flops as he knows that this particular deal is not good for you and will put you in a financial mess but you are trying your best to beat God with your impatience.

A newborn sucking on his mother's breasts never doubts whether the milk is warm enough, whether it is pasteurized and whether all the vitamins have been added to it. As long as the child depends upon his mother he is fine. He falls, she picks him up, he cries, she feeds, and she gives him love and food when needed. The child has a faith around the mother, but as he starts growing up and starts understanding the devious ways of life he tends to lose trust. It starts very early in life; a unruly child is promised a gift if he or she starts behaving; when the time comes to buy the gift the parents back out or another promise is made to buy even a better gift. The pattern continues and the child grows up on broken promises and has developed a lack of trust in his parents and in his own self as well because you are his role model. How can he grow up and trust his very best friends when he is asked for help?

When we do not even have a simple feeling of trust in others, or in ourselves, how can we ever have faith? Which falls in the spiritual category—have you ever seen a dollar bill—it says very clearly "In God we trust." You take that bill to the grocery store with a piece of trust, that you can buy what you want because it is not that piece of paper you are carrying but the trust of the U.S. treasury. The only difference is that when you have faith you are not provided with legal tender from the office of God which says, "My faith is in the divine force" that you can cash in your next prayer. Trust we use for logic and faith is the blossoming of the heart. The seed of trust is planted in the land of patience and we nurture it with our love and start our journey into the realm of bliss beyond this mundane happiness. We only experience this bliss when the rosary of faith has started blossoming in our hearts.

Faith is nothing but a natural source of divine energies which nourishes our inner self, and in order to keep the flow of this natural source, we need to clean it with our tears.

We drink water and that water goes through our body and in the process the whole body is cleansed. The waste the body throws out is converted into urine and then it is thrown out of the body; the same goes for food. Just as water cleans our body of toxic waste, tears clean our heart chakra of negative emotions the same way. We go through tons of experiences every day and the stronger our heart center is, the more we are able to withstand negative experiences, but then our heart reaches a stage where it overloads and at that moment we need crying. Our bio-energies stay clean just because of the heart center. To keep our heart center clean is not only necessary but also the most integral part of our survival in this mad-mad world.

Men need more crying than women because man's heart center is a negative pole and is not active like his sex area, whereas a woman's heart area is active so it is very easy for a woman to cry. She can have tears rolling down her cheeks in 3 seconds. For men, it can take hours and days. For the majority of men, it is hard to cry because of the programming they get while growing up: "Don't be a sissy, Johnny! Do not cry like a girl, you are a boy." It is very dangerous for society to say that a man should not cry; if men stop crying, they will start destroying. So cry if you need, you are not being a sissy, you are being human, and always remember that the more you are able to cry with ease, the more stable you will find yourself and you will stay free of emotional diseases.

When I was growing up my dad used to say that laughter is the best medicine. Laughter keeps the sex area balanced. Have you noticed that it is not easy for women to laugh? Their laugh is very flimsy and local; they are unable to laugh from the core of their bodies, but they are good at crying; they can "Cry their heart out." On the other hand, men can even lose their breath while laughing. Laughter is the positive polarity and cleans the sex center of the man. Just make the sound hoh-hoh and it will hit your sex center. Look at a woman laughing—she will go haaaheeehaaa and it will be very musical as it is only hitting her heart center located between the breasts and returning. Her laughter is not coming from her vaginal area which is a negative polarity. If you can make a women laugh like a man, chances are she will run to the bathroom to pee or will lose control of her bladder, and if the women is very sexual she could have an orgasm. Most women can only laugh deeply like a man at the time of having an orgasm; at that moment she is really laughing. The reverse is true for men; men will only cry when their heart center has opened up or when the cycle is complete at the time of the sex act. If the two partners are involved in sex and they really care for each other and love each other, as soon as the man gets the energy back from her breast area he can have tears rolling out of happiness and bliss. The reason the man and woman are unhappy is because one of them is not receptive for the energy to flow in a circular motion. Men cannot cry their heart out; their crying is very flimsy because their mind is in operation at that moment and they are thinking about the next step, whereas when a woman cries she is just crying; she can go on crying for hours. Men cannot cry for more than a few minutes as their minds will jump in and break their crying mode. If you are a man do not hold tears, and if you do, you will be holding at stake the future of your emotional health.

Does happiness lie in one's freedom? Each one of us is a slave; unless and until man goes beyond this slavery we are not free. Any notion like: I am living in the USA, which is a free country, is falsifying the fact of life. Any idea of freedom is a white lie. You feel hungry—you are a slave to your body. If you are an obsessive thinker—you are a slave to your mind. You want to buy an expensive car—you are a slave to your desires. You are no more than a slave—a slave to your body, not to mention the outside world. You are a slave to your company, your boss, your automobile, your telephone, the appliances you use, the electric company, the government, your religion, your gender; your consciousness is locked behind this jail called a rib cage. As long as you have this body, you are bound by the laws of this dimension and cannot leave your body and wander in other dimensions unless you have meditated for years and have come a step closer to enlightenment.

The "I" within you has no choice; the day this "I" drops, that very day all your chains will break and you will achieve freedom. Until then we should call ourselves "at liberty"; we have the liberty to do this or do that but we are not free and there is no freedom. The English language is very fascinating but we have misused it and abused it according to our liberty; otherwise, the English language is very whole and holy since we have a word for every emotion.

Awareness is the key to the garden of happiness. What is awareness? Awareness is the ability to look at others and at the same time look at one's own self. If you cannot think beyond your small world, you are not aware. I am Steve and I love my dog, my girlfriend and my car and I make tons of money. That means you have not known life and awareness has not opened its door to you. You are locked in the mindset of Steve who is successful in this material world. Your life is no better than a puzzle where the dog, car, house, girlfriend, etc., fit perfectly, and if one day you find that a piece is missing from your puzzle, you will not have the awareness that this life is a mere toy and you will start crying just like a baby with a broken toy.

Who are you? Are you a reality or a mere illusion? Are your dreams reality or is your waking state reality? Awareness is exploring the inner and the outer world. Being in a state of no awareness is being lost in your world of fantasies, your desires, dreams, wants and liking. Most people are just attentive; any sensible person is attentive and mindful, observing, watchful, but when you observe and the observer is also observed, you jump on the bandwagon of awareness.

The majority are lost and belong to the herd; they are just following others, thinking the other knows the way. But the other is as confused as you are. Have you seen a herd of sheep? All are yelling and pushing each other and are being directed towards the farmhouse by dogs who have been trained to control the sheep. Look at your life. Whether you are being paid $5 an hour or $50 an hour, you are part of this herd, the only difference being that the one who is making $5 an hour is at the end and the one who is making $50 is at the front and will have a cozy place in this worldly farmhouse.

Once you know what awareness is, you will not like to waste your time in useless gossip and discussions, because with awareness comes the realization that you are born with limited energy and that energy needs to be conserved and not to be wasted trying to prove your point among friends and relatives; then you will not stretch a small episode into a soap opera of life. Too much talking is not good for emotional and physical health and one should be as precise as possible. When you talk too much you attract people towards you or make people run away from you; either way you are inviting loneliness. Either you are making people addicted towards you or you are hankering for their company and in the process you lose the gift of existence you are born with, which is your aloneness, your inner self.

In your aloneness you get a chance to be friends with your inner self, but if you keep on looking for friendships outside of you, you are befriending your own self; you are losing a friend who will never leave you even if the whole world turns their backs towards you, and who is your inner self? Your awareness, the speck of God, which resides within you. And he never leaves you, even if you have to discard this body.

If you have not cared for your own self, how can you care about others? If you have not been fair to your own self, how can you be fair to others? If someone has fallen in a well you can only rescue him if you are in a safe position. If someone needs money you should have extra money to help that person. Unless you are in a safe position, and unless your cup is overflowing, how can you even think of helping someone else? If you are unhappy within how can you spread happiness to others? You can only create an illusion of spreading happiness. If you want the world to be happy, the seeds of happiness must be sown within. Once you start flowering, then the pollen of your happiness will spread on its own in the world around you.

Tips on Happiness:

1. Always find time to relax and get in touch with your inner self. Your inner self is a source of fresh energies and you can only dive in that source provided you are in your aloneness, and you will always come out of it refreshed, ready for the world.

2. Follow the proverb "Trust in God but be on Guard." It sounds very contradictory because if you trust God then why be on guard? What it means is be aware. You have been given the power to weigh things and make your decisions and if you are on guard, there will be no need to blame others at the end.

3. There is an old Indian proverb; I will just give you the translation: Fragrance creates a blissful future, whereas a bad odor brings bad luck. When you translate a proverb, it is bound to lose its original meaning because proverbs are rhymed and when the rhythm is broken, the meaning loses its fragrance. What the above proverb means is that good energies are attracted to cleanliness and to the aroma of the perfumes (I am talking about natural perfumes and not the synthetic ones that are made from cats' placentas). If your body is clean and smelling fresh and your house is clean and smells fresh, then you will automatically feel blissful, and if you stay dirty and messy, your dirtiness will attract negative thoughts, people and circumstances. What happens when you smell a bad odor? Instantly you plug your nose and run towards fresh air. Good vibes and bad vibes are attracted towards respective frequencies.

4. Humbleness and being down to earth is the current that keeps the happiness growing. Be humble; be grounded so that no one can shake you off your feet.

5. Do not repent, brood or dwell on past errors and mistakes. Follow the rule of forgive and forget, and this rule applies to others as well as to your own self. You must forgive your own self first and then you will be able to forgive others.

6. Live in the moment; the past is gone and the future has yet to arrive; this very moment belongs to you. Take a deep breath, breathe out through your mouth and feel this moment in its totality. You have the key to happiness; now go within and open the doors of awareness that will lead you to the unending source of bliss.

15

Religion

In the times of the cavemen, survival was their religion. After thousands of years religion has become our survival tool. No wonder we have entered the phase of holy wars. The future of mankind is left to "Jihads" and Crusades. People are sacrificed in the name of religion and people are sacrificed in the army. It seems religion and army are the two edges of the same sword that cuts and divides.

Christianity, Islam, Hinduism, Buddhism, Judaism, Sikhism, and we can fill the whole page with all the others in the list. We have more variety when it comes to religion than our choices of onions at the local grocery store. By the way, if you keep on peeling the onion you are left with nothing. I respect your personal beliefs in whatever religion you were brought up, but do we need all these religions and have they been successful in resolving all the questions mankind has? Have these religions contributed to the happiness of man? Or in fact have they been catalysts into directing the course of humanity towards hate and fanaticism leading to holy wars?

We were born in a particular religion for a reason, or maybe it is a mere coincidence, but then we should have lots and lots of love for the people belonging to the same religion, should it not be so? Then why do Protestants hate Catholics and Catholics cannot agree with Jehovah's Witness? There are so many divisions within Christianity that very soon it will supersede the number of religions on the planet.

It is not worth discussing Hinduism because there are hundreds of Deities and Gods and people have created a religion around each God and Deity. Moreover, I have not heard anybody fighting over Krishna or Shiva—a Krishna lover will respect Shiva as well, with no superiority factor involved.

Within Islam there are just two divisions, Shias and Sunnis, and they are dire enemies. Isn't that strange that one religion has two divisions and so much hate that they are always ready to kill each other in the name of Allah? Sufis are better off as they do not associate with either and have their own sect under the umbrella of Islam.

We have Jainism in India which came into existence near the time of Buddha, and within Jainism we have Digambars and Pitambars who do not agree with each other but agree with the philosophy of Mahavira.

Fine! We can leave all these alone by pointing that these are very old religions and down the line things became distorted.

Let's take a very modern religion, the religion I was born into: Sikhism. Sikhism is just 300 years old. Ten gurus from Guru Nanak who believed in universal brotherhood and he was neither a Sikh, nor a Hindu, nor a Muslim, though he was born to a Hindu family, but he denounced religion and said we are all brothers and sisters of one father, GOD. The chain moved on and ended at the tenth guru: Gobind Singh, who was the founder of Sikhism, which was created out of Hindus and Muslims to protect them from the invading Moguls (ancestors of Bin Laden). When Guru Gobind Singh left his body, he left the holy book Guru Granth (Guru's encyclopedia) that was compiled by the fifth guru. Guru Gobind Singh's final word at the time of leaving his body was that there will not be any physical guru after me and the encyclopedia should be treated as your guru.

This holy book of Sikhs contains wisdom of the chain of gurus as well as from other sources from the saints and seers belonging to Islam and Hinduism with some mention about Jesus Christ. The teachings of Sikhism are based upon universal brotherhood and one God concept. Three hundred years ago, Sikhs were very few and there were just Muslims and Hindus in India and the surrounding areas, and it was a custom to convert the first son born in any Hindu family to be a Sikh, as Sikhism was a sort of army of people to protect the Hindus and Muslims from the Mogul invaders, and Sikhism was taken as a bridge, bonding Hindus and Muslims as both would worship Guru Nanak in their own ways.

When the British invaded India, this army of Sikhs was adopted by the British. They were given a special place within the British Army until the smart ones started realizing that the British were robbing India of its culture and material wealth, and another army was created consisting of Sikhs, Hindus and Muslims to fight the British. In 1947, when the British left India, they divided India into two, with one part becoming Pakistan.

So, returning to the subject of Sikhism, the religion is very young, with all its history intact and uncorrupted as of yet. Since the west is exploring new areas of spirituality, lately there have been additions to this religion from all over the world because of one man, Yogi Bhajan. He has a strong following among westerners that includes American whites, blacks, and Jews who have adopted Sikhism.

As a result we have American Sikhs and Brazilian Sikhs and Japanese Sikhs and so on. But even before Sikhism had these additions there were already two divisions within this religion. Jats (farmer community or land owners) and non-Jats, and within Jats there were low caste Jats and high caste Jats. Then we have divisions within non-Jats; again we have low caste and high caste. The dilemma is that all teachings of the first guru to the tenth guru were focused on eradicating the caste system. In order to remove the caste system, the tenth guru gave a discipline that all men will have their last name as "SINGH" and all women will have their last name as "KAUR" so that no one should feel "holier than thou." Surprisingly the trend has always been that non-Jats never let their sons and daughters get married in Jats and vice versa, and in case a girl and boy from these two communities fall in love the drama could end in bloodshed. Even though both communities sit under the roof of one temple called Guru-dwara (the door of the Guru), eat together and sing the praises of God sitting next to each other, when it comes to making critical decisions pertaining to Sikhism or their lives, the two seldom agree. The distortion has reached a point where the Jats and non-Jats have formed their own places of worshipping under the banner of Sikhism.

Even though the first guru's message was universal brotherhood, the traditional Sikhs who are born in Sikhism are very much against Yogi Bhajan and his followers who have adopted Sikhism. These traditional Sikhs disagree with Yogi Bhajan for bringing people from other religions and skin colors into Sikhism because they consider these people impure, as the message of the tenth guru was that Sikh is one who is "Khalsa," meaning pure. Do you know what the word Sikh means? You are in for a shock. It means student, one who is always ready to learn.

Man is so cunning that he comes up with his own interpretations, which fits his thinking. This religion was created just 300 years back. Looking at the consciousness of mankind and the social structure we can see both have changed drastically.

I can visualize Christ, Mohammed, the Hindu gods, Sikh gurus crying like a child and saying why me! Where did I go wrong? I had never thought that my message would program mankind that one day they would kill each other using my name. They all must be wondering if there was any way to erase their identities from the history of the earth so that man is not involved in the foolish behavior of fanaticism.

If you agree with me on the concept of abolishing the concept of marriage, then you will agree with me on the concept of abolishing all religions from the face of the earth, as religion has caused more damage to our mind, body and consciousness than any other concept or dogma, even marriage. With the break of marriage, you lose wife or husband and the kids, but adopting a different religion than one you were born in, you lose all your friends and family, sometimes even your parents, who are supposed to be with you whether you are a criminal or king because you are their product, their own mirror.

The social structure has changed; people want power, companies are merging because they are sick of fighting in this competitive market— how about having a merger in the religious market? I do not think it will happen soon looking at the state of people's consciousness. Let's be practical and realistic; let's merge all the divisions of Christianity and make every Christian a Christian and not a Catholic, Protestant, Jehovah's Witness, etc. Let's merge Shias and Sunnis within Islam. It should not be difficult; one religion, many divisions, and the competition goes on to prove who is the best. The focus of all religions is to increase their number. What for? God? Is God a commodity that the more you have the richer your life will be?

Man is as freshly foolish as when Jesus was nailed to the cross, and there have been additions to his foolishness—when Socrates had to drink the poison, and when the Moguls boiled the Sikh gurus alive in hot water and they were made to sit on hot sand under burning fire because they refused to adopt Islam. Anybody who is a non-Muslim is known as "Kafer" (rejected one). All of Islam's teachings are based upon this concept which Mohammed never said, nor did Jesus say that a non-Christian is not the son of God. What they meant was that if you reject the existence of God, you are a "Kafer" and one who becomes one with the divine is the Son of God or "pure" as Jesus and the tenth guru of the Sikhs said.

According to Quran, the highest form of Jihad is a person's fight against the temptations of evil and his struggle to lead a good life. But for the majority of Muslims in the world, "Jihad" means to fight for the religion and protect it from "Kafers." And who are these "Kafers"? They are the people who do not agree with Islam.

These innocent spiritual masters forgot to put the warning label on their spiritual medicine: "Caution: Keep away from childish people and only take when in a very aware and loving state."

Man wants freedom; this is the inborn desire of every being who is born on this planet; animals, birds, fishes, they all want freedom. They would rather be killed in the jungle by their predators in freedom than live in security in the cages of a zoo. Freedom is the sole purpose, the sole desire, and these poor animals do not have any religion because their freedom lies in the free movement of their physical bodies, but man on the other hand, realizes that he is locked behind this rib cage and his freedom does not lie in his free will but his freedom lies beyond this "I." The dilemma is that this desire of wanting to be free has got stuck on the "I" concept.

I am a Christian, I am a Jew, I am a Hindu, I am a Sikh, and the list goes on. Ask these people who the hell this "I" is: the kind of clothes you wear, your body, your mind? Ask a young American kid: "what is the meaning of religion?" Do you think he has time to think about this mundane spooky stuff? For him, God is a "Ninja Turtle" who can fight everyone. How can he be influenced by someone who was nailed to a cross? For a kid, it will be emotionally disturbing if his "Ninja Turtle" is nailed to the cross or is put on hot sand or made to drink poison, because his upbringing is based on fictional characters who are the best of the best, be they Ninja Turtles, Spider Man, or Superman.

Religions are nothing but roadmaps that lead you to the same destination.

Let's presume you want to go to Bombay from Chicago; you have the choice to go the Atlantic route, which is via Europe, or you have the choice to go the Pacific route, which is via Asia. You have been given the choice to fly on different airlines or you could take a ship, or if you are an adventurer, you could go by land and sea, but the sad story of humans is that they are just holding the route guides—the majority do not even have the awareness which can buy them a ticket to the beyond, and they are fighting for the route maps that the Bible has the best way or the Koran has the best route and their religious company is the best. Our religious airline takes you straight to heaven where you enjoy what you have been denied on earth.

All religions say it very clearly that unless you die from this "I-ness," you will not attain real happiness nor will you know your real identity, and the naïve, foolish man has interpreted that unless you die and make others die for this "I," you will not attain, and what is this "I"? I am a Christian, I am a Muslim, I am a Hindu, and I am ready to die for my religion and kill others who will go against this "I."

Just as you cannot open a can without the help of a sharp metal, and just as you cannot dig the ground without a sharp object to prepare the land to sow the seeds, you cannot break these false doors of ego without sharp words. Thus, if you belong to one of the above, accept my challenge: take off your clothes and just go stand in front of the mirror and have a good look at yourself; check every body part to see if you will find any stamp that says "Product of Islam," or "Product of Christianity," or "Product of Hinduism," and see what part of your body represents your religion. Is your nose Christian or your eyes Islamic or your head Hindu? If tomorrow you died in a plane crash your Christian body could lie next to a Hindu's body which could be next to a Muslim's body at the disaster site, and if there were not enough space available to transport your body to your home city, you could remain lying face to face in an embrace with another body whose religion you hated all your life and from whose hands you would not even drink water. Today your "I" has gone back into the queue, waiting for a new identity for returning to Earth. Only God knows that this time you might be born in a Christian family while your Islamic body rots in the grave in which this "I" hated Christians all his life. Your "I" drops out of your mother's womb with a new identity in a Christian nation and your fight continues for the religion, this time for Christianity against Islam and the drama continues. No wonder the ancients called this world "Maya" or illusion.

16

From Religion to Spirituality

New Age holistic music, meditations, chanting mantras, spiritual retreats, having a guru. Being spiritual has become more of a fashion than a way of life.

It seems humanity is in transition. The west has been obsessed with capitalism, sex and technology for a long time and now they are moving towards spirituality. On the other hand, the east has been obsessively religious and sexually repressed and now they have adopted the ways of the west. People have started changing lanes on the road of life.

Westerners are getting fed up with Jesus because Jesus does not intrigue them any more. Living a fast-paced life with all these technological toys and the glamour of fashion, Jesus seems like a person who did not know how to have fun. Being the son of a carpenter, Jesus was hardworking and lived an honest life, but in today's dishonest world where money has become the God, Jesus has no place in the business world and has become a poor man's scapegoat.

The west is slowly moving away from Jesus, and now they want Krishna and Buddha, because Krishna seems more wholesome, logical, and fun loving, and Buddha gives them mental relief from all the noise this technology has created. On the other hand, Krishna lovers in India are sick of the duality of Krishna's philosophy, as he had all the fun in his life, whereas these people have a hard time getting ends to meet. Jesus seems like part of their existence, born and brought up in a poor family who sacrificed his life for others, so half of South India has embraced Christianity and the other poor countries have followed the same pattern. Parts of China, Philippines, Korea, Vietnam—the list is long and getting longer day by day.

Blacks in the west and in Africa followed Jesus for a while but when they felt that Christianity was not doing anything about racism and

Hinduism was quite confusing for them, they decided to adopt Islam as it matched their radical way of thinking and moreover Islam is not bothered about the color of the skin.

From Krishna to Mahavira to Buddha to Jesus to Sikhism—too many religions, too much information, nothing fits in the lives of modern man and all we see and experience is turmoil, desperation and exhaustion on the spiritual level. Some religions allow you to drink and be merry and some forbid alcohol and have strict rules about living this life. While one religion forbids cutting hair, the other wants you to shave off your head. I am sure the spiritual masters were not into fashion, nor did they have any fetishes about hair.

With all these religions on our small planet the big question arises: Have we reached anywhere? With all the holy wisdom we have on our planet, why is humanity in chaos? How come these religions are not producing a Jesus, a Krishna, a Mohammed or a Buddha every day or maybe every month or every year?

You will be shocked to know that, on average, one enlightened master comes into existence every 40 years, even though we have over six billion people on our planet. This divine flower emits a new aroma with the undercurrent of fragrance, and repeats what others have said in the past but with a new approach, as there is nothing new to be said. He dies and leaves behind his words and his words give birth to a new religion; for people to bow in front of this new holy book, worship his pictures and are ready to fight and defend their master and his philosophy.

It seems mankind is more interested in reading the map every day and defending the map, and very few have the guts to walk on the inner path because there is darkness inside and man fears darkness, because darkness is representative of death and each one of us is scared of death. But amazingly we are always ready to push others into this darkness by killing them in the name of religion. Thousands are sacrificed every year in the fire of communal violence.

Do we really need all these religions? Taking birth in a particular religion is a mere coincidence; moreover, 99% of the people follow a religion just because they are born in it and the whole family is involved in it. They do not have the consciousness and the guts to explore what others have said. A Christian cannot go to a Hindu temple and vice versa because the family is not going to accept him. It would be very insulting for the family and the person will be taken as a traitor.

I have a headache and my dad works for the aspirin company but I am allergic to aspirin—taking an herbal medicine will be an insult to my dad. People have followed religion for the same reasons. Billions of people, hundreds of religions and the sects within these religions, and tons of books all tell you to live life in a certain way in order to achieve God.

Every enlightened person who ever existed on the planet has said very clearly that each one of us is unique and cannot (and never will) be duplicated. If this is true, then each one of us must have been born with our own unique way to communicate with our divine being, because the journey must start within and end within.

What is religion? A master like Krishna, Socrates and Jesus appears on the planet and tries to direct the course of mankind towards the source in a way that fits with the state of the current social structure. Looking at the state of their consciousness, their wants and needs, he tries to open their doors to the beyond, to give them something which is more potent than what they have, and one day he leaves his body and his words, his body dissolves in the earth, but his words are stored and made into a religion.

Have you ever watched a cowboy movie like "Machena's Gold," "Indiana Jones" series, or the movie where Clint Eastwood has half the piece of a map for a treasure and he searches for the gold for the next two hours on the screen. If you look with deep awareness, religions are nothing but pieces of maps pointing towards divine treasures. But sadly, times change and minds change, too. Hundreds of years ago Jesus said, "Love your neighbor." Today in the west, you do not even know who your neighbor is. At the time he uttered these words of wisdom, people were living in a commune type of setup; everybody knew what was happening next door, people were poking their dirty noses in each other's affairs, everyone knew what their neighbor ate the night before. There was too much judgment, people were not involved in their own lives but were more interested in the activities of next door, and Jesus had to say, "Judge ye not." Today after thousands of years that map has to be redesigned and represented because one is not interested in one's neighbor anymore. His words, "Love thy neighbor," do not fit in today's world where people hate their own selves. The western way of life is making the words of Jesus redundant.

Thousands of years pass, the social structure changes, the consciousness changes, and so should the holy book, but we have been trying to follow these holy books that were written thousands of years ago, forgetting that times have changed and so has the social structure. The words of the past masters cannot fit in the modern world and cannot be implemented as they were uttered.

For a common man whose struggle starts for food and shelter with the sunrise and ends at sunset in a tired body and mind with few papers which we call currency in his pocket. Do you think he has the time to mess in his neighbor's life when his own life is messed up? His tired and exhausted body needs food and rest so that he can fight the world for his survival the next morning. He is left with little energy that is enough to wind his day up and take him to bed. The reason Christianity has been able to convert these poor countries into being Christians is because for a poor man food is everything and someone who can provide food and health to them is the "Son of God."

Either we have to redefine the Holy Scriptures or we have to look for a new master, new guru or new religion that fits with our present state of mind. If mankind was smart enough they should have researched into all the so-called holy books, and with all the technology we have, we could have come up with a new holy book, selecting the best from all religions that have existed in the past, that would fit with the modern-day life man is living. Then we would not have any conflict and no one would have to defend this new religion and kill thousands in the name of Allah, as "Moguls" were doing 300 years ago. Their followers are still butchering humans, ordering "Fatwas" using the same old principle, though the means to kill have changed. Swords have been replaced with suicide missions.

Times change and people come up with their own rules to fit their state of mind, and as time passes these rules become religious laws. Sikhs are forbidden to cut or shave their hair, alienating them from the masses. On the other hand Jews do not shave their beards but instead cut the hair on their heads in a certain way so that they have bangs on the sides. Muslims cut their hair and their mustaches, but keep their beards, while Krishna people shave their heads, keeping only a tag of hair hanging from their heads, and the Buddhist monks shave all of their heads and beards. Their mindsets all stay the same, making them act nuts when it comes to defending their religions.

It reminds me of a famous story that once a young boy and an old man were traveling from one city to another, along with their donkey. While the young man was sitting on the donkey as they passed through a village, the villagers commented that look at that poor old man who is walking while that young robust lad sits on the donkey. So the young lad felt ashamed and got off the donkey and asked the old man to sit on the donkey. As they approached the next village the villagers said look at that grown up man sitting on that donkey while the young child walks. So listening to this, the old man got off the donkey. They were passing by the third village and someone commented that look at the fools, even though they have a donkey they are walking on foot. Listening to this, both the young and old sat on the donkey. As they were crossing a river the donkey could not take all that load and panicked as the bridge started shaking and all three fell in the river. The old man and the young lad swam to shore but the donkey was washed away.

The motto of the story is that when you listen to too many people you end up losing your ass.

Too many religions, too many disciplines to follow. It seems that the emphasis has always been on the outward and not on the inward. If it were the right way, then science would have found the soul by now because it has dissected every cell in the human body and looked at it under very powerful microscopes. There is so much confusion that unless and until one comes across the right information or the right guru, one is bound to discard religion or give up on one's passion to find the real meaning behind this human life. Very few among these frustrated souls would start looking within. Who would venture into the dark realms of one's consciousness or inner self? The one who has a thirst; but most start being very religious and end up being fanatics or atheists.

In 1988, two young women knocked at my door. They introduced themselves as Mormons and asked if they could come in and talk with me for a while. I invited them in and they started talking about God and how much they loved God. I asked them, have you ever been in love with a man? Both answered with a no. I said that if you have not been in love with a man, who has been created in God's image and is very much available, how can you be in love with God who has not been seen for ages but has always been talked about? They left without replying to me.

The west is hungry for spirituality while the east is hungry for the material. The east has known some secrets relating to the inner world and the west has known some secrets relating to the outer world. The west has used the east in the past and now the east has started following the west. The east is full of knowledge and wisdom relating to the inner world. When it comes to the inner world, the west is lacking. The western world has limited understanding of the spiritual world. I do not blame the west, because when your day starts with eating some poor animal's dead body and the rest of the day is wasted in winning the game of money and when one comes home one needs alcohol or drugs to relax the mind, then some entertainment in the form of sex is needed as well. In this kind of busy scenario who has the time to venture into spirituality. Who cares about the past lives, the future lives, karma, God, inner light? The west is living a robotic life and robots do not have souls and neither do they have hearts. Spirituality has seeped into the west quite recently and that also through "Beatles" and "Grateful Dead." If "The King" had not died, the west would still be rock 'n' rolling in sex and drugs.

Unfortunately most of the eastern philosophy that has seeped into the west talks of the beyond but withholds the crucial information of exploring the beyond. The clear reason is that most of the easterners who have brought the Vedic knowledge from India into the west have used it just to capitalize on it using the western strategies of logic and capitalism. The aim of the majority has been to cash in on the ignorance; no wonder an Ayurvedic weekend massage retreat costs around $3,000 and the Yogic flying technique costs around $8,000—it will cost you less to be a licensed pilot.

I feel sorry for the west when I see that people have lost their life savings in the search for wisdom and in the process all they learned was how to fly sitting in a lotus position.

Here is another beautiful story: There lived a disciple and a guru and they had been together for years. When they would go to the river for their daily bathing, sometimes the guru would walk on water but never taught his disciple the secret. The disciple was getting impatient because he was desperate to supersede his guru, but you know a guru is a guru because he has gone beyond all those issues of life. So the day came when the disciple could not take it any more and left the guru, challenging him that one day he will come back and show him that he can also walk on water. Nine years passed and one day the disciple came back to the guru, took him to the river and walked on the water to the other shore and came back, and told the guru, "Look, I can do the same thing and I have practiced for nine years just to show you that you are not the only one who can walk on water." The guru said calmly: "Son, you could have taken a boat across for few coins. There was no need to waste the precious nine years of your life in mastering this simple technique."

The west has become crazy about the eastern gurus and I do not blame them because eastern gurus can do more than the Las Vegas magicians: Materializing Ash, Rolex watches, gold rings, and they are yours to keep; there is no trick to it like the Vegas magicians. It beats the western logic. The east is full of such mysteries and revelations because the east has explored the inner world and has gained insights into the hidden mysteries of our existence. In the west, very few people stumbled upon these mysteries using their faith in Jesus Christ but out of the fear of logically obsessed society. They were only able to release their pressure by coating it as non-fiction, and quite recently these people have come out openly in the form of faith healers. A few others who went through these magical experiences used drugs, like LSD, altering the human chemistry, and in the process a few chakras got jump-started, speeding up their drugged lives and proclaiming them new age gurus. On the other hand, the east dived into "self" using meditation, devotion, following a strict discipline of celibacy, by eating a strict vegetarian diet consisting of certain foods only, and came to the realization of these mysteries in an aware state of mind and was able to document them. As a result, these formulas and techniques have been practiced over and over again by many and have produced many enlightened men and women. In India divine wisdom has been passed on from master to disciple for centuries.

In the west, logic is supreme—mind is the master and logic his disciple. The west has been chanting the mantra of positive thinking for many years now. Since logic is the disciple, which is part of the mind game, it is always involved in praising one's own self. Since the emphasis has been on the mind, the heart chakra or the emotional center has not been explored in the west. Interestingly, the heart chakra is the turning point and all logic ends at the heart center. From there, man starts moving inwards, towards spirituality.

Here is another eye-opener. Look at the color of the lips belonging to westerners and you will find that the majority have pinkish lips. Now compare it with men and women from the east and you will find any color from pink to black. According to the science of body features, pink lips means that one is still in the kindergarten stage in the school of life and will have to gain more knowledge and wisdom (not just information), hence the heart center has not been explored yet.

In India, you will find very few people having pink lips and their lip color changes as they age. This change can only be seen in the east, where people exchange the emotional energies or the "Hraday shakti," because, in the west, only heart-shaped candies and balloons and greeting cards are exchanged on Valentine's Day and the real heart is always protected by the excellent logic the western mind has. As a result, the lip color seldom changes and stays pink all their lives even as they grow old and die.

The west is not emotional; it is logical to the point that an easterner will call a westerner heartless. The east has not explored logic in the past; the whole of the east is based upon emotions. The east is heart-oriented and the west is mind-oriented. So, in the east, the reason people's lips are mostly black is because they are emotionally burnt and their heart chakras are in bad shape, whereas, in the west, people are logical. They are not touchy and they do not allow their emotions to interfere in their logic. Their logic has a good filtering system, but just as the eastern heart that has been burnt due to being overused, the western mind is burnt with being overused. Psychologists and psychiatrists are in abundance in the west and they have a good track record of having the highest suicide rate as well as colon cancer. The emotional release is missing from the western consciousness; as a result, the health care industry is booming. If only we could make the west emotionally sensitive, help every westerner explore his heart chakra, we can create a heaven on the planet.

Just tell an American that he is an SOB and he will respond in equal or more derogatory language. His way of responding will be very rational and his emotions will not be touched by the harshness of the sound of SOB. On the other hand, when an Indian is told that he is an SOB, he will be ready to kill you because there is no filtering system and you have touched his emotions and abused his mother who is an integral part of his emotional dominance over his mind.

The heart chakra is intact and not used at all in the west. The dilemma for the west is that the concept of Christianity is based upon Bhakti or Devotion, which relates to the heart chakra. The west, being logical, cannot be involved in Bhakti as their way is meditation; in order to walk on the path of spirituality they must start their journey on the path of meditation. So Buddha, Krishnamurti, Socrates, Osho will be more helpful to the western man.

The journey must start within whether it starts at the heart center or it starts at the mind level and cannot be goal-oriented. In the physical world you might work for a few years and attain your goals, but in the inner world, no goals can be set and all desires of attaining the unknown or accessing the unknown will prove to be futile and bound to frustrate you.

On the path of spirituality there are only two ways: Meditation or Devotion, and both lead to grace, and when grace is showered your kundalini shakti opens up. The serpent power starts rising upwards, which in turn opens up the chakras, and each chakra has its own secrets, so one is bound to come across many mystical experiences.

False gurus from the east have started selling these tricks to the spiritually starved west on the pretext of spirituality. The west robbed the east of their heritage when the British invaded India, and it seems now the east is ready to rob the west using spirituality. What goes comes back. Since the east was made poor, it has become hungry for wealth. The west has experienced the luxuries and is hungry for inner wisdom as people in the west have reached the heights of logic. If logic were so powerful, then half of the western civilization would have been enlightened by now. In the last few years the west has started feeling the futility of logic; as a result, there is spiritual exhaustion.

When it comes to spirituality both the east and the west are poor in their own ways. The east has the caste system and the west has racism. Thinking in terms of black and white is not being spiritual. Thinking in terms of race is associating one's self with the Angel group or the Devil's group. If you want to walk on the path of spirituality you will have to let go of color. You will have to close your eyes to the outside world and turn your focus inwards on the screen of your consciousness. When you start looking inwards you will have to be friendly with the black color, and if you are going to love the inner black, then the outer black is no different because he carries that flame of God that you carry within your white skin. If you are shipwrecked in the ocean, the person who saves your life becomes your God, even if he belongs to the skin color you have hated all your life. Fighting the darkness within or outside of you will not take you anywhere—you will have to make it your friend until the light appears.

In order to enter the temple of spirituality, we need to leave our shoes of judgment at the door and start walking barefooted. We need to forget that we are black, white, or proud to be an American; ask a Texan whether he is a proud American! Kids are not racists but the adults program the innocent minds with thoughts of duality. That is the dilemma of mankind.

I will emphasize again—there are just two ways to explore the inner world: Devotion or Bhakti which is the path of the heart center, and the other way is of Mind or Meditation which is the path of intellect. Fascinating it may sound, but one reaches the other in the end and jumps into the beyond as again both devotion and meditation are part of this duality and are mere tools.

One who starts with meditation has to drop the mind and the heart center opens up. On the other hand, one who starts with devotion eventually finds the gates to ultimate wisdom. It is very important for you to know what is the best path for you; otherwise, you will be wasting your time and become frustrated and dejected in the process.

I would strongly suggest that women should not follow meditation. Until a woman has reached menopause, she should not try to meditate. The east has been very smart, as from a very young age girls are programmed in such a way that their bent of mind sways towards Bhakti or devotion and they are not involved in the games of the mind. In the east, woman is more motherly, more feminine, compared to the west where woman is becoming father-like, and these feminine fathers are not only losing love but their emotional balance, too. The gay population is an outcome of these masculine mothers. The position of the man in the west is very pathetic.

The first step towards spirituality is to become human, as that is the turning point. If you belong to the Angel group you have to learn to accept things as they are without trying to change them in your favor. You are not holier than thou. Since you have tremendous confidence and are very positive by nature you must spread that to the Devil's group without picking up their negativity, as the Devil's group are power hungry, cruel and selfish on one hand and always wanting to make this world a better place to live on the other hand. The Angel group people are very giving but jealous, possessive and perfectionists at the same time. They must break their connection with being overconfident as the way they live their lives is by destroying the confidence of others so that they are always ahead in the game. Their ways of controlling others are very subtle and devious.

Knowing your type and bringing your state of mind to right in the middle is a very important factor and it will give you a tremendous jump and will bring you a step closer towards being in the state of no mind which is the final goal whether it is angels or devils, whether you start with meditation or devotion.

Before we go into meditation, let's look at the mind. Our mind is so powerful that it is busy even in our sleep. Our mind creates these dreams for us without our conscious knowledge and plays them on the screen of our consciousness when we close the doors of our eyes to the outside world, just like a movie theater. When we sit in a movie theater we are watching fiction and the doors to reality are closed for us. We could be watching a comedy, and outside of the movie theater people could be killing each other, and we do not know. We have connected our present time to this illusory reality that is playing on the screen for us, and as soon as we are out of the theater we come to the real world and have left fiction in the movie theater.

What is meditation? Just presume that you are sitting by the opening of a tunnel and cars are rushing out of the tunnel. All of a sudden you see this beautiful sports car and your mind jumps in the car and you start riding in a fantasy land of thoughts connected with that car or its driver. This is the state of not being in meditation. Let's put this example to work. You, the "I" within you, that "I am" within you, is watching the drama of thoughts on the screen of your mind. A thought is displayed on your conscious screen. You have two choices. Jump on the thought, power the thought with your emotions, feed it with your awareness, and let the thought take you on a ride. But if you want to dive deep into meditation, you will diffuse the thought by not allowing it to nurture on your emotional energies. As soon as it pops on the screen of consciousness you will be aware and prepared to wipe it off using your awareness and wait for the next one and you continue the process for days and months until the traffic has stopped and you have become thoughtless. But if you have become thoughtless you haven't reached yet because the thought of being in a thoughtless state is another thought. As a result you are not yet in a meditative state of mind. The "I am" is still there at the opening of the tunnel, and the road is there and the tunnel is there, so you work on dissolving the tunnel, the road, and then just you are left, so being in that state where just you are left, you have started on the journey of meditation. At this point all you can do is have patience and be a watcher and a point will come when the watcher will become the watched or both will not be there and the rest is your own individual experience.

Men should always start with meditation and one day they find the futility of this whole Maya or illusion. Women should not meditate and you can see that Buddhist monks are always men. In the Muslim religion, women are banned from the holy place of Mecca. Just a few years back, women were not allowed to be priests in Christianity. These are all religious distortions, as no one knows the real meaning behind not allowing the women to meditate.

If a woman starts meditating, the human species will become extinct in less than 200 years, as most of the children born will be insane. There is no need for the woman to watch her mind or mess with it as she has been created with a purpose that is higher. Her way is devotion, whether it is art, dance, serving her family, mankind, or giving birth or giving love to the newborn that becomes her natural meditation.

A woman will become insane if she starts watching her mind. In a nutshell, no matter what group a woman belongs to she should stay away from meditation. The reason women have started having premature babies and handicapped kids is because woman has started working in the office place and has started using her mind for mundane issues, not realizing that her purpose of taking this birth as a woman is divine, and she is losing the sensitive balance very fast. What will happen if you drive a race car in the bumper-to-bumper traffic every day? It will lose its potential to compete in the races. If a woman wants to have kids, I would suggest that she quit her work from conception to until the child is two years old and just involve herself in enjoying life so that we have newcomers who are already in a joyous state.

Men who belong to the Angel group are best suited for Bhakti or devotion, the reason being they have too much confidence and positivity, and that can only be transformed into humbleness by serving others, whether it is the guru or humanity.

The purpose is to be human-like where one starts moving forward instead of moving upward or downward. When they start serving the unlucky ones who are not so blessed as they are, they will realize the futility of the mind, which will open their doors to devotion.

On the other hand, men belonging to the Devil's group should start with meditation because meditation is going to bring them to a point where they will start moving upwards towards being a human, since these kinds of people live hopeless and helpless lives. They must explore their mind in order to understand the functioning of the mind, the thought process and the powers of the mind.

For men belonging to the human group, it does not matter as they have taken birth with a balanced state of mind and it is up to them whether they want to swim in a river or the ocean.

It is about time that we start looking inwards. We do not need any more wars on this planet as we have caused enough damage to the sensitive ecological system. We have too many diseases on this planet and the clear reason is that man is losing his touch with the earth, thus losing his connections with the sky. Symbolically speaking, men are the trees and women are the earth, and if earth becomes dry and loses its balance, the tree becomes uprooted and dries out, and if many trees become dry in a jungle then we run the risk of forest fires because each dry tree is a potential fire hazard. Woman is man's ground, since woman is losing her connections with the earth, which is her faith in herself and the power of love. As a result men are losing their love moisture. No wonder breast cancer is becoming the No. 1 killer disease in the world as more and more women lose their connection with the "Hriday Shakti" or the heart energy. On the other hand, men are dying with heart diseases. If we want the world to survive and if we want people of this planet to be happy, women should stop their obsession for beautifying their bodies, which is a mental act, and they should work on being in touch with their heart energies. If the woman loses her connections with her love center, "heart chakra," which is her center of love (not lovemaking), it will be very sad for humanity as I foresee nothing but more chaos on the physical and emotional level since emotions are our driving force to live this life.

Our salvation lies in our becoming aware of lives, in knowing our purpose that we are here to learn, experiment, understand and move on as this world is like a bridge and we should not plan to make homes on it. We have been given another chance to break the chains of the past and the future and live in the moment. The decision is yours whether you want to live a life of white lies or seek the truth, which lies hidden within your darkness.

Tips on Bhakti Devotion:

1. Even though devotion is the easiest way, it needs a lot of trust and gratitude. If you have trust and gratitude for your parents, who brought you into this life, then it will be easy for you to trust your guru. If this basic trust is missing, then you will have to start with your parents. At least be grateful to your parents for giving you this opportunity (your body) and for bringing you into this life, equally for both parents. You may not realize it, but the only connection you have with God or existence is not through your church but through your parents. Even if your parents were not good to you, make them understand their mistakes and let go of the past; your parents are human and to be human is to err. The west has more hate than love for the family, in contrast to the east, but then the west is logical and there is no problem which cannot be solved with logic, so it is easier for the west to let go and forgive and forget. Once you start with gratitude towards your parents you can move on to being thankful to Mother Earth and then towards the existence for giving you this opportunity to enjoy this drama of life. As you become humble, faith will start showering on you, and then miracles and grace will become an everyday routine, as the path of devotion is very sweet and heavenly.
2. It would be better if you keep your faith or devotion to yourself and not say a word about it to others. There are more people out there to hamper your progress than help you. Your faith in the unknown should remain 100% secret, and not even your parents should know about it, as it is your link with your inner self, the unknown.
3. Chanting is an excellent way towards devotion. You can choose the universal sound "AUM" or you can take any other word from your religion that fits with your mindset and chant it for a few hundred times every day.
4. Serving the poor, sick or even serving the animals is another form of devotion, provided you are not being paid for it.

Tips on Meditation:

There are hundreds and thousands of way to meditate and you will have to choose the one your heart goes for. Here are a few ways you can choose from:

1. Start with your breath. Your breath is the chain that links the body and the being. Every time you breathe in you are taking in life

energies and every time you breathe out you are dying to your past. Breathing in is your future and breathing out is your past and you exist right between the two breaths. Go in with your breath and count to 8, hold your breath for 8 counts and then release with 8 counts and then again hold for 8 counts. Practice this for a few months and the rest is your own experience.

2. Sit in front of the mirror and start looking into your eyes with love and affection and say to yourself that "I love you" with a lot of sweetness. Follow this every day until you do not find the need to say it with words. If you are a self-hater, you will have a hard time looking at yourself for more than two minutes, but as you start loving yourself day in and day out, your time will increase and so will your state of mind as well as your relationship with the outside world.

3. Always meditate either early in the morning or towards the evening using the same place. Your surroundings should be very quiet and you should not be disturbed while meditating. I find 2 AM to 4 AM to be the right moment as all energies are quiet and everyone is sleeping. After 2:00 AM the darkness has started the task of handing over this world of duality to light. These few hours of meditation can have similar effects on your inner darkness and light.

4. If you start having experiences that are beyond our dimension—such as feeling out of body or feeling that your body is not being pulled by the gravitational forces of the earth and you tend to levitate, or you see light—do not fear the experiences or get attached or obsessed, just continue your efforts; you will only experience the above after a few months of regular practice. These are just indications that you are progressing on the path. Again, do not discuss these experiences with anyone; otherwise, people will call you crazy and you will become disheartened and drop the practice.

5. Just like we eat every day and have a bowel movement every day, the same way our mind eats all the thoughts and we need to meditate everyday in order to clean our psyche.

6. Go to the ocean or the woods or by the river if you are the lucky one to live by a riverside, watch the water, listen to the sound, and try to concentrate on the void between the two sounds.

7. The most immediate and easy experience one can have after a few days or weeks of meditation is that one starts flying in one's dream or one becomes aware in one's dream that this is just a dream. Be thankful to the existence for giving you such an experience in the shortest possible time and just move on and continue meditating.

Whether it is devotion or meditation, be innovative and try to find new ways so that you do not get struck and keep on flowing; otherwise, the mind will be bored; the purpose is not to bore the mind but to sharpen your intellect and make it into a razor's edge.

17

Guru or Master

"Be your own light." Buddha
Live in the state of a student until you have arrived. Live this life with an
open mind and open heart because the guru can come in any form or shape.
The doors to your willingness to learn and experience should never be shut.
As soon as you say, "I know," you have shut the doors to your own future.

In ancient times people were seekers—they still are but the goals have changed. So one such seeker decided to look for the perfect guru. He had read many books, listened to others who were on the path of divinity, he went to numerous saints, practiced their ideas but always found himself in doubt. After years of searching he found a man who was in precise alignment with his thoughts of a perfect master. So the seeker said to the man: you seem to be the perfect guru, the kind I had been looking for and my journey is at an end. With great reverence he asked the guru to accept him as a disciple. To his amazement the guru said that it is not possible because he was seeking the perfect disciple.

Over six billion people on the planet and almost 99% are seeking happiness in the form of health and wealth. Then there are a few who are seeking fame and a small percentage are seeking divine knowledge out of which a very few are seeking the divine light.

In the last 50 years or so, the market for gurus has expanded. We now have gurus from the east and gurus from the west. We have gurus who have made financial empires and we have gurus who are not interested in even meeting the common man and whose material is available on the Internet, for anyone to go through, and at no charge.

Some gurus have already left their bodies and very few people really got the chance to meet them in person. Then there are gurus who are divine magicians and there are magicians who claim to be gurus. We have gurus in three-piece suits and we have gurus in various color robes.

If you get a chance to go to India you will find gurus in birthday suits as well.

Some gurus give hugs, some whisper the sacred mantra in your ears, some will jump start your kundalini, some will blast open your third eye or give you a glimpse at the unknown. It all depends upon the guru and the state of your consciousness. Look on the Internet and you will come across hundreds of such gurus with their so-called wisdom, information, and new techniques; some work and some don't. It boils down to many gurus, multiple choices and more confusion.

People are jumping from one guru to another in search of the right one who can give them a technique to follow precisely for x numbers of days and time, so one day you wake up enlightened and start your own guru business—no need to follow any guru. Enlightenment has become the goal for a great majority of seekers.

When making a selection, it is easier for you to choose the right washing powder to wash your clothes bright clean than to find a guru who can help you with your karmic laundry. Chances are that by accepting a faux guru you might wash off your bank balance and also ruin the sensitive threads of your emotional chakra as many gurus are greedy and acidic by nature. Overall the guru business is too risky a venture for both guru as well as the disciple.

What to do? Are you really searching for a guru or just looking for some answers? What can the guru do for you? Oh! So you are one of those people who do not know where to start in search for spiritual wisdom and someone talked about his guru in a new age book store or café, but this guru does not intrigue you and you want someone who is your type and has a good track record, no Rolls Royces, orgies, mass suicides, or financially ripped-off disciples.

I ask you, what are you really trying to achieve? Calmness, peace of mind, getting rid of your abused childhood, your guilt, your anger? Or is your goal enlightenment? Do you know that most of the gurus who come from the east have no or little demand back home? If you go and visit them in their home countries, you will find maybe two or three easterners around them who are their relatives or business people who will help you arrange for your flight reservations, get your dollars exchanged for you in the black market or help you buy antiques to take back.

In the east, astrologers and good doctors are in greater demand than gurus because the east is sick, physically and financially. They do not have many emotional problems because they have a family system, and if they run into problems, it is taken care of by other members of the family or blamed on God and a few coconuts are busted in a temple at some idolized demigod's feet.

The east is physically poor because fresh air, clean water and a good sewage system are hard to find and the body is unable to cope with all the bacteria it has to fight, so the body is in constant demand for a good doctor. The east does not have an abundant source of swimming pools or health clubs as we have in the west, and not many can afford it either; these luxuries are limited to the rich class. The east is in search of a guru who can heal their financial and physical problems or a guru who can help them get a visa to one of the rich countries in the west. If you were to find such a guru, he will have a hard time marketing himself in the west because you do not need a green card to live in India and a visa to India is as available as a pack of beer to westerners. All you need is a few thousand dollars and a passport for your ticket and expenses.

The west is financially affluent. In the west, if you have a physical problem, the chances are you will live because of the advancements in the medical science. Even if your mind gets a divorce from your body, your body will survive for many years on life support system. Whereas, in the east, you have less chances of living because there is lack of awareness with regard to the physical body.

On the other hand, the west is mentally sick because of being unemotional. There are hundreds of unibombers, anti-abortion activists, rapists, serial killers, snipers, child abusers, white heads, skinheads and anti-government activists contemplating their next move in their lonely cabins and rooms. The day is not far when the government will have to create a department to look for kids and adults who have the potential to become a threat to the government and society.

The west is very logical but mentally suffocated and emotionally dehydrated, making every man a potential maniac and a threat to the masses. The east will kill in the name of religion but the west will kill for the heck of it. There is no solid motive behind the majority of homicides that take place in the western countries.

In the west, people who have reached this realization and are feeling suffocated, jump to the spiritual side and their search starts with these gurus who are in big demand. Very few really get a chance to be with a real master who has gone beyond the illusion of life, and how will you know whether you are with a real guru or a fake one. Fake ones will influence you more than the real ones. Fake ones need to compensate with their eloquence, their magic tricks. Once you surrender to their gimmicks, you will be taken as their close disciples, and when you have beén sucked of your hard-earned money, the guru will tell you that now it is time for you to go and explore on your own, and you find yourself in the middle of the intersection not knowing which way is the right way for you, and—wait a minute—you are carrying a bigger bundle of frustrations and also you are alone, tired, and in a financial mess.

Poor you! If you were born in the east, your parents or relatives would have taken you back and helped you get back with your life. But, being born in the west, your parents hate you now for condemning their beefy lifestyle vs. your inclination towards eastern philosophy, and they have found a good excuse to enjoy their wealth in their old age. They will not only die guilt-free, but they will leave their estate to their cats and dogs and have an expensive funeral and a tomb where you can go and drop tears every year asking the void why they did that to you. Your girlfriend has also left you, or your wife has married a rich tycoon and does not even want to see your face. Talking of relatives, your brothers, sisters, or cousins will not even return your phone calls. They are in an unavailable state or out of town on a business trip as they have been forewarned about the state you are in.

I really feel sorry for the west and my eyes get filled with tears when I look at the western system that has become part of my experience too. On the outer level we have 24-7-365 hot and cold water, uninterrupted electricity, gas stations, repair shops, hospitals, restaurants, highways, police; everything is so perfect, life is so comfortable as long as you are chanting the cruel mantra of capitalism. But as soon as you detach yourself from the capitalistic God, it gets mad at you and sucks its resources from your life; your life equates the dog living by a slum in a Calcutta neighborhood. Lost, angry, hungry, frustrated, helpless, hopeless, and you can add your experience to it as well. Unless you are Bill Gates, Bill Clinton, Michael Jackson or Mariah Carey reading this book, then your miseries fall in different categories: Anti-trust lawsuits, another sex scandal, bad nose job performed by your incompetent cosmetic surgeon, or it could be nervous exhaustion due to too much fame and money, more than the mind can handle. Then you are not bothered by the fleas or ticks of poverty, but your experience is very similar to the dog that has been left in the brand new SL500 in the parking lot of Saks Fifth Avenue on a hot summer day while your mistress shops in a temperature-controlled, state-of-the-art shopping mall. You are gasping for cool air; at least the slum dog has the option to sit under the shade of the tree. Poverty carries a certain freedom while richness takes all your freedom away, even the hope of being free some day. On the day of judgment the poor have nothing to lose, whereas the so-called rich have a lot to let go of.

So coming back to gurus, few genuine gurus from the east who are frustrated with the illogical and uneducated east flock to the west with a desire to change the course of the spiritually depleted west, but the pressure from the Christian fundamentalists is so much that their communes are destroyed very methodically and the guru is either framed in a sexual lawsuit, killed, or is left with no choice but to flee the country. The ones who are very smart keep a low profile and never come in the limelight as they know that the media in this country is no more than a roller coaster ride and you get dumped in the end. ISCON movement is one example, Bhagwan Rajneesh or Osho is another example. While Osho was leaving the country, he was asked by a reporter: "Bhagwan, you say that you are enlightened, how come you were unable to realize what was happening around you," and Bhagwan replied, "Enlightenment only means that I have known myself."

Mankind is very smart; they killed Jesus and they killed Socrates and they killed many others, and I can guarantee you that you will be added to the list if you get enlightened and want to help the masses taste the divine nectar. You will be exterminated by the so-called "intelligent ones," by this unaware humanity, unless you take my advice and pack your bags and flee to a third-world country, because in a third-world country, you will not be put behind bars and poisoned. Either you will be loved, respected and cared for, or they will just think that you are crazy and will leave you alone.

Are you ready to face the darkness? Truth is hidden in the darkness of your consciousness and the majority are scared of the dark and fear the genuine master, but once the master is gone, there is no risk. Then we can create a religion around him because it is easier to live your life by the book than by the side of a real master. A real master lives in totality and you will find all tastes around him, i.e., anger, love, compassion, even cruelty, but his cruelty will carry an undercurrent of compassion. At times he has to be cruel because you have given him the responsibility to heal you of your past and direct you towards a higher state, and he is going to break all your concepts and will kill your "I," whereas the holy book will strengthen your "I."

In a nutshell, it is really hard to find a real guru, and even if one stumbles across one, it takes years of trust and love to get something out of the guru. Love and trust are missing from the majority; people do not even trust their own selves. As a result, the majority act like sheep in the herd, ready to be directed by someone who can install that small piece of trust coated with words of sweetness.

Preachers know this secret and they use it to their benefit. I ask you, what is the need of preachers in our world? If you are hungry, can you satisfy your hunger if you sit in front of the TV and watch Mr. Wong cook? The only way you can satisfy your hunger is if you walk to the kitchen, cook on your own and eat.

If you are spiritually thirsty, I suggest that you pack your bags and make a trip to India. Rain or shine, stay there, do not run away from the heat, dust, pollution, pickpockets, and con men. Just by living in that country, your inner self will start opening up and you will find a new meaning to your life. I guarantee you that once you visit India and live there for few weeks, you will become a misfit in your own western culture; the west will appear to you as a ghost town. The same happens to easterners who settle in the west. They go back and everybody tells them back home, "You have changed, you have lost your culture, you are westernized, you don't have a heart any more, your words are hurting, you have become unemotional." You will lose your western programming once you stay in India for few months. This is only possible if you move around and visit the so-called holy places. But if you stay in the metropolitan cities in your air-conditioned hotel room, then you will be better off going to the book store or your local library and getting few books on philosophy and yoga because you are not thirsty yet. Your thirst is not for water but for a soft drink.

Go look at the poverty, the helplessness and hopelessness, and the frustration of these poverty-stricken eastern countries—despite all these, the majority carry a tint of peace and calmness on their faces. Despite the poverty, they have not become cruel to themselves or to others, and they are very much in touch with their inner selves. They will give you if they can without asking anything in return whether it is knowledge, guidance or service. While you are in India, try this: approach a private citizen, rickshaw driver or a taxi driver, anyone who has an automobile and tell them that you have been robbed of your money and you are hungry, you need to go to your country's embassy. I guarantee you that five out of ten people will be ready to buy you lunch, chat with you and drop you off at the consulate at their cost. Their happiness will be if you write to them from home that you are back home safe and sound. Try the above in any metropolitan city in the U.S. and the taxi driver will laugh at you or you will be showered by the "F" word.

You have seen one side of the coin and you always thought that the coin has only the head; you will be shocked when you find the tail. The east is very tail-oriented, whereas the west is very head-oriented.

On the other side, the story is just the reverse. When the majority of easterners come to the west, you will find their tails between their legs, as they feel very insecure, but living in the west for a few years, they find that they carry a head too.

So how does one know whether the guru is real or not? Logically speaking, you can search the Internet to find ratings for these gurus or flip a coin. Before I tell you what to look for in a guru I would like to ask you a question: Do you know why in the ancient times idol making was so popular? You might not know the answer; hence, take my word. The science of body features was very popular. The east knew the secret of how the mind works. The east started creating symbols in the shape of idols so that the eye picks up the hidden mysteries in these idols and an image is created in the subconscious of how a perfect human looks. Idols were created to direct the course of the masses towards a higher state of mind and to save humans from unnecessary hardship, because whenever man is going to involve himself in an inhuman act, the idols will pop on the screen of the conscious mind and will distort the negative thought pattern. There was no law in those times and neither was there any crime. The science of idol making was used to diffuse the negative thought patterns from taking over both sides of the mind.

If you go to India you will find hundreds and thousands of these idols of a perfect man and woman. There is a God and Goddess behind each area of human thinking—God for wealth, God for knowledge, God for creativity, God for health, God for destruction, God for protection, and so on. With the Mogul invasion, the social structure became distorted and the invaders destroyed thousands of these idols. Quite recently a 1500-year-old idol of Buddha was destroyed by the Taliban regime in Afghanistan.

These idols are still working on the principle they were planned for and have been saving the east from a social disintegration. Even when a real guru was absent or the holy books started taking the responsibility of gurus, these idols were working as silent gurus. Now singers and actors have replaced these idols in programming young minds. Look deeply: a child who is brought up around toy guns, violent movies and Halloween stuff is not going to grow up as an enlightened master because his guru was the bad man in the cartoons he had been watching all his childhood, the toys of destruction he played with, the violent movies he watched and the violent video games he played and the posters he saw every night before going to the bed. The ugly masks he wore on Halloween are going to rule his mind for the rest of his life. For him life will be a replication of Halloween where everyone is ugly and thirsty for his blood and it is quite logical to follow the rule of thumb, "When in Rome, do as the Romans do." If you look at the young generation, the fate of mankind is doomed unless a politician who has a spiritual background comes forward and changes the course as Singapore did with chewing gum. It is one of the products which is banned by the government, and there is a strict punishment for smuggling chewing gum into the country. With drugs they are even stricter and the punishment is the death penalty.

Pieces of art are not mere shapes but mathematical symbols at a very higher level only the subconscious mind can understand. Just pay a visit to a Hindu temple just for the sake of curiosity and look very closely at the idols; just forget the people who are worshipping them and you will stumble upon the hidden secrets. You will come to know that these idols were created to install an image in the minds of people as to what a perfect human looks like.

An idol of Buddha would tell you exactly the state of a man who has reached an enlightened state. The ancients knew these secrets that if the state of one's mind changes, they start appearing on your physical features. Since the mind is the controller of the body, these idols were created to reach the subtle using the gross.

Here are some tips for finding a genuine guru.

Before you start your search for the right guru, make sure you have looked into the eyes of a carnivorous animal, i.e., lion, tiger, wolf, etc., and also into the eyes of a cow or deer. With that, memorize the traits of both these animals. Now you can safely start your search. Here are the indications.

Just visualize that your face is like a bud that has not bloomed into a flower yet. What happens when a bud transforms into a flower? Everything expands. Exactly the same way every feature will carry expansion on the face of a guru. His face will look blissful, you would want to keep looking at him for hours, the lower lip would have expanded like a rubber band is stretched. His eyes will have the calmness of a cow, and if you see the wolf's eyes, just run because he is still looking for his next prey. The ears will be very fleshy, because if the ears are paper-thin, he has not even come out of his cruelty yet. All his nails will be shining like pearls, as nails show the state of one's bio-energy; there will be a glow on his skin, face, as well as on his feet. He will look happy and will carry the divine smile; his cheeks will be full blown just like a high-cheeked woman or a happy toddler; you will find him very receptive, compassionate and caring. He will be intellectually very sharp but as innocent as a child.

The "I" will be missing from his every breath. If you are a real disciple, you will want to surrender to him and become like him because his aura will influence you and will give you a taste of totality.

Gurus are not made to order; they are born as one is born to be a musician or artist, one cannot train one's self into being a guru or teacher. The day you reach enlightenment your physical features will expand just as I have described above but the problem is that we have lost trust. One who has never seen a flower and you take him to a bud and then show him the picture of a flower and say this bud will open up one day and be as beautiful as this picture, the other is not going to take your word as truth until he has experienced the process with his own eyes.

I can assure you that there is hope as I am not a pessimist; I have seen the pictures of masters and have been with them when they were not enlightened and I have seen and been with them when they had arrived at the doors of existence and their whole body was dancing with the divine play. Each one of us has the potential to reach the highest state man can ever achieve but you need to have the right chemistry within you. People like you and I have reached that state in the past, people like Krishna, Jesus, Socrates, Buddha, Nanak, and many others—they were people like you and me before they arrived.

But if you are stuck with the religion you are born in, 99.9% chances are you will die with your unexplored and forged mindset. But if you use your mind and carry a passion within your heart and start searching, the day is not far when you will find your path.

Start the search by looking into the religion in which you are born, and if you stumble upon the mysteries, you are bound to start respecting others who have walked on the path. Then you will not say that Jesus is the only Son of God or non-Muslim are "Kafers" (rejected ones). If your own religion does not fit with your mental chemistry, then expand your search. Search in the Vedas, venture into Greek philosophy, into Zen, look into the lives of Sikh gurus and read the Guru Granth Sahib, explore Hinduism, read Gita, look into the lives of Sufi masters or Buddha and see what works for you, maybe you will come back to your religion with a new understanding.

Until you find a guru who fits the above description, be your own guide. It is you who will have to decide based on your understanding of a real guru or teacher. He is not going to come and introduce himself, " Hi, I am the enlightened master from India and here are my credentials; can I get a job being your guru?" A real guru is not interested in MLM (multi-level marketing). He is not in search of followers; he will not advertise that you can join now and be among the top ones as the commune is fresh with an unlimited potential. A real guru is not interested in promoting himself.

Always remember, a perfect guru is always in search of a perfect disciple so that he can sow the seed of knowledge in order to get a healthy harvest of wisdom. If you are given a bucket of seeds and told that this is the last bucket of seeds left on the planet and if you waste it you will die of hunger, would you sow the seeds in a desert or in a marshland? Or will you look for the right land to sow the seeds to your survival?

Do not use religion as a blind man's stick; do not expect the guru to become a guide dog for you and walk you to the altar of God. By the way, even your dog can take you to the altar of God provided you have great reverence for him and realize that the same energy circulates within your dog that runs your life. Be open and responsive and you will find each and every moment of your life to be a stepping-stone for you. If you have decided to live this life in awareness, even a three-year-old can become your guru at times. Life is short; do not waste your time searching for gurus or for spiritual wisdom; there are no 7, 9 or 10 laws towards attaining your being. All laws, notions must be dropped, start looking within. You cannot find God because God must find you. Be open and become aware, transform yourself into a fertile land and sow the seeds of your consciousness into the land of knowledge, or it could be the other way too and one day you will dance looking at the harvest, and if a guru who has tasted God comes along to help you, be grateful. Until then, be your own guru.

18

Death and Beyond

One who has taken birth will have to die one day; nothing is more certain than death on this planet. We are so scared of death that we never think that one day we will be facing that final moment when the life energies will start leaving this body and there will be no "I" left behind. Even before the body starts rotting, one's kith and kin are going to dispose of the body so that it does not pollute the atmosphere. The ones who claim to have loved you, the ones who have used you, manipulated you on the pretext of loving every part of your body, will be in a hurry to bury or burn. You will be left to your burning pyre or made to rest in your grave where all the five elements will dissolve in the Earth and no trace left of that man or woman who commanded such power. Death will dissolve everything and all your attachments and belongings will wither away into the unknown realms of death.

If we are expecting a baby we always plan ahead and prepare for it; even before the baby is born we do medical tests to know the sex of the baby so that we can buy new clothes and paint and decorate the baby's room accordingly, and we even decide the name. When we are flying from one city to another, we plan and prepare in advance. We book our tickets and make sure we get our choice of food and seat preferences. We pack our bags and make a list of things we will need for our trip and we make a checklist so that we do not forget anything. But when it comes to Death, we do not plan ahead even though each one of us starts getting messages in the form of dreams, thoughts, and through many other mysterious ways that very soon death is going to knock on our door, which starts happening exactly nine months before the actual death happens.

It takes nine months from the time of conception to birth and many women become aware of the moment when the soul enters the fetus and makes it alive. It takes exactly the same amount of time for one to die.

The seed of death is planted within you by the existence nine months before you die and you become pregnant with death and stay pregnant with death until the life force leaves your body.

People who are very aware and have reached a very high state of consciousness know this secret. As soon as the seed of death is planted in their beings they come to the realization that the time is coming and start getting ready for the final act in this drama of life.

But for a human who has lived a mundane life, obsessed by the hunt for money and power, he will not pay any attention to very sensitive messages his unconscious mind is throwing into his consciousness, into his dreams, and he will not even realize that the tip of his nose is not in his vision any more as his eyeballs have changed position. Normally if you look straight, the tip of your nose always remains in your vision and it depends upon the dominance of the brain as to which side is visible to you, as not everyone will see their right side or their left side. Each individual will see only one side of the nose, but as soon as you become pregnant with death the eyeballs change their position, and as the time comes closer and closer, the tip of the nose starts disappearing and one day you cannot even see the tip of the nose anymore nor can you see the blue sky.

Dreams are another channel where you are warned about the future events. Any dream that is being repeated many times is an indication of an event that will impact you on a deeper level. The type of indications of the coming of death depend upon the state of one's consciousness as well as past karma. Of all the indications, the best indication is given by the body, as even though one is eating normally no longer is the food being enjoyed by the body as one's strings with the earth are being uprooted. This indication is also experienced when one is going to change the place one is living or if one is going on a trip for few weeks; the same is experienced just before the body is going into a sickness mode.

If ever you have gone to camp in the wilderness you must have realized that it takes more time to set up your tent than to uproot it. Have you been through the experience of a woman giving birth to a baby? It takes nine months for the baby to develop but takes only a few minutes for the baby to come out of the womb. It will take even less time for the actual death to happen only if your karmic records are clean and you do not have any derogatory remarks on your karmic report; otherwise, every single moment of your last nine months will be felt as lifetimes of torture; it all depends upon your past history.

Unless you have prepared for death all your life, this tent of your life will be uprooted as if a tornado hit you, and as you have never remembered the actual moment of your birth you will never realize the experience of death. If we have missed life, death is the only moment left to us where we are given a last chance to know the mysteries of this existence before we start all over again in a new body and under new circumstances.

Life is a mysterious journey and death checks you in to the retreat center where your being can relax and enjoy itself until you become ready for the next adventure. Similarly, you work hard all day long and go to sleep at night, and your body gets refreshed at night and you wake up to a new morning. Someone who has lived his day in totality will sleep in totality and is bound to wake up to a new sunrise. But one who has missed life, how can he not miss death?

All our lives we keep on fighting for power and money, not realizing that one day we will have to discard all this and move on. This everyday struggle makes us so weak that one day we are unable to face death at all, not to speak of welcoming death and making it into a celebration of what's beyond it. For most people life is wasted on puny and mundane issues that do not get solved while people are in their physical bodies, and then their astral bodies are so eager to apologize to their families on "The Beyond" show.

I have never figured out why humans feel happy when a baby arrives and why they cry when he/she, after x number of years, dies. It should be the other way around, because for the majority, birth is the start of a miserable period whereas death is the end of such a period. Very few enjoy this so-called life.

There is an interesting story about death. Once in Tibet there lived two laughing monks. Wherever they went, they would make people laugh; crowds would roll on the ground laughing as the laughter would turn into tears rolling out of the eyes and people bending with stomachache. Shopkeepers would forget to sell and buyers would leave the shops to join the crowd on the street. Such was the power of these two monks. You have not laughed unless your whole body starts laughing, unless every single cell in your body has joined the laugh. Society has suppressed laughter to preset laughing sounds. That was funny! And you get back to work. Since people cannot laugh, people cannot cry either, as crying and laughter are two sides of the same coin. So one day, one of the monks died and everybody was sad as they took his body to the pyre. As his body started burning, a big firework started just like the Fourth of July fireworks in the USA. As the monk knew about his death, he was very aware about the time of his death, his being pregnant with death, as all his life he celebrated, and since his life was a celebration, he wanted his death to be a celebration too, so before he died, he had wrapped firecrackers around his body and the whole sky lighted up as if the whole existence was celebrating his death. Looking at the fireworks the whole town started laughing.

Unless we prepare for death every single day, we will not be ready at the time of death. Just before we go to sleep, we need to prepare for sleep as sleep is nothing but a reminder to us that one day we will go into a deep sleep where we will not wake up in this body. Unless we welcome sleep in a very aware state, we will never be able to wake up to a new morning, because if we go to sleep with a tired body, we will be waking up to another tiring day or another life not knowing why we are here and what the purpose of our life is, then we will keep on taking births and dying as we have done in the past for millions of lifetimes.

Here is another story from India that will give your life a new meaning. It happened in the times of King Janak. The king was sitting on his throne while all his advisors were seated at their respective places. They had a long day and the king was tired, so he dozed off. Everybody became silent because the king had dozed off.

The king goes into a dreaming state and in that state he is in a war with the neighboring country. Unfortunately he loses the war and is caught by the enemy. Since he was a very powerful king, the enemy king says that I am not going to kill you or jail you, and he orders that all his expensive clothes and jewelry be taken off and he should be given just a shirt and a pajama to wear and should be allowed to go wherever he wants to. The enemy king also makes sure that he is not helped by any citizen or that person will have to face severe punishment.

Poor Janak starts his journey barefooted out of his kingdom. Two days pass and he is still not out of his kingdom's boundaries. He reaches a place where a rich man is offering food to the poor from his kitchen. He joins the long queue and to add spice to his misery the food is finished by the time his turn comes. He requests the man in charge to get him some food as he is extremely hungry. The man looking at his pathetic situation suggests that he scrape the food from the walls of the pot and also help him wash the pot. Janak scrapes the food and washes the pot and the man puts the food on his hands. Janak leaves the place with the scraped food in his hands. An eagle that is flying above him sees the food and dives on the food, grabbing a piece. In the process the rest of the food is dropped in the dust and Janak's hand is scratched by the sharp nails of the eagle. He cries out loud and wakes up abruptly, only to see that he is sitting on his throne, his advisors looking at him with reverence waiting for him to say something. He narrates the dream to his advisors and questions them as to which is the real dream? What he saw few minutes ago or what he is seeing now. No one could answer to his heart's satisfaction, so he called on his young guru Astaka-vakra and posed him the same question. Astaka-vakra answered: King Janak, what you saw in the dream was true for you at that state and time; that was your reality as you had forgotten that you are still a king who is in power. What you are watching at this moment is your reality for the present time, but this too will be lost one day at the time of death. But the watcher within you never dies; know that watcher and you will conquer every state including death.

Most people fear death and do not want to even talk about this grave issue. For most people, life is lost in illusions and fantasies, and while alive we make every arrangement so that we never come to the realization of what death is. Since we fear death so much we have decorated death with flowers and ceremonies to make it look less horrible because it is always someone else who has died and not us.

In the east, society has made death into a catastrophe: women, men, and kids cry and yell their hearts out, food is rejected by the close members of the family for days, and the sadness continues until the last rites are performed and the ashes are scattered into a holy river, a period that could take weeks. They do not even stop at this, as every year the anniversary of the death is sad-i-brated. The departing is taken as a unrecoverable loss for the family.

The story is entirely different in the west; in the majority of cases the hospital, insurance company, government, or friends take care of burying the body, unless the person is rich enough to leave a will, in which case the family will be around. The body is gift wrapped and the coffin, burial ground, last rites, etc., are planned to give the final goodbye to the dead and his or her body. You burn or bury the body, come home and talk about the person and about how good or bad he or she was, and with every passing day your mind starts focusing on your ongoing issues in life until the time comes when you no longer think about it.

Question yourself: Have you ever thought, visualized, envisioned, contemplated, chewed over, mused or meditated about the moment when this "I" who is reading this book will have to leave this body and move into an unknown world beyond death?

Here are some tips that will help you prepare for the last moment when your "I" will have few breaths left and you will be ready to leave this elemental body and move on:

1. You are not the body. A continuous understanding is needed that this body is not mine and will have to be discarded one day. In other words, remember that this body will die one day. Drop your attachment with this body as well as with this material world. Life is a bridge; don't make a home on it.

2. Physical pain is the best tool given to mankind to prepare for death. When in pain do not associate with pain, do not feed pain with your awareness, do not think, feel or say that I am in pain. No! The body is in pain and not you. This understanding will give a new meaning to your life.

3. Breath control is another way of taking charge of your life. Breathe in for 8 counts, hold for 8 counts and release the air for 8 counts. Go on increasing the counts as you become comfortable. Your span of life is determined by the number of breaths you take which is based upon your karmic record; if you want to expand your life, breathe slowly and rhythmically.

4. Staying quiet for a few days and not uttering a word will help you calm your mind. Once you have taken control over your chatterbox, you have taken a major step towards conquering death.

5. Watch your breath go in, the sound it makes when you breathe in is soooooooo. When you breathe out it makes the sound of hummmmmmmm. Just remember that each moment you are living and dying, each moment you are breathing in your future and dying to your past and the moment in between the two breaths is the moment of the "here and now." Watch this so-hum cycle and in a few months you will be amazed at the results.

6. Keep track of your dreams and the sensitive messages your unconscious mind is sending you, and try to understand your dreams.

7. Do not associate yourself with worldly experiences as they are not yours but belong to the material world. Practice detachment and keep your calm and stay centered within your awareness in extreme moments of happiness and sadness. If laughter comes, be a watcher; if tears fall, stay aware.

8. If you feel you are closer to death, visualize that you have left your body and the body is lying there dead. Visualize that your body is being burned on the pyre and is left to ashes. This meditation will not only help you with death but might take you beyond death while you are still a guest in this body.

9. You will be better off and it will save your being from going through a horrible time if you make sure that after death your body is burned

within 3 hours of your death rather than buried, as it takes a longer time for the soul to transition from this dimension to others if the body is buried. If the body is burned to ashes, the connection of the being is instantly broken with the body as it turns into ashes. Just as we are connected with an umbilical cord with our biological mother, an invisible cord links the astral body with the physical body; if the dead body is burned to ashes this invisible cord is instantly dissolved but if the body is buried in a grave it can take days, months and years for this invisible cord to dissolve. If we want to eradicate darkness from the planet the first step we can take is to burn the bodies instead of burying them.

Beginning

Let's start this life with a new awareness, a new promise to stay awake no matter what price we have to pay. This drama called life is nothing but a play of thoughts, emotions, and actions on the merry-go-round of breath.

Anger comes; become aware and go to the root of the anger and see where it is coming from and you will be amazed to realize that it came from nowhere and it gets dissolved into nowhere. Hate is an experience; go into hate and see whom you are hating. Is it the other person? What if this other person dies in a few minutes, will your hate continue? If it does, you are, in fact, hating your own self, as the other no longer exists.

Thoughts and emotions are nothing but traffic on the road of one's consciousness, and when we rush towards a particular thought we get into an accident. As a result we jump to conclusions. But if we go slowly, we can ride on a particular thought, experience it, and then get off the thought. Are we not patient with positive thoughts and circumstances? Do you ever rush towards positive thoughts? If you do, then you are never able to enjoy the positive thoughts or experiences. Rush and you miss, slow down and you start enjoying life. Patience is the key towards being into an aware state of mind—with this increased awareness one can enter the realm of wisdom.

What is meditation? Slowing your chattering mind, calming your thoughts to the point where the traffic of thoughts is no longer experiencing a rush hour. As you go deeper and deeper, there are no thoughts left, except for the thought of meditation or the thought of your I am-ness. One day this dissolves too for a split moment and you start experiencing a new awareness that you have never experienced.

We take from society but seldom give back; share your life with others. Enjoy people without judging them; everyone is fine the way they are. Be compassionate towards yourself and others.

Always stay on guard, there are tons of negative people out there who want to fleece you of your spiritual wool and offer your body and soul to the dark energies.

The past is gone and the future has not yet arrived; learn to live in the moment and you will know the difference. Drop your guilt and your fear; guilt belongs to the past and fear to the future. Guilt is also connected with failure—you failed in the past and you are guilty. Don't you want to be successful in the future? Death is in the future and if you can overcome the fear this very moment, you have already won.

In 1993, my flight took off from Los Angeles and within 15 minutes we were facing bad turbulence. Everyone started screaming as the plane lost altitude in an instant. People started feeling nauseated; it happened again, and when we landed at JFK we saw emergency vehicles next to the runway. This experience of the fear of death was very enlightening for me and gave me a tremendous transformation. Looking at the situation and hearing people's screams, I became more aware at the time and asked for divine help to save us from this horror.

This life does not belong to you—each breath you are taking is being forced into you and sucked out of you after a few seconds. Try holding your breath for few moments and your whole body will go into a mayday situation; you will be gasping just as a fish without water. Always remember this life is a gift from God to you, to experience the joys and sorrows of the illusions and go beyond it. Play, enjoy and learn from it, that's all existence wants from you.

The choice is yours: enjoy and grow or fret and fall. You have been given the freedom to be happy or die sad. You are the engineer of your life; make the best of it or make the worst of it. If you live in the moment, then there is no happiness or sadness, there is only void, the God.

It's your choice to either allow the negative energy or the positive energy create the roller coasters for you. If you let your thoughts plug into your emotions and nurture on your bio-energies, you are being a slave to this illusionary life. If you are aware, you will only nurture thoughts that will help you grow in life; otherwise, the thoughts become your master and you remain a slave for lives to come, until a master comes and out of compassion knocks on your head to wake you up from your eternal sleep. Until then you are on your own.